Aesthetic and Myth in the

POETRY OF KEATS

AESTHETIC AND MYTH

IN THE

POETRY OF

KEATS

BY WALTER H. EVERT

PRINCETON, NEW JERSEY

PRINCETON UNIVERSITY PRESS

1965

❖

Publication of this book has been aided by the Ford Foundation
program to support publication, through university presses, of
works in the humanities and social sciences.

Permission of the Oxford University Press to quote the H. W.
Garrod translation of a passage from Aristophanes' *The Birds*,
which appears in Garrod's *The Profession of Poetry and Other
Lectures*, and to cite Keats's poetry from the Second Edition
(1958) of *The Poetical Works of John Keats*, edited by H. W.
Garrod, is gratefully acknowledged.

❖

Printed in the United States of America by
Princeton University Press, Princeton, New Jersey

for

MARILYN

KATHY

and

MIKE

Preface

THIS book is concerned with Keats's aesthetic ideas and with the effects of those ideas on his poetry. While it includes discussion of a great many poems, major and minor, its purpose is to survey not the poems but the turns and counterturns of the creating mind as these are reflected in the poetry. It is, in effect, the history of an internal warfare, and the poems that are discussed most fully are those which remain as monuments of battles won or lost in that anguished conflict. Given this orientation, it necessarily follows that there are other kinds of commentary, equally interesting and valuable to a study of the poems, that will not be found here because they lie outside the scope of my intentions.

Since a full-length study of a poet, however oriented, might reasonably be expected to treat all his major works, I have provided an appendix for the discussion of poems which, for one reason or another, did not seem relevant or necessary to the main argument. If it seems somehow disrespectful to place such a poem as the "Ode on a Grecian Urn" in an appendix, I can only say that I have not felt it so. Nothing has been "relegated" to the appendix, nor are any poems placed there because of a possible embarrassment to my main argument. I consider the Grecian Urn ode, for example, to sustain very well the argument of the whole. But it does not add anything to what we can learn from the "Ode to a Nightingale" about Keats's frame of mind at the time when both were composed; it lacks the demonic metaphor which conveniently binds the Nightingale ode to other major poems having a similar theme; and it is less directly related by context and allusion to Keats's earlier poetry. The decision to place the "Ode on a Grecian Urn" and other poems in an appendix was thus based on relevance and on an aesthetic preference in the organization of my own argument which I hope will be allowed me, if not forgiven.

Not all of my aesthetic preferences could be indulged, however, even by me. I would have preferred the treatment of *Endymion* to bulk less hugely than it does in the whole, if only for the sake of visual proportion. But trim as I might, I have been unable to reduce it drastically. I can only put forward for excuse the facts that the poem does constitute, after all, very nearly half of all the poetry that Keats saw fit to publish in his lifetime, that it does embody by far the most extensive and coherent representation of the aesthetic ideas with which I think Keats to have been centrally concerned, and that its problems have by no means been so thoroughly laid to rest by the frequent and full discussions of previous writers as to render cursory treatment adequate.

While mentioning previous writers, I might add that I decided, after some hesitation, not to include recurrent summaries of the positions of scholars and critics whose interpretations agree with or differ from mine in various particulars, if they *merely* agree or differ. While there may be some inconsistency in my practice here, I have tried to limit my references to writers whose statements bear directly on points at local issue. As it has seemed to me most likely that anyone reading such a book as this either will be already familiar with Keats scholarship, or will be in the process of becoming so, it has seemed unnecessary to reproduce here what can be found elsewhere with more satisfaction to both the reader and the original authors.

In the sixteen years during which Keats has been my major literary preoccupation, I have of course learned a great deal from other writers—much more than I could disentangle and acknowledge in footnotes. While

PREFACE

I have tried constantly to remain independent of critical traditions, and to see Keats, as it were, for the first time, it would be untrue and ungenerous not to confess a feeling of kinship with and deep indebtedness to all who have written on Keats before me—if only for the stimulus often of silent argument. I regret that the recent critical biographies by Walter Jackson Bate and Aileen Ward appeared too late for integral use in my own study. I have found much of interest in them but have been able to insert only occasional reference to them in my text. It does not particularly disturb me that we sometimes disagree with one another radically. We will all be judged finally by the extent to which we agree with Keats, and not with each other; and meanwhile, we can perhaps shed different kinds of light on the problems that concern us all.

For various kinds of help I should like to acknowledge debts of gratitude to the late Professor Madison C. Bates, of the Newark Colleges of Rutgers University, who aroused and fostered my earliest interest in Keats, and to Professors Charles T. Davis, of the Pennsylvania State University, Earl Leslie Griggs, of the University of California, Santa Barbara, Glenn O'Malley, of Northwestern University, and Carlos H. Baker, of Princeton University. To Professor Baker, let me add in deepest gratitude, my further indebtedness is of such variety and long standing as to beggar the formal limits of a preface. The readers for the Princeton University Press also gave me generous and often humbling counsel. Where error and folly remain, it has obviously not been for lack of the very best advice.

My thanks are also due to Miss Edith Lufkin for her patient and flawless typing of the manuscript, to the Research Committee of the Academic Senate in the University of California, Los Angeles, for financial assistance

PREFACE

in the later stages of research and composition, and to my editor, Mrs. William Hanle, for all the things that she knew best how to do. And finally, for many kinds of help, wisely and humanely given, I should like to thank Miss R. Miriam Brokaw, of the Princeton University Press.

Contents

Aesthetic and Myth in the
POETRY OF KEATS

I went to the Isle of Wight—thought so much about Poetry so long together that I could not get to sleep at night. . . . Another thing I was too much in Solitude, and consequently was obliged to be in continual burning of thought. . . . (May 10, 1817)

I think a little change has taken place in my intellect lately— I cannot bear to be uninterested or unemployed. . . . (January 23, 1818)

What a happy thing it would be if we could settle our thoughts, make our minds up on any matter in five Minutes and remain content . . . but Alas! this never can be . . . for as the material Cottager knows there are such places as france and Italy and the Andes and the Burning Mountains—so the spiritual Cottager has knowledge of the terra semi incognita of things unearthly; and cannot for his Life, keep in the check rein— (March 24, 1818)

I find that I can have no enjoyment in the World but continual drinking of Knowledge . . . there is but one way for me—the road lies th[r]ough application study and thought. (April 24, 1818)

Then I should be most enviable—with the yearning Passion I have for the beautiful, connected and made one with the ambition of my intellect. (October 24, 1818)

. . . if I am not in action mind or Body I am in pain— (December 18, 1818)

. . . it was written with no Agony but that of ignorance; with no thirst of any thing but knowledge when pushed to the point though the first steps to it were throug[h] my human passions—they went away, and I wrote with my Mind— (March 19, 1819)

I think if I had a free and healthy and lasting organisation of heart and Lungs . . . so as to be able [to bear] unhurt the shock of extreme thought and sensation without weariness, I could pass my Life very nearly alone. . . . (August 24, 1819)[1]

---

[1] All the above citations are from *The Letters of John Keats, 1814-1821*, ed. Hyder Edward Rollins, 2 vols. (Cambridge, Mass., 1958), consecutively as follows: I, 138-39, 214, 254-55, 271, 404; II, 12, 81, 146. Unless otherwise specified, this edition will be used for all references to the letters hereafter, and will be designated simply *Letters*.

The Mind and the Means

DURING the past half-century it has become increasingly respectable to discuss Keats as a thinker—or at least it has not seemed patently absurd to do so. This has been, of course, distinctly a development of our own time. While nineteenth-century critics did occasionally assert his seriousness of intent in particular works, the Victorians tended for the most part to look for other qualities in Keats than they did in the philosophic Wordsworth. None of the great Victorian poets was untouched by Keats, but they studied him for his tone and technique, while the reading public responded directly and primarily to his evocative power.[2] Matthew Arnold both reflected and summarized the quality of the general response when he praised the "fascinating felicity" and "natural magic" of Keats's poetic diction, while reluctantly concluding that there was less to be said for the matter so expressed.[3]

The shift in critical orientation, the willingness to find intellectual as well as emotional and artistic integrity in Keats's poetry, was signalized, if not consummated, in _The John Keats Memorial Volume_,[4] published 100 years after the poet's death, in which a significant number of

[2] The indispensable volume for this phase of literary history is: George H. Ford, _Keats and the Victorians: A Study of His Influence and Rise to Fame, 1821-1895_ (New Haven, 1944).

[3] Matthew Arnold, _Essays in Criticism: Second Series_ (London, 1888), pp. 119-21. See also Ford, _Keats and the Victorians_, pp. 31-32.

[4] London, 1921.

INTRODUCTION

contributors addressed themselves directly to the matter
of Keats's thought. When C. D. Thorpe a few years later
devoted a whole book to the subject,[5] the revolution in
attitude had for all practical purposes been accomplished.
Since that time there has been inevitable disagreement
as to Keats's intellectual kind and competence, but those
serious students of the poet are rare today who still
think of him chiefly as a facile word-smith or precious
celebrant of sensuous delight. This is not to say, of course,
that Keats is now read as a homiletic poet, or that there
has been any decrease of interest in or response to the
magic of his utterance. It is to say, simply, that he is
acknowledged to be a poet in the full sense of the word,
and that it is therefore taken for granted that what he
says to us is shaped no less by his mind than by his heart.

As one tends to recall only the two or three familiar
passages of self-conscious cerebration in Keats's letters,
it might be as well to call attention to the brief extracts
which stand at the head of this chapter. Culled more or
less at random from letters written throughout the literarily important years of his life, they sound, in varying
contexts and with differing qualifications, a single recurrent note. In the period over which these comments
are spread, the intellectual bent of Keats's mind took a
very sharp turn, as will appear hereafter, but at every
point the letters manifest the same evidence of mental
drive. The general impression is of an unquiet, restless,
searching mind, intensely earnest and at times almost
compulsive in its activity. The reliability of this impression is confirmed by Charles Dilke, one of Keats's closest
friends, who commented on the first of the passages
cited here: "An exact picture of the man's mind and character. . . . He could at any time have 'thought himself
out' mind and body. Thought was intense with him, and

5 *The Mind of John Keats* (New York, 1926).

[4]

seemed at times to assume a reality that influenced his conduct—and I have no doubt helped to wear him out."[6]

As further evidence of a propensity for hard thought, there are such plainly allegorical poems as *Endymion*, *Lamia*, and *The Fall of Hyperion*. And to these in turn may be added, as touchstone, the poet's declared belief in the essential unity and coherence of diverse human experience: "I find there is no worthy pursuit but the idea of doing some good for the world—some do it with their society—some with their wit—some with their benevolence—some with a sort of power of conferring pleasure and good humour on all they meet and in a thousand ways all equally dutiful to the command of Great Nature";[7] and, "Every department of knowledge we see excellent and calculated towards a great whole."[8] The mental activity which takes place within such a context, or which eventuates in such conclusions, is clearly not random. Indeed, when a person writes lengthy allegorical poems, and sees all varieties of human conduct "equally dutiful to the command of Great Nature" and all human knowledge "calculated towards a great whole," he is not only a thinker but also, in native tendency at least, a systematic thinker.

It is easy to be thrown off the track when such a person remarks, "I have never yet been able to perceive how any thing can be known for truth by consequitive reasoning,"[9] but we should fairly take into account the hesitant acknowledgment that completes his sentence, "—and yet it must be." We may find an attitude of condescension toward the dry, logical mind when the poet writes to his publisher, of one of his poetic passages, "The whole thing must I think have appeared to you,

---

[6] Quoted in Maurice Buxton Forman (ed.), *The Letters of John Keats*, Third Edition (Oxford, 1947), pp. 25-26n.
[7] *Letters*, I, 271.　　[8] *Ibid.*, 277.　　[9] *Ibid.*, 185.

who are a consequitive Man, as a thing almost of mere words";[10] yet the "thing" he refers to is one of the most famous (if also perhaps most equivocal) systematic constructions in English poetry, the "fellowship with essence" passage in *Endymion* (I, 777-842). When one considers such public performances as this, and such private adventures in speculative activity as the "vale of Soul-making"[11] and the "Mansion of Many Apartments"[12] hypotheses in the letters, to take only the most familiar examples, one is obliged to acknowledge that we have to do with a mind which habitually and characteristically assimilates experience into comprehensive epistemological and metaphysical structures. It is a mind, moreover, not idly playing with ideas, but firmly calm and trustful of its own sufficiency: "I have great hopes of success . . . but. . . . I am in no wise dashed at a different prospect. I have spent too many thoughtful days & moralized thro' too many nights for that, and fruitless wo^d they be indeed, if they did not by degrees make me look upon the affairs of the world with a healthy deliberation."[13]

Still, Keats's reiterated aversion to "consequitive" thought is part of the record and deserves more than dismissal as momentary aberration or self-deception. He clearly chose between alternatives, though it may be that the alternatives are less mutually exclusive than many people wish to think. Actually, the conflict is not between reason and unreason but between methods of perceiving coherent relationships among experiential elements within a rational framework. Keats's adjective merely defines the difference between the logical and the poetic processes: in logical (i.e. "consequitive") thought, one thing *leads to* another; in poetic thought, one thing is perceived to be *like* another in its essence or

---

[10] *Ibid.*, 218.   [11] *Ibid.*, II, 101-4.   [12] *Ibid.*, I, 280-82.
[13] *Ibid.*, II, 128.

its configuration or its effect on the perceiver. In neither case does the individual fact have meaningful existence outside some context of relationship. Both modes may be said to be rational processes in that the assimilating and ordering medium is human reason. While the logical method is consecutive, and the poetic associational, both can be, and often have been, schematized into comprehensive value systems.

It will be one of the arguments of this study that Keats did systematize his perceptions and that he was governed, through much of his poetic career, by the system he had formulated. It was primarily, however, a system rooted in analogy, and, while it pretended to a certain consecutiveness at its upper levels, its logic was built upon analogies among data not properly comparable.

But Keats's indifference to, or skepticism of, this sort of objection is implicit in such of his observations as: "Can it be that even the greatest Philosopher ever . . . arrived at his goal without putting aside numerous objections"[14] and, "it is an old maxim of mine . . . that eve[r]y point of thought is the centre of an intellectual world—the two uppermost thoughts in a Man's mind are the two poles of his World he revolves on them and every thing is southward or northward to him through their means—We take but three steps from feathers to iron."[15] Both of these statements doubt the possibility of a comprehensive objectivity, the first by supposing a goal whose achievement has priority over integrity of means, the second by supposing a limitation of human capacity to escape the initial frame of speculative reference. In making such statements, Keats reveals, of course, something about the characteristic bent of his own thought processes, something which finds expression in the tenor of his poetry throughout its whole extent.

[14] *Ibid.*, i, 185.   [15] *Ibid.*, 243.

INTRODUCTION

The tendency to which I refer is that of the religious
mind. There is a practical difference between the working methods of the uncommitted and the committed
metaphysician, between the pursuers of "truth" and of
"Truth." Both operate in the same area of transcendent
value, but the conclusions of the uncommitted philosopher are *merely* true, carrying desiderative but not pre-
scriptive implications for human behavior, while the conclusions of the religious philosopher are *absolutely* true,
and hence establish imperatives for personal behavior.
The uncommitted philosopher may conclude that all effects originate in a purposive deity, but he feels no necessity to conclude so, and he will carry his argument only
so far as, and in whatever direction, his evidence leads
him. The religiously committed philosopher begins with
the supposition of purposive deity and explains known
effects in terms of the given cause. He will omit evidence
that leads to other conclusions on the ground that the
inadequacy of his human understanding to assimilate it
properly should not be allowed to obscure the fact that
such effects as he is dealing with demand such a cause
as he has posited. He has a "goal" and will "put aside
numerous objections" to reach it; he has his working pos-
tulates, and "every thing is southward or northward to
him through their means."[16] The phrases used by Keats

[16] One is tempted to cite, by way of illustration, Newman's fewer
than three steps from feathers to iron, "*if* there be a God, *since*
there is a God, the human race is implicated . . ." [*Apologia pro
Vita sua*, ed. Wilfrid Ward (Oxford, 1913), p. 335], which rapid
progression from doubt to certainty he justifies precisely on the
ground of there being so little objective evidence of God's existence in man's wretched world that it is necessary to postulate
Him as the Creator from Whom man has *fallen away* into his present misery [*ibid.*, pp. 333-35]. In charity, one might recall that
Kingsley had challenged Newman to prove, in effect, not the being of God but the extent of his actual faith in that Being—in
which context a weak argument is tactically more effective than

[8]

in expressing what he takes to be axiomatic in speculative activity reveal unmistakably the essentially religious quality of his own mind.

In saying so, however, I find myself directly opposed to the only scholar who has tried to evaluate Keats's work in the light of specifically religious criteria. Professor Hoxie Neale Fairchild repeatedly denies that anything like an authentic religious attitude finds expression in Keats's poetry. He grants Keats a certain exuberant paganism but insists that "Even when most earnest and intense, his paganism is much more aesthetic than religious. . . ."[17] Unfortunately, one feels throughout Professor Fairchild's monumental study a blurring of the necessary distinction between general religiosity of outlook and specific sectarian commitment. On this point I find interesting the remarks of an Anglican clergyman and professor of theology who distinguishes centrally between "having a religion" and "being religious." He sees the latter as of first importance, since it is the spirit, and not the outward profession, that performs the essential religious function of integrating and directing the whole life of the individual. In the light of this distinction, he accepts as genuine, if inferior, modes of "being religious" any sincere and wholehearted submission of the self to a purpose outside the self, including such seemingly remote concerns as programmatic political action and the search for scientific truth.[18]

Such latitude of definition is likely to have more appeal for psychologists, however, than for theologians or

---

a strong one, faith being the more remarkable and the more necessary as rational grounds for belief diminish. Regardless of occasion, however, the method is revelatory.

[17] Hoxie Neale Fairchild, *Religious Trends in English Poetry* (New York, 1949), III, 462.

[18] A. C. Bouquet, *Comparative Religion* (Pelican Books, 1945), pp. 13-14.

even the general laity. In the ordinary understanding of what it means to have a religious mind, we would, of course, expect to find something more, something which is no doubt implicit but yet not expressed in this objective distinction. Whatever the object of one's devotion, we expect to catch in the treatment of it a strain of reverence. And I submit that only a gross insensitivity to poetic tone could miss that abounding reverence which is almost the hallmark of Keats's poetry. Much of his aesthetic pleasure, indeed, even in paganism's artifacts, was rooted in this anterior disposition. To Joseph Severn, and it was typical of him, he once used the immutable eternality of the Holy Ghost as a conceptual referent for the spirit that he felt to be expressed in Greek art.[19] Absurd or offensive as some Christian communicants may find the comparison, it nonetheless demonstrates Keats's instinctive frame of reference.

Other critics, as different from each other as they are from Professor Fairchild, have found in Keats's poetry what he did not. Frances M. Owen, one of the first to undertake a full-scale study of the poet, noted a "curious silence throughout the poems on the subject of religious *belief* . . ." but found in *Endymion* and *Hyperion* "a diffused spirituality which gives . . . the impression of a mind liberated from the desire of definite religious expression because permeated with its essence. . . ."[20] M. H. Abrams has been struck by Keats's "almost priestly consecration . . ."[21] and G. Wilson Knight, compelled toward the same terminology, feels that Keats's poetry has the quality of ritual, the poet being seen through it as the priest-like celebrant. From my own experience of the

[19] William Sharp, *The Life and Letters of Joseph Severn* (New York, 1892), p. 29.

[20] Frances M. Owen, *John Keats* (London, 1880), pp. 178-79.

[21] M. H. Abrams, *The Mirror and the Lamp: Romantic Theory and the Critical Tradition* (New York, 1953), p. 328.

[10]

poetry, I must agree with Knight's conclusion that "His whole work moves to this point, challenging our limited sense not of the beautiful but the sacred."[22] One may quite properly decide that one does not feel the same experiences to be sacred that Keats did, but this ought in no way to diminish awareness of that capacity for reverence, or awe of the not-self, which is manifested throughout Keats's poetry and in which religious experience may be said to begin.

None of this is intended to suggest, of course, that Keats was either consciously or unconsciously a "good Christian." To be sure, one could find worse models than Keats for the conduct of life, but Christianity, while it has promulgated a great social ethic, would mean very little if it were no more than a social ethic. And whether we find shocking or amusing those romantic enthusiasts who are wont to find parallels between the lives of Christ and Keats, we must be concerned finally not with ex post facto typology but with the essential quality of a major poetic career. The only question that is immediately relevant is that of Keats's attitude toward doctrinal Christianity, the deepest intellectual and spiritual current of that European culture in which his poetry had its origins and of which it was to become not the least significant part. The answer to the question is that, while he absorbed the cultural effects of its symbols and values, he found himself unable to subscribe to its doctrines and strongly opposed to its force as a social institution. He often used its vocabulary as a means of expressing supernal absolutes, but he rejected its theology and authority.

[22] G. Wilson Knight, *The Starlit Dome: Studies in the Poetry of Vision* (London, 1941), p. 304. Knight's remarks originate in a discussion of the "Ode to Psyche," but he makes similar judgments throughout his discussion of Keats (pp. 258-307), the general tenor of which is indicated by his chapter title, "The Priest-like Task: an Essay on Keats."

Should one argue that the catechistic letter to his sister Fanny[23] and the confidence in immortality which he expressed after his brother Tom's death[24] show at least a rudimentary knowledge and implicit acceptance of Christian doctrine, it is only fair to point out that these were both "occasional" expressions, written under circumstances in which he would scarcely be expected to speak (or, in the latter case, to know) his everyday mind. His outbursts at the time of his own approaching death are more revealing: he felt the "horrible want of some faith"[25] and reflected bitterly on his incapacity to have "this last cheap comfort—which every rogue and fool have," the consolation of sincere Christian belief.[26] Throughout his recorded life he never had a kind word to say for the Christian Church. He was opposed to its interposition of what he considered to be a humanly fallible but nevertheless authoritarian sacerdotal institution between man and the object of his reverence. He tended to see the institution as conspiratorial, engaged, for the profit of the ecclesiastical hierarchy, in the suppression of natural passion and right reason through the propagation of superstition and the dogmatic forcing of individual conscience.[27] His objections, in other words, were

23 *Letters*, II, 49-51. 24 *Ibid.*, 4.

25 *The Keats Circle Letters and Papers, 1816-1878*, ed. Hyder Edward Rollins (Cambridge, Mass., 1948), I, 181. This work will be cited hereafter as *Keats Circle*.

26 *Keats Circle*, I, 197.

27 For a representative sampling of Keats's comments on Christianity, see *Letters*, I, 137 (concerning the report of a contemporary Austrian sect who practiced human sacrifice, "—and do Christians shudder at the same thing in a Newspaper which the[y] attribute to their God in its most aggravated form?"); I, 178-79 (the mean abuse of authority within the Church hierarchy); I, 179, (the desirability of a natural religion, uncontaminated by institutional authoritarianism); I, 281-82 (the historical superstition and cruelty of the Church, only partially purged by the Reformation); I, 319-20 (the emotional impoverishment of the people by the

not to reverence but to what he conceived of as its cynical exploitation and perversion. Much of this anticlerical attitude probably reflects his revolt against the authority, and consequently the values, of his guardian, the "bigoted puritan"[28] Richard Abbey—a revolt which was nourished by the antiauthoritarian political liberalism imbibed, as early as his Enfield School days, from the Hunts' *Examiner*.[29] But, wherever his views were acquired, they were constant throughout his life.

Here then was Keats's dilemma: Inclined toward speculative activity and a basically religious view of life, yet out of sympathy with the dominant metaphysical mode of organizing experience in that culture to which he must address his poetry, how was he to proceed? The problem was by no means uniquely his,[30] and it is unlikely that

Church, here the Scots Kirk); ii, 63, 70 (the intellectual and moral vices of the clergy); ii, 80 (the splendor of the man Jesus obscured "by Men interested in the pious frauds of Religion."); ii, 101-104 (a system of salvation [the world as a "vale of Soul-making"] which, unlike Christianity, "does not affront our reason and humanity" because it takes account of the human heart).

[28] This characterization of Abbey, which has been echoed in various ways by most Keatsians, is from Claude Lee Finney, *The Evolution of Keats's Poetry* (Cambridge, Mass., 1936), i, 14. Cf. the similar views of Keats's most recent biographers, Walter Jackson Bate, *John Keats* (Cambridge, Mass., 1963), pp. 29-30, and, more gently, Aileen Ward, *John Keats: The Making of a Poet* (New York, 1963), pp. 20-21.

[29] The best treatments of Keats's political views are Clarence DeWitt Thorpe, "Keats's Interest in Politics and World Affairs, *PMLA*, xlvi (1931), 1228-45; and Herbert G. Wright, "Keats and Politics," *Essays and Studies by Members of the English Association*, xviii (1932), 7-23.

[30] The general dilemma has been widely recognized. Earl R. Wasserman, for example, has observed that "with the nineteenth century almost all accredited systems of ordering experience had broken down," with the result that the individual poet "had to make his poetic world before he could make his poems, because first he had to work out the functional relations of his experiences" [*The Finer Tone: Keats' Major Poems* (Baltimore, 1953), p. 228].

he ever formulated it in precisely these terms, but it did exist, and it did have to be met.

Like others of his time, but none more conspicuously, Keats met it by turning to a cultural taproot which had been largely neglected in the poetry of the Neoclassic age, the mythology of classical antiquity. Here he found, in the very origins of Western cultural history, a ready-made vocabulary and symbolism of those natural forces and ideal concepts on the balance of which he believed the cultural health of the individual to depend, and which he thought to be artificially stifled by the prevailing Christian culture. Perhaps it is inaccurate to imply, with the word "found," that he suddenly discovered this mine of elemental poetic ore, for his fascination with myth antedated his poetic career. But at some point very early in his writing life, certainly before he had firmly settled upon poetry as a profession, he had discovered the utility of myth and had constructed a fairly elaborate aesthetic upon its foundation. The outline of that structure, its effects on Keats's poetry, and its place and fate in his developing artistic thought, will occupy much of our attention in the following pages.

For the present, we might consider some general aspects of this mythological concern. Although he alludes

---

T. S. Eliot implies that the expectations of the poetic audience aggravated the problem, for the "decay of religion, and the attrition of political institutions" led the public to expect "religious aliment" from its poetry, so that the poet had tacitly to accept the status of lay-priest [*The Use of Poetry and the Use of Criticism* (London, 1933), p. 16]. No doubt the peak of this expectation came later in the century, at about the time Matthew Arnold was urging, in "The Study of Poetry," that poetry was the inheritor of a defunct religion's obligation. That Arnold could urge such a claim testifies indirectly to the success with which the earlier Romantics had met the problem of aesthetic communication in a fragmented culture. If it also testifies to a radical confusion of Victorian values, that is not a question to debate here.

frequently to the human heroes of classical story, Keats's primary interest was in the deities, and these are extraordinarily prominent in his poetry. His earliest known poem, the "Imitation of Spenser," contains references to Morning (his name for, presumably, Aurora) and Flora. *Endymion* and *Hyperion*, the two "long" poems upon which Keats expended perhaps the greatest efforts of his brief career, are entirely given to the celebration and elaboration of myths centered in deity. Within *Endymion* are embedded separate hymns to, characterizations of, or addresses to Apollo, Bacchus, Cupid, Diana, Neptune, Pan, and Venus. In the remaining body of his work there are odes to Apollo, Maia, and Psyche, apostrophic sonnets and odes to Autumn, Fame, Hope, Peace, Sleep, and Solitude, all conceived in the vein of classical personification, and virtually innumerable allusions to and inclusions of Olympian matter, throughout. Needless to say, this remarkable concern has not gone unnoticed in critical writing.

Among his contemporaries, Leigh Hunt, who shared and sometimes engendered Keats's sympathies, recognized and approved of the centrality of myth in Keats's poetic imagination. For him it was sufficient commendation to say of the poet that "he never beheld an oak-tree without seeing the Dryad."[31] The same tendency in Keats's poetry was observed in another light by John Clare, the "Peasant Poet," with whom, through their mutual friend and publisher, John Taylor, Keats appears to have carried on a sporadic critical debate.[32] Clare objected to Keats's "constant alusion or illusion to the gre-

[31] Leigh Hunt, *Imagination and Fancy; or Selections from the English Poets*, A New Edition (London, 1891), p. 283.

[32] The debate, such as it was, is summarized in June Wilson, *Green Shadows: The Life of John Clare* (London, 1951), pp. 85-86.

cian mythology . . . when he speaks of woods Dryads & Fawns are sure to follow & the brook looks alone without her naiads to his mind yet the frequency of such classical accompaniment make it wearisome to the reader where behind every rose bush he looks for a Venus & under every laurel a thrumming Appollo. . . . he often described nature as she appeared to his fancies & not as he would . . . had he witnessed the things he describes."[33] Clare's objection to the overuse of mythology was echoed by Byron, whose objection, however, was less to the purported falsification of nature than to the impropriety of a relatively uneducated Cockney's presuming to poetry at all, and especially to an allusive poetry oriented toward classical antiquity. Keats's verse, he sneered, consisted merely of "versifying Tooke's Pantheon and Lemprière's Dictionary."[34] But after Keats's death, and under persistent pressure from Shelley,[35] Byron relented to the rather grudging extent of acknowledging, in as public a place as *Don Juan* (XI, LX), that in *Hyperion* Keats had "without Greek / Contrived to talk about the Gods of late, / Much as they might have been supposed to speak."

Contemporary comment was primarily given to such expressions of approval or annoyance, and it was not until later scholars began to examine Keats's work that any serious attempt was made to explain, evaluate, or interpret the infusion of myth in his poetry. His first biographer, Richard Monckton Milnes,[36] set the tone for what

[33] *The Prose of John Clare*, ed. J. W. and Anne Tibble (London, 1951), p. 223.

[34] *The Works of Lord Byron: Letters and Journals*, ed. Rowland E. Prothero, 6 vols. (London, 1901), v, 269.

[35] According to Thomas Medwin, *Journal of the Conversations of Lord Byron: Noted during a Residence with His Lordship at Pisa, in the Years 1821 and 1822* (London, 1824), p. 294.

[36] I discount the brief "Life" by Keats's friend Charles Brown, which was delivered as a lecture before the Plymouth Institution on December 27, 1836, and was subsequently transmitted to

has become, on the whole justly, the general conception of Keats's orientation toward classical myth. Noting that the poet had a thorough but not vast command of Latin, and no Greek at all, Milnes commented, "Yet Tooke's 'Pantheon,' Spence's 'Polymetis,' and Lemprière's 'Dictionary,' were sufficient fully to introduce his imagination to the enchanted world of old mythology; with this, at once, he became intimately acquainted, and a natural consanguinity, so to say, of intellect, soon domesticated him with the ancient ideal life, so that his scanty scholarship supplied him with a clear perception of classic beauty, and led the way to that wonderful reconstruction of Grecian feeling and fancy, of which his mind became afterwards capable."[37] Various attempts have been made to broaden the acknowledged base of Keats's direct familiarity with classical literature,[38] but most subsequent studies have agreed that the poet succeeded in revivifying the old mythology through a natural sympathy with the spirit in which it originated.[39]

In his monumental, and in many ways excellent, history of English poetry, W. J. Courthope later struck a note, not dissenting but critical, which is still occasion-

---

Milnes, with revisions, for his use in preparing his own work on Keats. Since Brown's memoir was not published for a hundred years after its composition, it had no direct effect on the poet's reputation. It can now be consulted in the following editions: Dorothy Hyde Bodurtha and Willard Bissell Pope (eds.), *Life of John Keats By Charles Armitage Brown* (London, 1937); and *Keats Circle*, II, 52-97.

[37] Richard Monckton Milnes, *Life, Letters, and Literary Remains, of John Keats* (New York, 1848), p. 17.

[38] E.g. Herbert Warren, "Keats as a Classical Scholar," *The Nineteenth Century and After*, XCIII (1923), 62-68; and Douglas Bush, "Notes on Keats's Reading," *PMLA*, L (1935), 785-806.

[39] With the exception, as in so many other matters, of Amy Lowell, who maintains that "Keats never had the slightest knowledge or comprehension of the true Greek spirit." *John Keats*, 2 vols. (Boston and New York, 1925), I, 346.

ally heard. Courthope contended that Keats's natural feeling for "the mythological spirit of pagan times," combined with "a voluptuous perception of beauty in natural things, and a brilliant fancy which enabled him readily to abstract ideal forms from the objects presented to his eye," led him toward a mythologized nature poetry which was essentially pictorial, and therefore static, and that his motive was the creation of an ideal atmosphere, free from the dynamic social flux of his own age.[40] There is surely some element of truth in this argument, reluctant though one may be to grant it, and difficult though it may be to measure its extent. It can certainly be said, however, that flight was not Keats's conscious intention, and I think it will not be too difficult to show that his ideal vision comprehended more than mere verbal statuary.

Full acceptance of Keats as a major poet has led, of course, to special studies of particular qualities in his work, and his use of mythology has been the subject of several of these. Before the end of Keats's own century, a French critic had questioned the extent to which his extraordinary employment of myth conveyed any of the values associated with the culture from which it was derived. He concluded that Keats's mythologizing, through *Endymion*, exists for its own sake, and, while embodying great intensity of feeling, is revelatory of nothing profound enough to warrant the use of its machinery;[41] but that, in his mature work, Keats's acute sensitivity to external form[42] and his perception of the earth- and life-

[40] William John Courthope, A *History of English Poetry*, Volume 6: "The Romantic Movement in English Poetry" (London, 1910), pp. 323, 350.
[41] Joseph Texte, "Keats et le néo-hellenisme dans la poésie anglaise," in *Etudes de littérature européenne* (Paris, 1898), p. 116.
[42] *Ibid.*, p. 141.

centered quality of the Greek spirit[43] entitle him to be
called "the most Greek of the English poets."[44]

Much the best treatment of the subject, and one of the
best essays on Keats ever written, is Margaret Sherwood's
excellent discussion of Keats's mythological orientation.
Its essential statement is that myth was a necessary
mode of utterance for the young poets of Keats's time,
who required a new poetic vocabulary for the expression
of a new view of man's nature and destiny,[45] and that the
special role of myth in Keats's work was its provision of
a means by which he was enabled to interpret and express his insights into the operative processes of nature,[46]
the principle of harmonious unity in all life,[47] and the
fulfillment of individual destiny through obedience to
nature's laws.[48]

Douglas Bush's invaluable survey of mythology in
romantic poetry finds in Keats's work "a progressive adaptation of myth to humanitarian symbolism,"[49] sustained
by a native "myth-making instinct,"[50] an ability upon occasion to draw together into unity the separate strands
of myth, nature, and literature,[51] and a willingness to
alter received myth freely, accepting any of its post-
classical accretions in order to make it serve the poet's
own ends.[52] Perhaps too much has been made, in Keats
scholarship generally, of the poet's purported growth toward humanitarian sympathy, and consequently of the
effective means for its expression, but the intention is

[43] *Ibid.*, p. 142.   [44] *Ibid.*, p. 130.
[45] Margaret Sherwood, "Keats' Imaginative Approach to Myth,"
in *Undercurrents of Influence in English Romantic Poetry* (Cambridge, Mass., 1934), p. 206.
[46] *Ibid.*, pp. 211-12.   [47] *Ibid.*, pp. 215, 263-64.
[48] *Ibid.*, pp. 218, 264.
[49] Douglas Bush, *Mythology and the Romantic Tradition in English Poetry* (Cambridge, Mass., 1937), p. 84.
[50] *Ibid.*, p. 105.   [51] *Ibid.*, p. 106.   [52] *Ibid.*, p. 118.

pious and must not be deprecated. Professor Bush's insight into Keats's expansion and adaptation of received myth is, however, of the very first importance in understanding the poet's working method.

Romantic adaptation of received myth verges on a chapter in the history of poetry and ideas that has only recently been receiving the attention that it deserves, the mythological syncretist movement of the eighteenth and early nineteenth centuries. Engaging the energies of serious theologians, lay scholars, and a fascinating assortment of the lunatic fringe, it had an intellectual vogue that has perhaps been underestimated simply because its primary assumption has been discredited (i.e. that all the world's religions and mythological systems derive from an ur-myth which embodied a universal system of natural religion). There are hints, in his mythographic eclecticism, that Keats was aware of, and in some casual ways influenced by, this activity, but the attempt to interpret his major poems in the light of it has so far been more suggestive than revelatory.[53]

A recent tendency in literary criticism, perhaps more relevant to the history of criticism than to our immediate purpose, is yet of tangential interest. The mode here is to establish a dialectic of some familiar antithesis (pain-

[53] Edward B. Hungerford, *Shores of Darkness* (New York, 1941), pp. 106-62, discusses *Endymion* and *Hyperion* at length, the former with unpleasant condescension and baffling irrelevance to the main topic of his study, though with generally convincing argument respecting hitherto unsuspected "sources" of narrative detail; the latter with more attention to his thesis and a plausible conjecture about the poem's over-all design, but with what sometimes strikes me as a far fetch in the details.

Other useful contributions to the literature of the historical phenomenon, though more remote from our immediate interest, are: Albert J. Kuhn, "English Deism and the Development of Romantic Mythological Syncretism," *PMLA*, LXXI (1956), 1094-1116; and Frank E. Manuel, *The Eighteenth Century Confronts the Gods* (Cambridge, Mass.), 1959.

pleasure, action-contemplation, real-ideal, time-eternity),
give it a two-headed mythological name, and then discuss
some poet's work in terms of the mythologically denom-
inated pairs. Thus, Allen Tate, observing Keats's interest
in the semantic and experiential ambiguities of love, locates the center of the poet's concern in an attempt to
reconcile the claims of the Uranian and Pandemian Aph-
rodites.[54] Robert Wooster Stallman fixes upon Keats's
preoccupation with time, finding it his "cardinal theme,
figuring either as the total intention of his poems or as
the obsessive motif of his minute particulars."[55] This he
discusses in terms of Spengler's Apollinian-Faustian dialectic (i.e. the static, disengaged, momentary sense-pres-
ent vs. the dynamics of temporal and spatial infinity),
concluding, as his title indicates, that Keats is at his characteristic best when Apollinian. Dorothy Van Ghent sees
the theme underlying the whole body of Keats's work as
the struggle of the Dionysian character (compact of unreconciled opposites) to become Apollinian (balanced),
through a process of dying into life.[56] Dorothy Van
Ghent, indeed, takes the final step into cultural anthro-
pology and views all the poetry (though she is chiefly
concerned with Keats's "epics") as ritual externalization,
on familiar archetypal patterns, of those human instincts
that produced the very mythology upon which Keats
drew.

Although Mrs. Van Ghent uses Keats's own mythological characters as representative of his Apollinian ideal
(Adonis in *Endymion*, the Titans [!] in *Hyperion*), it is

[54] Allen Tate, "A Reading of Keats," *The American Scholar*, xv
(1945-46), 55-63, 189-97.
[55] Robert Wooster Stallman, "Keats the Apollinian: The Time-
and-Space Logic of His Poems as Paintings," *UTQ*, xvi (1947),
143.
[56] Dorothy Van Ghent, "Keats's Myth of the Hero," *K-SJ*, iii
(1954), 7-25.

clear that in this recent phase of criticism we have moved away from Keats's mythology to the more catholic pantheon of his commentators. The one fact that emerges from the whole survey, however, is that no one considers Keats's mythography, except in some of his apprentice poetry, as merely incidental, decorative, exotic, or imitative. There is a variety of opinion about its precise function and meaning for him, and about his dexterity in its use, but general agreement that it is a truly organic element in his poetry. In the pages that follow, I hope to confirm that general impression and to show in detail the place of this mythography in his aesthetic and its effect on the poems he left us.

ONE

Imitatio Apollinis

IT IS commonly assumed that Keats in his early poetic career was intellectually tentative, uncertain, and exploratory, dominated by a powerful desire to be a poet while as yet unable to arrive at a conceptual view of either life or art adequate to give substantial body to his aspirations. This phase, one understands, lasted through, and some months beyond, the composition of *Endymion.* But by about late summer 1818, we are told, Keats had somehow acquired a clarity of mind and maturity of artistic vision that enabled him to produce, within little more than a year, a significant number of superbly wrought, enduring poems.[1]

[1] One may take as representative of this dominant attitude Claude Lee Finney, *The Evolution of Keats's Poetry,* II, 741: "There was considerable storm and stress in Keats's mind before he attained a balance and harmony between the different faculties of his mind. The chief problem of his life consisted in his endeavor to develop a philosophy of life and poetry which would satisfy every faculty of his mind in its reaction to the facts of his experience. . . . [In] the spring of 1819 he established [his philosophy of negative capability] upon a sound empirical basis. This philosophy, which satisfied every faculty of his mind, ushered in the great creative period of his poetry." In an earlier attempt at full-scale evaluation of Keats, Frances M. Owen, *John Keats,* pp. 29-30, set the tone in asserting that the poet did not until 1820 reconcile his conflicts, but then came to realize "that the sense of beauty . . . is incomplete until it . . . allies itself with . . . reality. . . ." Sidney Colvin, *John Keats* (New York, 1917), p. 52, agreed that the poet underwent an intellectual maturing process in which, "as time went on, delighted sensation became more and more surely . . . transmuted and spiritualized into imaginative emotion . . . and symbolic suggestion." Ernest de Selincourt, "The Warton Lecture

There is considerable warrant for seeing Keats's career in these terms. One has only to compare the early "Calidore" fragment with the two Hyperion fragments, the early lyric ode "To Hope" with the odes of 1819, or the narrative *Endymion* with the narrative *Lamia* in order

on Keats," in *The John Keats Memorial Volume* (London, 1921), throughout his remarks assumed such a development, asserting, for instance, that "twelve months of strenuous intellectual effort" produced a *Hyperion* which was superior to the earlier poetry because its heroic theme "gave little scope to the weaker side of his genius which had luxuriated in the mazes of *Endymion*" [p. 11]. Hugh I'A. Fausset, *Keats: A Study in Development* (London, 1922), p. 118, says that Keats only "in his last days" came to know that it is "the poet's highest duty to enter by a sympathetic understanding into the life not only of nature but of man, and by that complete identification with the universe . . . win the power to vision for man a world of higher harmonies." B. Ifor Evans, *Tradition and Romanticism* (London, 1940), p. 137, and Aileen Ward, *John Keats: The Making of a Poet*, pp. 178-80, are among those who see Keats coming to intellectual maturity in the two versions of *Hyperion*. Walter Jackson Bate, *John Keats*, pp. 323, *passim*, in his own way follows the majority lead to the discovery, well on in Keats's writing-life, of a "new self-clarification, indispensable to the poetry of his final year and a half. . . ."

Dissidents from this general view would seem to include Clarence DeWitt Thorpe, *The Mind of John Keats*, p. 25, who maintains that "Almost from the first he was thinking hard on the nature of poetry and the poetic art." But Thorpe is principally concerned with aesthetic, at this point in his study, and he allows that, in the wider sphere, it was not until "after the failure of *Endymion*" that "there began to take place in the mind of Keats a clarification process in which the eternal facts of poetry in their relation to life were to have proper perspective" [p. 27]. Amy Lowell, *John Keats*, throughout, and H. W. Garrod, *Keats* (Oxford, 1926), prefer not to think of Keats thinking. The *locus classicus* of their position (and it is perhaps the only point on which Garrod could have brought himself to agree with Miss Lowell) is probably Garrod's "I think him the great poet he is only when the senses capture him, when he finds truth in beauty, that is to say, when he does not trouble to find truth at all" [p. 61]. Raymond D. Havens, "Unreconciled Opposites in Keats," *PQ*, xiv (1935), 290, believes that Keats was not necessarily moving in any direction intellectually, whatever might have been his movement poetically,

to mark an extraordinary growth in vividness of articulation and firmness of control. There is, moreover, the poet's own later admission to Shelley that, through the writing of *Endymion* at least, his "mind was like a pack of scattered cards."[2]

The trouble with this view is that it tends to judge the *nature of the mind* by the *quality of its achievement*. We are, of course, interested in the mind primarily because of its achievement. But great poetry results from the successful fusion of many elements, only one of which is its conceptual orientation, and we risk being seriously misled if we equate successful communication with conceptual vigor and failure of communication with con-

---

and that many have been deceived about the poet's mental life because they failed to see that "he passed rapidly from one position to another . . . and then back again," but "felt and expressed the opinions of the moment as if they were the inalterable convictions of a life-time." More recently, David Perkins, *The Quest for Permanence: The Symbolism of Wordsworth, Shelley and Keats* (Cambridge, Mass., 1959), has asserted that "as Keats developed, no major tendency of his imagination was dropped" [p. 192]. What he means by this is that the central fact of Keats's poetry is the desire for escape from the experience of flux, which is expressed early in the isolated contemplation of suburban prettiness and late in a recurrent death-wish. The antique flavor of these conclusions belies those gifts of observation and analysis which are evident whenever Mr. Perkins feels free to exercise them. Many years before all these commentators, and in an entirely different spirit, Elizabeth Barrett Browning had presented an idealized Keats, emancipated from the normal human developmental process, in "Aurora Leigh" (i, 1003-1006), as:

> . . . the man who never stepped
> In gradual progress like another man,
> But, turning grandly on his central self,
> Ensphered himself in twenty perfect years.

Such argument as there has been, then, is between those who see no real intellectual development and those who see the poet as unintellectual in his early career but firmly in control of his ideas at the end.

² *Letters*, ii, 323.

ceptual vacuity. The mind of Keats's brief poetic maturity was indeed significantly different from that which sought expression in the poetry through *Endymion*. But I believe it can be demonstrated that early in his career the poet conceptualized far more widely, firmly and deliberately than, with intermittent exceptions, he did during the period of his major work. I suggest, further, that the brilliance and intensity (and in some cases even the existence) of the later poems is to some extent the result of a loss of faith in what had been for him a guiding conceptual rationale, and that this loss of faith was accompanied by a radical shrinking of the poet's philosophic horizon.

The misleading factor in assessing Keats's intellectual development is the superb rhetoric, or diction, of the later poems—what Keats called, in the letter to Shelley cited above, "the Poetry" or "Mammon," as opposed to the "purpose" or "God" of a poem. This part of the letter is important enough to be recalled in full: "I received a copy of the Cenci, as from yourself from Hunt. There is only one part of it I am judge of; the Poetry, and dramatic effect, which by many spirits now a days is considered the mammon. A modern work it is said must have a purpose, which may be the God—*an artist* must serve Mammon—he must have 'self concentration' selfishness perhaps. You I am sure will forgive me for sincerely remarking that you might curb your magnanimity and be more of an artist, and 'load every rift' of your subject with ore. The thought of such discipline must fall like cold chains upon you, who perhaps never sat with your wings furl'd for six Months together. And is not this extraordina[r]y talk for the writer of Endymion? whose mind was like a pack of scattered cards—I am pick'd up and sorted to a pip. My Imagination is a Monastery and I am its Monk—you must explain my metap^{cs}

to yourself."[3] It is evident from the distinction, both figuratively and literally made, between "purpose" and "Poetry," and from the Spenserian image which follows, having to do with loading every rift of the *subject* with poetic ore, that as late as mid-1820 (i.e. to the very end of his active writing-life) Keats habitually divorced poetic form and content. I say "habitually" because this is not the first example of such a separation in the poet's view of his craft. During the writing of *Endymion*, three years earlier, he had made a significant comment in the same vein: "I must make 4000 Lines of one bare circumstance and *fill them with Poetry*."[4] What one had to say was one thing; the way in which one said it was another. Both were parts of the process of creating poems, but they were separable parts.

One might take as symptomatic of Keats's relative concern for the two parts his comments on them at different stages in his career. It was while he was revising the proofs of *Endymion* that he tossed off the axiom, "if Poetry comes not as naturally as the Leaves to a tree it had better not come at all."[5] The context of the remark suggests that he was speaking not of complete poems but of "Poetry" as he used the word to Shelley and as he used it in connection with the filling of *Endymion*'s 4000 lines, i.e. as pictorial and verbal texture. While he had definite ideas about the effect a poem should make, he does not show here any great concern for poetic surface, such as he so earnestly urged upon Shelley at a later time. He takes it for granted. And it has often enough been lamented by later commentators (especially of *Endymion*) that he did not sufficiently discipline himself in the earlier poetry, all too often losing his subject under the variegated verbal cover with which it was overlaid.

[3] *Ibid.*, 322-23.   [4] *Ibid.*, I, 169-70, italics mine.
[5] *Ibid.*, 238-39.

Keats did, in fact, admit that most of his early work had been "dash'd of[f] . . . in a hurry."[6] However, in the writing of the "Ode to Psyche," in April 1819, when he was just short of the peak of his achievement, he claimed to have worked at a "leisurely" pace, to have taken "pains," and he felt that the poem read "the more richly for it."[7] Should there be any doubt about what precisely he took pains with, the temper of his mind at the time is clearly indicated in the sonnet "If by dull rhymes" where, urging a new form for the English sonnet, he counseled his fellow poets to

> inspect the Lyre & weigh the stress
> Of every chord & see what may be gained
> By ear industrious & attention meet,
> Misers of sound & syllable. . . .[8]

This was copied, a mere three days later, into the same letter in which he commented on the pains he had taken with "Psyche." Quite clearly he was preoccupied with "sound and syllable" in a way that he had not been when he made the cavalier pronouncement about "Poetry" coming as naturally as leaves to a tree. Given the separable elements of a poem, as he defined them, his lesser concern for "Poetry" at the earlier period and his urgent preoccupation with it at the later time may be taken as at least minimally indicative of a greater and lesser interest in "purpose" during the same two periods.

In any case, it has not been sufficiently emphasized elsewhere that it is in the context of this heightened attention to integrity of poetic form that his remark to Shelley, about having had a mind like a pack of scattered cards, must be understood. For one thing, the "mind" he speaks of is not philosophic but poetic, in Keats's special

---

[6] *Ibid.*, II, 106.   [7] *Ibid.*, 105-106.
[8] I use the text in *Letters*, II, 108.

sense, as the next sentence shows, where "Imagination" is used as a synonym for it. For another, he had been upbraiding Shelley for concerning himself too much with intellectual content and too little with poetic form. He was reminded by Shelley's letter before him that the other had recently been rereading *Endymion,* and he felt obliged, in defense of his position, to disavow it as an example of his precepts. If it is "extraordinary" for the author of *Endymion* to counsel less attention to "purpose" and more to "Poetry," it must be because *Endymion's* faults are similar to those he is criticizing in Shelley. Concerned primarily with its "purpose," he had allowed his imagination to burgeon with whatever came "naturally" to it. He had not disciplined the "Poetry"; he had used it as mere filler, and not always of the purest ore, and the poem was therefore a failure. This self-critical admission of former weakness functions tactically as an assertion of present strength, which in turn qualifies him to give advice about poetic finish—not conception but finish—with which, as we have seen, he had been increasingly concerned. It is this matter of finish—call it diction, rhetoric, or what one will—that chiefly distinguishes the later from the earlier poetry. And it is the magic and majesty of it that delude us into believing that Keats was thinking more comprehensively and deeply in his later poetry than in that of his apprenticeship. He was thinking differently, and perhaps better, but he was not thinking more; and he was by no means more content with the conclusions to which his thought led him.

The truth appears to be that in his early poetry Keats was looking, not for a substance to embody in poetic form, but for a form amenable to the intellectual formulation of the relationship between life and art that he had possessed from the very beginning of his poetic career. Such a form he thought he had found in *Endymion* and, at the time of its earliest conception, in *Hyperion*. Until then, he experimented with imitations of Spenser and the eighteenth-century ode, with verse epistles expressing the height of his aspiration, with narrative verse, with didactic-descriptive verse essays which seriously attempted, but failed, to embody his central conception, and with, of course, the sonnet. Fragments of, and therefore clues to, the poet's central conception are embedded in most of these pre-*Endymion* poems, as examination will show. In several places the poems, or parts of them, are unintelligible without an understanding of this conception. And a very few of them, quite unambiguously, tell the reader what the poet's basic assumptions are.

In order to provide a framework for the particulars with which we shall be concerned from now on, it might be helpful to sketch in at this point the outlines of Keats's central formulation. As the poet never gave it complete expression in any one place, it has been inferred from partial explanations and repeated allusions throughout the early poetry and from occasional hints in the letters. That Keats held such a view one infers from its touchstone quality, for virtually everything he wrote, through *Endymion*, conforms to its pattern, and some passages that have baffled commentators are reduced by its means to perfect comprehensibility—without, of course, becoming better poetry by that means. In outline, then, the poet's metaphysical and aesthetic hypothesis was as follows:

The complete spiritual cycle of individual human life and growth is comparable to the annual cycle of physical life and growth in external nature. These cycles are not only comparable by developmental analogy but are harmonious with each other because identically subject to the influence of a single beneficent power, or law, which manifests itself in and through them. This power is the law of universal harmony, by which all existing things are held in a balanced interrelationship with each other, and initially discrete elements are fused, through an assimilative growth process, into new, organically integrated entities. The power is best exemplified concretely in the late-Greek conception of the god Apollo.

As god of astronomy Apollo presides over the universal system of physical harmony; as god of medicine he maintains harmony among the physical elements of the human organism; as god of the sun he marks the passage of time and presides over the ripening of the fruits of earth; as god of song and poetry he presides over the ripening of human intellect and brings it to comparable fruition in a harvest of harmonious expression.

The process of intellectual ripening, however, is confined in its direct operation to those who acknowledge the god and are peculiarly able to perceive his power and influence, i.e. the poets. It is the poets' function to receive, interpret, and transmit knowledge of the god to men who ordinarily feel his influence less directly and who, without the poets' aid, do not properly understand it. The source of the poets' illumination, as it is the visible and demonstrable sphere of the god's activity, is the natural world. In it is found a concrete external reflection of that unifying and ripening activity which takes place concurrently, under the influence of the same power, within the maturing human soul. The world of nature therefore confirms the validity of, and serves as the understanding's bridge to, that ideal perfection of experience which the soul intuits with increasing clarity as it anticipates the further stages of its own growth.

The agency of fusion, in which all physical and spiritual elements of experience are comprehended by the poets as complementary aspects of a single harmony, is the imagination. Since the imagination perceives the world of idea to be a correlative half of the experiential whole, it is free of time and space and not bound to frame its visions within the relational limits of normal human reason. The imagination is fed by knowledge of the sense-world, whose elements it transmutes into their ideal counterparts. The imagination is therefore the mediating agency between the worlds of the mundane and the divine. Since the poets' function is mediatory, their role is variously priestly and oracular, in the immediate service of mankind and the ultimate service of the god. The poets' necessary medium of revelation to man and of homage to the god is song, for it is the nearest possible human approximation to the divine harmony which they have recognized in the natural world as the self-revelatory and tutorial voice of the god.

Although this notion of the god's speaking through nature is to some extent metaphorical, an important element in much of Keats's poetry is lost if we fail to recognize that, at least for purposes of expressing his conception, it is often understood quite literally by the poet. In order to see how this operates, and to introduce more concretely the conceptual synthesis outlined above, let us look at a particular poem, the "Ode to Apollo" of February 1815. As the clearest statement of his mythological aesthetic that Keats ever made, and as the gathering-place of most of its attendant associations, it is too important a work to be reproduced in anything less than its entirety.[9]

9 I cite the text of H. W. Garrod (ed.), *The Poetical Works of John Keats*, Second Edition (Oxford, 1958), hereafter to be cited simply as *Poetical Works*. Unless otherwise indicated in the notes, all subsequent quotations of Keats's poetry will be from the text.

ODE TO APOLLO

In thy western halls of gold
    When thou sittest in thy state,
Bards, that erst sublimely told
    Heroic deeds, and sang of fate,
With fervour seize their adamantine lyres,
Whose chords are solid rays, and twinkle radiant fires.

Here Homer with his nervous arms
    Strikes the twanging harp of war,
And even the western splendour warms,
    While the trumpets sound afar:
But, what creates the most intense surprise,
His soul looks out through renovated eyes.

Then, through thy Temple wide, melodious swells
    The sweet majestic tone of Maro's lyre:
The soul delighted on each accent dwells,—
    Enraptured dwells,—not daring to respire,
The while he tells of grief around a funeral pyre.

'Tis awful silence then again;
    Expectant stand the spheres;
    Breathless the laurell'd peers,
Nor move, till ends the lofty strain,
Nor move till Milton's tuneful thunders cease,
And leave once more the ravish'd heavens in peace.

Thou biddest Shakspeare wave his hand,
    And quickly forward spring
The Passions—a terrific band—
    And each vibrates the string
That with its tyrant temper best accords,
While from their Master's lips pour forth the
      inspiring words.

[33]

A silver trumpet Spenser blows,
    And, as its martial notes to silence flee,
From a virgin chorus flows
    A hymn in praise of spotless Chastity.
'Tis still! Wild warblings from the Aeolian lyre
Enchantment softly breathe, and tremblingly expire.

Next thy Tasso's ardent numbers
    Float along the pleased air,
Calling youth from idle slumbers,
    Rousing them from Pleasure's lair:—
Then o'er the strings his fingers gently move,
And melt the soul to pity and to love.

But when *Thou* joinest with the Nine,
And all the powers of song combine,
    We listen here on earth:
The dying tones that fill the air,
And charm the ear of evening fair,
From thee, great God of Bards, receive their
    heavenly birth.

The slight narrative element of the ode elaborates a
fancy derived from several classical sources.[10] Having
completed his daily task of driving the sun's chariot,
Apollo takes his evening ease in the poets' Elysium,
where dwell for eternity the great poets of past time.
Several of these poets (Homer, Virgil, Milton, Shakespeare, Spenser, Tasso), each in characteristic vein, sing
for the entertainment of the god. Finally, Apollo himself
sings, in company with the Muses, and his song is the
most beautiful of all.

Were the poem to function only on this level, it might
deserve the impatience with which its critics have treated

[10] G. Giovannini, "Keats' Elysium of Poets," *MLN*, LXIII (1948),
19-25, discusses probable and possible sources for Keats's conception of a favored place reserved for poets after death.

IMITATIO APOLLINIS

it.[11] The narrative action, however, merely "carries" the solid substance of the ode. This substance begins to appear when it is observed that the song of each poet, while preeminent in its kind, represents merely a single quality of the whole poetic medium. Although there is some overlapping, and a general nebulousness of definition,

[11] In outward form the poem is imitative and seems hardly more than a schoolboy exercise, which is probably why Miss Lowell, who may in this instance be taken as representative of the commentators, contemptuously dismissed it as "somewhat pretentious . . . long and very dull" [*John Keats*, I, 66]. It is not directly imitative of Dryden, however, as Professor Bate has suggested [*John Keats*, p. 41], nor does it, as Colvin asserted, in "style and expression owe everything to Gray" [*John Keats*, p. 23]. Professor Finney, while recognizing Keats's poem to be imitative of the eighteenth-century ode as a whole, concludes that its particular indebtedness, in both theme and stanza form, is to Vansittart's "The Pleasure of Poetry" [*Evolution of Keats's Poetry*, I, 61-64]. Comparison of the two poems supports this conclusion beyond any reasonable doubt.

Ascertainment of a model is of special interest because it gives us a standard by which to measure Keats's poem and, therefore, a clue as to the relative seriousness of Keats's attempt. To acknowledge, first, the defects of Keats's ode, it must be granted that the key stanzas are the first and last, and that those intervening are, beyond a necessary minimum, mere filler. They could have been increased or decreased in number without materially affecting the idea that animates the whole. The intermediate stanzas, however, taken as a unit, do have an organic function in the poem, introducing significant action into the setting provided in the opening stanza, and establishing a thematic context for the important statement made in the concluding stanza. Granting a certain looseness within the stanzas themselves, the poem yet has a definite purpose which it adheres to throughout, in marked contrast to Vansittart's aimless meandering in the same form and on a kindred subject. Some of Keats's diction is careless; indeed, a few phrases seem to have no function beyond fulfillment of the demands of meter and rhyme. Yet the poem as a whole shows, again in contrast to Vansittart's, a deliberate and generally successful attempt to vary sound and movement to suit the qualities of poetry enumerated within the poem. In short, the ode's calculated improvement over its model strongly implies that its composition was undertaken seriously, and not as mere imitative exercise or *jeu d'esprit*. That it is still too undisciplined for the elucidation of so vital a subject I take to be the reason that it was left out of the 1817 volume.

[35]

these qualities, in the order of their introduction, might be abstracted as: vigor, melody, elevation, passion, variety, and sweetness. Each poet is supreme for composition in his own kind, but none is universal. The song of each is a *partial* representation, a facet merely, of the total beauty that poetry comprehends. As the first two lines of the concluding stanza make clear, the whole beauty of poetry is possible only to its god. The initial word "But" distinguishes (psychologically, if not grammatically) the song that follows from those preceding it; and the italicized *"Thou"* further separates this singer and his song from the others. Finally, the statement that all the powers of song are combined when Apollo sings leaves no doubt that they were not all combined before. Whatever exigencies led Keats here to include the Muses as contributors to the divine harmony, these goddesses need not be considered as functional in the central conception. They seldom appear in Keats's poetry and obviously held little significance for him, while Apollo is repeatedly invoked and alluded to as the source and inspirer of song.

The remainder of the final stanza, solidly prepared for by the mythopoeic setting and action of the first seven stanzas, brings the poem with a rush out of the fanciful area of its poetic kind and into the sphere of operative poetic theory, if not indeed of epistemology. We are told, in the stanza's first tercet, that when Apollo sings, "We listen here on earth," i.e. we on earth can hear this perfect, all-encompassing harmony. The natural question, "How?" is answered in the closing tercet: We hear the song of the god, not directly as from an anthropomorphic being, but in all the natural sounds of earth, mingled and combined, when the stillness of evening renders them audible. Quite simply, the voice of nature is the voice of God.

Fortunately, we need not wonder whether the "dying tones that fill the air" at evening are imaginatively heard projections of the poet's own mythopoea or, as interpreted here, are the sounds of the natural world at close of day, for there is a later poem that makes the point explicitly:[12]

How many bards gild the lapses of time!
    A few of them have ever been the food
    Of my delighted fancy,—I could brood
Over their beauties, earthly, or sublime:
And often, when I sit me down to rhyme,
    These will in throngs before my mind intrude:
    But no confusion, no disturbance rude
Do they occasion; 'tis a pleasing chime.
So the unnumber'd sounds that evening store;
    The songs of birds—the whisp'ring of the leaves—
The voice of waters—the great bell that heaves
    With solemn sound,—and thousand others more,
That distance of recognizance bereaves,
    Make pleasing music, and not wild uproar.

Here in unambiguous detail, the sestet elaborates the kinds of evening sound which the poet found pleasing, and which, intermingled in his consciousness like the verbal beauties of those great poets who came before him, inspired him when he sat down "to rhyme." It also provides, in its version of the *concors discordia* principle,

[12] Although Garrod's text lists "How many bards" as undated, Finney [*Evolution of Keats's Poetry*, I, 101] points out that Keats's friend, Richard Woodhouse, whose scrupulous recording and annotating of the poet's work has given us much primary information that would otherwise be irrecoverable, dated the sonnet as of March 1816, in his annotated copy of the *Poems* of 1817. Most editors accept this dating as authoritative. The date is of interest insofar as the similarity of image and idea in the two formally disparate poems, written more than a year apart, reveals the persistence in the poet's mind of an unchanging theoretical concept.

an implied rationale for the ode's attribution of undifferentiated nature sounds to Apollo. If all natural sounds
are perceived as components of an harmonious orchestration of nature, then their combined effect is not un-
reasonably attributable to the god whose special province
it is to regulate the universal harmony. And further, if
the divine harmony to which the individual poet tunes
his song, and of which his song is a fragmentary echo,
is expressed through external nature, then external nature
must be the authentic source and standard of all true
poetry and the medium through which the god of poetry
reveals himself to his servants.

Placing these poems of identical rationale together—
the sonnet, a straightforward poetic statement, and the
ode, a mythologized poetic fancy—gives us an interesting glimpse of the way Keats translated his experience
into the culturally established terms of classical myth. It
is quite clear that he did not merely accept Apollo as the
nominal god of poetry, in the spirit of the self-conscious
Elizabethan convention, but rather that he made the god
functionally representative of his own experience and
reflection. Before settling on the seemingly innocuous
lines at the end of the Apollo ode, the poet must have
gone through a considerable process of thought, of which
the more direct statement made in the later sonnet probably represents an intermediate stage. In the sonnet we
can see that two kinds of experience, literary and natural,
have been assimilated to each other in their ability
equally to stimulate the poet's imagination. We also note
that the individual members of each class are submerged
in a total harmony, and that it is awareness of this harmony on the most comprehensive scale that inspires the
poet's own creative effort. From here, on the rough-hewn
analogical principle that things emotionally equal to the
same thing are substantively equal to each other, it is

but a step to the inference of a higher principle of unity in which both classes of related members are joined, a comprehensive Idea in which both participate. Accepting the common premise that the classical deities were imaginative representations of natural experience, or forces in experience (which he might have encountered in many places and did encounter in Wordsworth's *Excursion*),[13] and finding his experience of harmony amenable to the concept of an harmonic principle working through all things and accessible to human perception, Keats could easily recreate the Greek poetic leap to anthropomorphic embodiment of the principle. Apollo, the generative god of nature and art, was the natural locus for the meeting of the collocations of experience—and the Apollo ode makes their meeting in the god explicit. Having arrived at this point in the objectification of his abstract ideas, the poet then could, and often did, adopt the Apollo figure as the symbolic equivalent of his entire complex of aesthetic values. And to the myth, as received with all accretions, he adapted successive theoretical ideas as they were formed.

But before developing any further the theoretical ramifications of this construction, it might be of interest to see how the properties we have already noted are deployed in other early poems. Although the complementary qualities of the two poems cited above lend substance to the hypothesis of a poetic theory centered in the god Apollo, the fact of its existence is significant only to the extent that its elements may be found to be actively operative in the poetry itself. And conversely, the dimensions of poems in which these elements have

---

[13] IV, 847 *et seq.* It will be recalled that Keats thought Wordsworth's poem one of the "three things to rejoice at in this Age." *Letters*, I, 203.

a place must by that means be conceptually enlarged.

Keats was never again as explicit about his poetic rationale as in these two poems, but, with the insight they provide, one can find the conceptual pattern submerged almost everywhere in the early poetry. More often than not, however, the idea is borne by imagery, situation, or some other allusive reference to the general organization of elements in the Apollo ode. For instance, the time at which the *concors discordia* in nature is heard by the poet, in both poems, is evening. Reasons, both mythological and naturalistic, are not hard to supply. During the day, while sacrificing none of his powers, Apollo is preeminently god of the sun; at evening, having concluded his labors on behalf of fruition in the physical world, he is free to assume wholly his role as god of poetry. On the mundane level, it is an observation of general experience that the "unnatural" sounds of man in his workaday world subside at evening, and the natural sounds may be perceived more clearly. It is possible, too, that for Keats evening was the best time to compose poetry, but he did not, or did not for long, prescribe it as the only time. Evening is frequently associated in the early poems, however, with the act of artistic creation, as in the following:

> . . . fain would I follow thee
> Past each horizon of fine poesy;
> Fain would I echo back each pleasant note
>
> . . . .
> Just when the sun his farewell beam has darted:
> ("To George Felton Mathew," 11-13, 16)

> Oh! how I love, on a fair summer's eve,
> When streams of light pour down the golden west,
>
> . . . .

IMITATIO APOLLINIS

Perhaps on the wing of Poesy [to] upsoar,
　　　　　　　　(Sonnet: "Oh! how I love")

Full many a dreary hour have I past,
My brain bewilder'd, and my mind o'ercast
With heaviness; in seasons when I've thought
No spherey strains by me could e'er be caught

. . . .

That I should never hear Apollo's song,
Though feathery clouds were floating all along
The purple west, and, two bright streaks between,
The golden lyre itself were dimly seen:
　　　　(Epistle: "To My Brother George," 1-4, 9-12)

It should not be overlooked that, in two of these three examples, the composition of poetry is represented as a process of echoing back a strain first heard from without, these lines thus further clarifying the Apollo ode's representation of the relationship between the singer and the source of his song.

But perhaps more immediately significant, for its diffusion over a wide area of Keats's poetry, is the concatenation in these examples of several other motifs from the Apollo ode. Because evening is the time of sunset, and the sun sets in the west, and its gold color is most vivid at that time, Keats repeatedly alludes to *poetry*, or to the *conditions* that make poetry possible, or to the *process* of creating poetry, or to the beneficent *effects* of poetry, by providing a setting or describing an object or action which makes use of the ideas of evening, sunset, west, gold. (All of these, it will be recalled, are associated with Apollo in the setting of the ode.) In the three examples given above—each concerned, in their contexts, with suitable conditions for the writing of poetry, and each designating evening as the time—one notes that the

[41]

period of sunset is given as the ideal evening interval in all three, and, in two of the three, gold and the west are superadded. The poetic relationship of these elements, however, is not uniform. In the second example, the quality of light seen in the west is golden. In the third example, the quality of light in the west is predominantly purple, but the gold color (naturalistically, of course, also a sunset color) is represented as originating in the lyre, thereby signifying Apollo's presence, and the presence of his inspirational power, in the grandeur of the natural scene. The significance of such shifts lies in the ease with which they are made. Although the lineaments of the situation presented in the Apollo ode are readily seen in the third example, it is not necessary to know the ode in order to perceive the sense of the passage. Nor, as the first example shows, is it necessary to include the whole nucleus of attributes in order to represent the underlying idea with which they are associated. In other words, once the principal lines of association were laid down, they were capable of being presented in any combination, with or without reference to the specific mythological and natural settings of which they were integral parts, and, in the poet's mind, still carry the same conceptual values.[14]

14 Very rarely, however, Keats's involuted allusions become too private, as in the sonnet "To My Brother George." The sonnet opens, "Many the wonders I this day have seen" and goes on to a catalogue of common nature phenomena which, one understands, are truly "wonders" to the poetic sensibility. But one line-and-a-half, "the laurel'd peers / Who from the feathery gold of evening lean," must appear to be gibberish to every reader of the poem who does not have a minute familiarity with all the early poems. The "feathery gold" is not hard to identify with sunset cloud effects, and, in any case, a gloss is provided in line 10 of the "Epistle" to George, which is often printed with the sonnet. But who are these "peers"? Why are they "laurel'd"? And what are they doing in an evening sky? They are, of course, the "laurell'd peers" of line 20, "Ode to Apollo," the great poets of the past, seen in their well-

This becomes most interesting when the associated attributes are cut loose from the parent situation and allowed to enrich another context, as in the sonnet "On
First Looking into Chapman's Homer":

> Much have I travell'd in the realms of *gold*,
>   And many goodly states and kingdoms seen;
>   Round many *western* islands have I been
> Which bards in fealty to *Apollo* hold.
> Oft of one wide expanse had I been told
>   That deep-brow'd Homer ruled as his demesne;
>   Yet did I never breathe its pure serene
> Till I heard Chapman speak out loud and bold:
> Then felt I like some watcher of the skies
>   When a new planet swims into his ken;
> Or like stout Cortez when with eagle eyes
>   He star'd at the Pacific—and all his men
> Look'd at each other with a wild surmise—
>   Silent, upon a peak in Darien.

Here we see, in the words I have italicized in the initial
quatrain, a familiar pattern which reveals a startling ad-

---

earned Elysium by the young poet whose imaginative identification
of art with nature finds objectification in this mythological image.
  Perhaps the first to find the reference in the sonnet unintelligible
was Richard Woodhouse, who inquired its meaning of Keats and
was directed by him to the Apollo ode for clarification [C. L.
Finney, *Evolution of Keats's Poetry*, II, 761]. Woodhouse at first
thought the coincidence due to the two poems' having been written
at about the same time [*ibid.*, II, 752-53, 761]. But Woodhouse
himself, in two transcripts, is our authority for dating the Apollo
ode February 1815, presumably on information from the poet, since
he did not know its date when he received the transcript of it from
his cousin Mary Frogley [H. W. Garrod (ed.), *Poetical Works*,
pp. lxix-lxx]. Of the sonnet, George Keats, to whom it was addressed, is our authority for the date, August 1816 [*ibid.*, pp. xlix,
39]. Keats's explanation to Woodhouse that the sonnet was to be
glossed with the ode written a year-and-a-half earlier provides another example of the remarkable persistence of his central conception, and its principal emblems, in the poet's mind.

vance in Keats's poetic maturity. Employing several of the associated elements of his private conception, in the poem's descriptive introduction to the subject of literary discovery, he has succeeded in translating what was for himself a symbol into what is for the reader a metaphor. Having discovered, in Chapman's rendering of Homer, a poetic performance which fulfilled his notions of what poetry could be, it was natural that his mind should have gravitated toward the Apollo symbol that had for almost two years comprehended all his ideas of poetic excellence.[15] The evidence that his mind did in fact move in that direction is seen not only in the italicized words of the first quatrain but in the relationship there established between Apollo and the poets. In the poem's medieval social geography, the power of the poets is inferior to and dependent upon that of Apollo, and the poetic territories over which they exercise that power are mere parcels of the whole area over which the god's power extends. The basic relationship of poet to god is therefore the same as that in the "Ode to Apollo."[16] That Keats succeeded in translating his private symbolism into the more public historical metaphor of the gold-seeking con-

[15] Twenty months, dating from the Apollo ode. The Chapman's Homer sonnet was written in October 1816, two months after composition of the poems addressed to his brother George.

[16] One is tempted to proceed from these demonstrable truths to the possible but undemonstrable. One might see the sestet as related to the octave, for instance, in the continuity of Apollo motifs, as well as in the obvious imagery of surprised discovery. As god of astronomy, Apollo governs the new planet that is discovered, in line 10, and the system of which it is a part. The poem closes with the discovery of a sea, and the sea's is one of the natural voices (in "How many bards" and various other poems, cf. below) through which Keats heard Apollo speak to man. However, since the typical reader could not be expected to know that Keats might so relate the elements of the poem in his own mind, and since there is no overt relationship of the sestet elements with the Apollo of the octave, these possibilities must be considered at best as latent.

[44]

quistador and Eldorado,[17] preserving all of the symbol's
essential elements and relationships without the distrac-
tion of reference to the poets' Elysium,[18] reveals the growing flexibility of the intellectual construct in the poet's
practice. It also foreshadows the subtlety of its later use,
where often the mere shadow of a clue, a single word,
reveals the depth of meaning that governs a whole passage or poem.

In the Chapman's Homer sonnet, the symbol linking
the conquistador framework to Keats's private system, and
perhaps the central symbol in the whole theoretical complex, is that of gold. Although, for a good reason that
will be discussed in its place, silver came to have its own
high position in Keats's scheme, gold is the property

[17] I believe the late John Middleton Murry was the first, as he
is the most lucidly explicit, to note this dominant metaphor, in his
article, "The Birth of a Great Poem," *Hibbert Journal*, xxvii
(1928), 93-110, most recently reprinted in his *Keats* (New York,
1955), pp. 145-65, with the specific discussion of this point on
p. 148.

In connection with this metaphor, which relates the end of the
poem to its beginning, another reference to Keats's personal system might be inferred. Just as the conquistador at the end of the
poem has discovered at the extreme western verge of his world
something more valuable than another mere realm of gold, has
discovered in fact a whole new world which was hitherto an unknown part of his own, so Keats, in reading Chapman, has discovered not merely another poem but a promontory on the extreme
western (i.e. ethereally inspirational) verge of his spiritual landscape from which he can see a whole new world of poetry opening
up. I doubt that this argument is more demonstrable than that in
note 16, above, but its logic is conformable to the logic of the
poem and imposes upon it a unity lacking in conventional discussion of it, which finds in the sestet mere analogues of the experience represented in the octave.

[18] G. Giovannini, "Keats' Elysium of Poets," pp. 20-25, reads
the whole octave as a rendering of Keats's mythical geography of
Elysium, a view which I find attractive, since it supports my own
in a collateral way, but which seems to me to misplace the emphasis, i.e. on the details of an antecedent intellectual construction,
rather than on the value of that construction for the poem.

most conspicuously identified with Apollo and therefore with poetry itself. Apollo's western dwelling, in the ode, is "of gold," and there is an almost definitive address to the god in the opening of another ode, or hymn, to Apollo from this period:

> God of the golden bow,
> And of the golden lyre,
> And of the golden hair,
> And of the golden fire. . . .

It should not escape notice that, in keeping with the reiterated association, but with violence to classical tradition, the god's bow, in the last example, has been changed from silver to gold. That is, Keats has deliberately amplified, and thus intensified, the identification.

Sometimes the association of Apollo and gold with poetry is made through direct reference to the god's musical adjunct, the lyre, as in the lines immediately above; the lines from the epistle to George (11-12), previously cited; the lines in *Endymion* (IV, 701-2), "I'll kneel . . . / to god Phoebus, for a golden lyre"; and through to *Hyperion* (in which "Apollo is once more the golden theme!" III, 28), where the as yet unfledged god, confronted by Mnemosyne and puzzled by his sense of acquaintance with one whom he does not recall having seen before, is told:

> 'Thou hast dream'd of me; and waking up
> 'Didst find a lyre all golden by thy side,
> 'Whose strings touch'd by thy fingers, all the vast
> 'Unwearied ear of the whole universe
> 'Listen'd in pain and pleasure at the birth
> 'Of such new tuneful wonder.
>
> (*Hyperion*, III, 62-67)

[46]

In Keats's numerous references to the lyre, it is always golden when associated with Apollo.

If we move closer to the representation of poetry and the Apollinian dispensation through reference to gold alone, we note that the pen used in writing poetry is made golden in the sonnet to Spenser, ". . . 'tis impossible / For an inhabitant of wintry earth / To rise like Phoebus with a golden quell," where the subject is the difficulty of achieving truly inspired poetry. When the mood is reversed (in the sonnet "On Leaving Some Friends at an Early Hour"), and, exulting in a sense of powerful inspiration, the poet sits down to compose, he begins a catalogue of extravagant correlative images with the command, "Give me a golden pen. . . ." In the second of these examples, unlike the first, that short step has been taken which divorces the gold symbol from its private Apollinian context and places it in the realm of common understanding as something that has very great value in its own right. This is entirely proper, because as long as gold is overtly associated with poetry, in whatever metaphorical guise, communication between poet and public is unimpaired, and the reader instantly recognizes that poetry is being represented as valuable. Thus the poet can allude to poetry itself or to the labor of artistic creation in terms that include some reference to gold and insinuate clearly, if incompletely, the high value he places upon the activity that he and the reader momentarily share. For instance, the poet is one whose "eye can reach those golden halls" where the imagination plays (Epistle: "To My Brother George," 35), one who strives to soar "with the bright golden wing / Of genius" ("To George Felton Mathew," 63-64), or one who, in the antiquity of time, won from his experience "some golden sounds" to pass in song to later generations ("I stood tip-toe," 203). The allusive nature of Keats's use of gold, and its specific

[47]

association with the god, is illustrated by a variant reading of the last example cited. The complete line, as published, reads, "So in fine wrath some golden sounds he won," but the reading of one autograph copy of the poem is, "So from Apollo's Lyre a Tone he won."[19] Both lines, in their context, represent the same action, the imaginative making of poems while inspired by the direct observation of nature.

Yet, unmistakable as the reader finds the general sense of these allusions, one may see how much of Keats's whole thought they left unexpressed. Despite the fact that these passages occur in contexts which associate poetry with either nature or humanity, the gold metaphor in no way suggests that one substantial value of poetry, acquired through faithful reflection of the highest principles operative in the external world, is its truth. And, while the idea of value is minimally present, the poet's own attitude of reverence is not conveyed by the common metaphor. These defects may partially account for Keats's ever-increasing tendency toward outright treatment of mythological themes in which the chief characters embody natural forces and powers and are known to have been, historically, the objects of worship.

It must also be pointed out that these examples, although they illustrate the utility and flexibility of the gold symbol, are limited in the sense that they are primarily concerned with the sphere of art. Each of the lines cited occurs in a passage of which the specific subject is poetry itself; and even if one were sufficiently familiar with the golden attributes of Apollo in received mythology to recognize his spiritual presence in the golden metaphors above, one would not readily see more than a subtle evocation of the conventional god of poetry. Keats's unconventionality, and the breadth of his inten-

[19] *Poetical Works*, p. 10n.

tion, are seen, here as elsewhere, in his verification of myth through naturalistic observation—a process culminating in the use of the gold symbol as a bridge between the two worlds of the god and the two modes of apprehending him. It is Apollo's other major role in late classical mythology, as "Charioteer / Of the patient year" ("God of the golden bow"), i.e. god of the sun, that fulfills the gold symbol. Here, visible to the eye, is all the goldenness of the mythical Apollo, so that the poet may speak unaffectedly, in the metaphor of ordinary speech, of "golden sunshine" ("Hence Burgundy, Claret, and Port") and the "golden day" ("Apollo to the Graces").

In such simple terms, however, nothing is conveyed but delight. There is no virtue, no power, no process. Actually, it was the sun's pouring of its own power lavishly into the earth to make it fruitful, fulfilling the destined ends of nature and beneficently providing a golden harvest for men, that instilled in the poet a sense of some divine agency operating actively in nature. Early evidences of this organic goldenness are the description of Apollo's chariot path "Across the gold Autumn's whole Kingdom of Corn" ("Apollo to the Graces"), the poet's desire, for purposes of poetical inspiration, to see, among other things, "high, golden corn wave in the light" ("To Charles Cowden Clarke," 92), the "universal tinge of sober gold" with which autumn is given a one-line characterization in *Endymion* (I, 56), and the "golden store / In Autumn's sickle" (*Endymion*, IV, 422-23), in which the whole season is represented in a single image. In each of these instances, in fact, the wealth of autumn is summed up in a single reference to gold. If ordinary observation would supply the reference and make unnecessary the supposition of a god who functions as a ripening agent, that same observation would supply the reds and browns that are not called upon in these lines. Gold does duty for all the autumn colors because Keats thought and continued to think of "reaped corn" as "heaped Autumn's wealth" ("Fancy," 41, 35), a treasure conferred upon man by beneficent nature. And the agency that brought it about was autumn's "Close bosom-friend" the "maturing sun" (Ode: "To Autumn"), as it was later to be designated in one of Keats's most serene and eloquent poems. In the earlier work, we come elliptically but firmly home to Apollo in the representation of the harvest season as that time "When . . . the sun his autumn tresses shook" (*Endymion*, I, 440).[20] The image is brilliant, perfect in its mingling of sun and harvest qualities; and yet, in terms of common understanding, its origin is virtually inconceivable. If one sees it, however, as the distillate of a mind that habitually conceived of autumn in terms of its golden harvest, and of that harvest as a wealth procured to man by a natural process which is presided over by the god "of the golden hair," the inconceivable image becomes the inevitable *mot juste*.[21]

As a sort of universal catalyst, then, the gold image probably functions more pervasively and variously than any other to suggest the cluster of ideas at the core of Keats's early philosophy of composition. It is, in fact, so

[20] It might be noted parenthetically that this image and several others in the passage where it occurs anticipate details, and to a certain extent the mood, of the ode "To Autumn."

[21] The golden hair image was used again in the first draft of *Endymion* (III, 44) to represent a natural phenomenon, sunset, "When thy golden hair falls thick about the west" [*Poetical Works*, p. 129n.], but was altered in the final version to "When thy gold breath is misting in the west." The person addressed is, of course, Apollo. A clumsier variant of the sunshine and golden hair motif was wisely canceled from "I stood tip-toe" (157 *et seq.*):

> One Sunbeam comes the Solitude to bless
> Widening it slants athwart the Duskiness
> And whert [*sic*] it plays upon the turfy Mould
> There sleeps a Nest of Hair wavy and gold
> [*Poetical Works*, p. 8n.]

often employed, and so seldom with the specific denotation of the bright metal with which it is normally associated, that its introduction in many contexts is almost irrelevant to the expository substance of those passages and serves simply for the ritualistic censing of the immediate poetic atmosphere.[22] For all of that, one recog-

[22] Such, for instance, is the passage that concludes the epistle "To George Felton Mathew" (76-93), a passage that has baffled and annoyed most readers. Colvin called it "queer" [*John Keats*, p. 110], Miss Lowell "dull" [*John Keats*, i, 82], and Finney "strange" [*Evolution of Keats's Poetry*, i, 79]. In these lines Keats, in all generous sincerity, flatters Mathew's delusion that he is a poet by fancifully outlining the process through which he is supposed to have become one. The process consists of multiple metamorphoses, reversing the customary direction of Ovidian transformation, however, and, in a lucky prescience of evolutionary dogma, passing Mathew through successively higher stages of organic life. He is first a flower, plucked by Diana as a sacrifice to Apollo and cast into a stream. There he is changed by Apollo into a "fish of gold," then into a swan sailing "O'er pebbly crystal, and o'er golden sands," and finally into a man. Since the passage climaxes a poem celebrating Keats's and Mathew's "brotherhood in song," and Apollo is the agent of transformation, there can be no doubt that the rather clumsy allegory signifies the making of a poet. All that holds the fancy together, however, in the stages between flower and man, is the repeated allusion to gold. (It is possible that an adumbration of *Endymion* is involved in the representation of the poet as one who passes through a natural identification with earth, water, and, in the imaginative faculty of man, the sky. For an additional reference to the poet's identification with all three regions, cf. the epistle "To My Brother George," 19-22.) Having been cast into the water as a gift to Apollo, and found by the god to be worthy of preservation, the flower is turned into a creature that can live in water, a fish; and, because sacred to Apollo, no ordinary fish, but a goldfish. There is no evidence that Keats knew anything at all about the extensive iconology of fishes, so one must assume that, because of the significance he himself found in gold, he "elevated" his conceit by changing his friend into this hapless variety. Then, bringing his friend from the deep to the surface, he makes him a swan, a bird given by Lemprière as sacred to Apollo. Again the created object fails overtly to manifest the god's purpose, so the context is enriched, in the poet's mind, by having the swan swim in a stream bedded on golden sand. The passage as a whole

nizes in ritual a fixity of conviction and a spontaneity of reaction to the objects of conviction that reveal unmistakably the bent of the subject mind. Wherever the central idea is present, one may expect to find it accompanied by the symbols of its ritual; and, more important for the scrutiny of a body of poetry, wherever the ritual symbols occur, one may reasonably hypothesize the presence of the idea that they customarily represent. The trick is to recognize the symbols, for if anything can be taken for granted in this sort of poetic thinking, it is that one symbol tends to breed another until the basic idea is represented by verbal elements that have no direct connection whatever with the original symbolic complex.

The first stage of development, as we see it in Keats's thought, is not hard to grasp. Apollo, the prime mover of his conceptual system, has a number of golden elements associated with his person in received mythology, his hair, lyre, etc. Further, as classical charioteer of the golden sun, he brings many of the growing things of earth to golden ripeness; and as inspirer of poetry, he brings forth the richest store of human thought in the brightest adornment of human language. Only a very small imaginative leap is required of the reader, therefore, to find the whole idea of the god's influence represented by some sort of gold reference. Keats's most explicit statement of the importance he assigned to the god occurs in the "Ode to Apollo," and, as we have already seen, not only gold but various auxiliary aspects of the ode's dramatic setting, such as evening and the west,

---

has been found vexing, if not embarrassing, by virtually all admirers of the poet, not only because it is rather silly, but because, lacking knowledge of the gold symbolism, they have just not found any consecutive sense in it. When one does see the golden thread that binds the parts together, its meaning is clear enough, but it does not satisfy because the references, outside Keats's conceptual imagination, are too obviously gratuitous.

serve there and in other poems as representatives of, or adjuncts to, the idea which is chiefly symbolized by Apollo.[23] But it is the concluding stanza of the ode which reveals the means by which the god communicates to men the sense of harmony he represents—and the particulars of this process are expressed, in limited exemplary detail, in the sonnet, "How many bards gild the lapses of time!" (And now we may note, "gild"—make

[23] There is a tantalizing moment at the end of the epistle "To My Brother George" (139-41) when, having considered at some length his reasons for electing the poetic vocation, the writer announces, "Now I direct my eyes into the west, / Which at this moment is in sunbeams drest: / Why westward turn?" We have the combination of west and sunset again, associated with a disquisition on poetry and climaxed by a rhetorical question which one feels certain was intended to introduce an exposition of the Apollinian rationale. Then, disappointingly, the whole thing is wrapped up with the laconic, " 'Twas but to say adieu! / 'Twas but to kiss my hand, dear George, to you!" The (perhaps unconsciously) reiterated " 'Twas," which places in the past tense an action introduced in the present, suggests the possibility of a time lapse between the writing of the two statements; and the reiterated "but" protests almost too much the inconsequence of the announced action. One can almost see the wheels turning, through the closing lines of the epistle. Much of the poem expressed an exalted, if not intoxicated, sense of the power of poetry in human affairs, and the poet had spoken of his "mad ambition" (110) to participate in that power. In such a mood he might well impart to his most sympathetic confidant his reason for believing himself fit to exercise such power, i.e. his consciousness of being already conversant with it at its source. The subject is elliptically introduced with the sunset reference, and then there is a long pause for meditation and organization of thought. But the hour is late, 140 lines have been already written, the fever of exaltation is wearing off and an exhausted reaction setting in, and the explanation is complex and difficult to frame. The attempt is therefore abandoned, the poet merely says goodbye, unconsciously slipping into the past tense in referring to something which is farther back in his time-sense than in the reader's, and unconsciously insisting, with the reiterated "but," that he wasn't really going to say anything important anyway. And so, one may speculate, a valuable piece of critical information was irretrievably lost to us.

golden—with their poetry.) These details, comprising constituent elements of the divine harmony, have in turn a symbolic function in other poems, sometimes in conjunction with other symbols of the basic complex, sometimes alone. The natural sounds enumerated in the sonnet are bird-song, the sound of the wind (in the sonnet rendered as a sound produced by the passage of the wind through leaves), and the sound of moving waters. In keeping with the rationale of the Apollo ode, i.e. that these are not mere casual sounds but the actual voice(s) of the unseen god, each is calculatedly presented in vocal terms: "The *songs* of birds—the *whisp'ring* of the leaves— / The *voice* of waters—" [italics mine].

There are fewer echoes of the last of these in Keats's poetry than of the others, no doubt because the inland setting of his normal experience removed him from continuous consciousness of open water. The sound of moving waters occurs frequently enough, but usually as part of a background to something else. The most characteristic use Keats makes of the effect is to reverse it, to create an atmosphere of perfect calm by introducing water preternaturally still. And yet, we have such evidences of its agency as an inspirational "voice" as the sonnet "To My Brother George," where, among the "wonders" the poet has seen that day, is

> The ocean with . . .
> . . . .
> Its voice mysterious, which whoso hears
> Must think on what will be, and what has been.

And Apollo himself, when about to assume his full deity, is subjected to its influence:

> Throughout all the isle
> There was no covert, no retired cave

Unhaunted by the murmurous noise of waves,
Though scarcely heard in many a green recess.
He listen'd, and he wept. . . .

(*Hyperion*, III, 38-42)

And there is, of course, the sonnet "On the Sea" as testimony of the poet's sensitivity to its "eternal whisperings":

Oh ye! whose ears are dinn'd with uproar rude,
Or fed too much with cloying melody,—
Sit ye near some old cavern's mouth, and brood
Until ye start, as if the sea-nymphs quired!

Indeed, on the occasion of this sonnet, it had sung to him at a significant place and time—on the Isle of Wight, where he had gone to begin composition of *Endymion*.[24] Further evidence of his continuing conception of the sea as a vital presence is its pairing with the wind, in close proximity to Apollo, as an obvious source of inspiration left unheeded by the poets of the century before his own:

[24] The letter in which the sonnet first appears is dated from Carisbrooke, which is inland, but Keats says that he had spent the previous day at Shanklin, on the island's east coast, where he would have had an unparalleled opportunity to experience the ocean sound not ordinarily available to him. That he was, in fact, powerfully impressed by it is indicated in his climaxing a description of Shanklin's picturesque prettiness with the exclamation, "But the sea, Jack, the sea—" [*Letters*, I, 131]. The point is worth making because the sonnet is introduced into his letter by a (mis)quotation from *King Lear*, "Do you not hear the Sea?" [*Letters*, I, 132], which might give rise to the suspicion that the sonnet was literarily rather than naturalistically inspired. To the contrary, however, it seems likely that the Shakespearean line was suggested to him by the impact of his own direct experience of the moment. For the effect on his poetry of immediate, nonliterary observation, if documentation is required, see his own comment in *Letters*, I, 301 (where, after a lengthy description of mountain scenery, he exclaims, "I shall learn poetry here . . ."), and Robert Gittings, *John Keats: The Living Year* (Cambridge, Mass., 1954), pp. 77-81, *passim*.

> . . . a schism
> Nurtured by foppery and barbarism,
> Made great Apollo blush for this his land.
> Men were thought wise who could not understand
> His glories . . .
>
> . . . .
>
> . . . Ah dismal soul'd!
> The winds of heaven blew, the ocean roll'd
> Its gathering waves—ye felt it not.
>> ("Sleep and Poetry," 181-85, 187-89)

But if the sea remained for Keats a seldom-heard, though authentic, voice of the god, the wind spoke to him everywhere:

> Happy is England! I could be content
>
> . . . .
>
> To feel no other breezes than are blown
> Through its tall woods with high romances blent:
>> (Sonnet: "Happy is England!")

In another place, at the end of a descriptive passage which includes "sun" and "golden corn":

> No sooner had I stepp'd into these pleasures
> Than I began to think of rhymes and measures:
> The air that floated by me seem'd to say
> "Write! thou wilt never have a better day."
>> ("To Charles Cowden Clarke," 97-100)

Its "balmy zephyrs" appear with a "summer's eve" and the "golden west" in the opening lines of the sonnet "Oh! how I love," and its "freshest breeze" soothes him as he lies on a cliff-top overlooking the sea, rejoicing in each "bright thought" that feeds the poetry which he values more highly than "hidden treasure" (Epistle: "To My Brother George," 113-25). It appears in a complex passage of "I stood tip-toe," where the sight of gold-colored flowers sets off a chain of associations which includes gold, poetry, Apollo as god of both song and sun, and the wind as his voice:

> Open afresh your round of starry folds,
> Ye ardent marigolds!
> Dry up the moisture from your golden lids,
> For great Apollo bids
> That in these days your praises should be sung
> On many harps, which he has lately strung;
> And when again your dewiness he kisses,
> Tell him, I have you in my world of blisses:
> So haply when I rove in some far vale,
> His mighty voice may come upon the gale.
>
> ("I stood tip-toe," 47-56)

There is an almost superstitious reverence in these lines, which might be paraphrased: "Don't weep, little flowers, for you are not forgotten. Poets are again obeying Apollo's command to celebrate the beauties of nature which you represent. When he comes to you again, as the life-giving sun, be sure to tell him that I value you properly so that he will continue to reveal himself to me, and inspire my poetry, by speaking to me through the wind." I suspect that, without the kind of insight provided by the Apollo ode and the sonnet "How many bards," even such a paraphrase would be difficult to make, and once made, would be difficult to understand.

As already suggested, one reason for the predominance of wind-sound over water-sound in Keats's poetry was no doubt their relative accessibility to his ordinary experience. Beyond that, however, it might be noted that the wind corresponded much more closely to his concept of Apollo as an invisible presence making itself felt in the human sphere; or, as one writer on the wind motif in romantic poetry defines it, "an entirely unseen power known only by its effects."[25]

It is well to remind ourselves that, whatever its final variants, Keats's original construction, as presented in its earliest and "purest" form in the Apollo ode, depends upon an unseen god who manifests himself to us through sound, not sight. Even in the myth's primary extension, Apollo, as charioteer of the sun, is not seen; only the sun itself, the power he directs, is visible. One wishes to emphasize this because of its peculiar appropriateness for the third of the nature-sounds mentioned in the sonnet "How many bards," i.e. "the songs of birds."

Although most birds sing, and one may properly understand that birds in general are intended here, Keats was usually more specific. More than a dozen species of birds are named in his verse, but four of these, the swan, dove, eagle, and nightingale, occur with considerable frequency, while the remainder appear no more often than casual observation or the requirements of particular poems would warrant. As their frequent occurrence implies, each of these four seems to have represented for the poet a special quality. In the majority of Keatsian contexts, the swan represents gracefulness, the dove sweet innocence, the eagle fierce and purposeful strength, and the nightingale song. From the natural circumstances in which the poet would have encountered the bird, as well as from received poetic tradition, the nightingale hap-

[25] M. H. Abrams, "The Correspondent Breeze: A Romantic Metaphor," *KR*, xix (1957), 129. Although Keats is not discussed, Professor Abrams' article is of particular interest here for its observation that "The poet Lucan said that Apollo founded the Delphic oracle at a huge chasm where 'the earth breathed forth divine truth, and . . . gave out a wind that spoke'" [pp. 122-23], a reference peculiarly apt to Keats's conception, and within his ken as a Latinist, though we do not know whether he ever did read Lucan.

pened to fit perfectly into Keats's Apollinian scheme (as
will appear presently), and hence became virtually the
personification of song.[26]

Perhaps we could most readily approach this concept
by noting the significant company of images that the
nightingale keeps in the following:

> Softly the *breezes* from the forest came,
>
> . . . .
>
> Clear was the song from Philomel's far bower;
>
> . . . .
>
> Sweet too the converse of these happy mortals,
> As that of busy spirits *when the portals*
> *Are closing in the west;*
>> ("Calidore," 152, 154, 158-60)

> Returning home at *evening*, with an ear
>> Catching the notes of Philomel,—
> ("To one who has been long in city pent")

> What is more gentle than a *wind* in summer?
>
> . . . .
>
> More secret than a nest of nightingales?
>> ("Sleep and Poetry," 1, 8)

[26] H. W. Garrod, "The Nightingale in Poetry," *The Profession
of Poetry and Other Lectures* (Oxford, 1929), p. 134, contributes
the interesting observation, "Homer calls the Nightingale by a
name which, in the Greek, is synonymous with poetry itself and
the poet. The *aēdon* is the 'singer', and once or twice in Greek
poetry the songs which the poet sings are called, prettily, his
'nightingales'." It would not have been necessary for Keats to
know this in order to assign the same value to the bird, but it
might have confirmed a subjective impulse to do so. Although a
Greek grammar was among Keats's books when he died [cf. *Keats
Circle*, i, 258], he had studied the language little, if at all, at the
time the nightingale first appeared in his poetry, for as late as
April 1818 he set the learning of Greek as one of his immediate
goals [*Letters*, i, 274]. Still, a tidbit like this might easily have
been picked up at almost any time in conversation with a more
learned friend who shared his interests—Clarke, for instance.

She did so breathe ambrosia; so immerse
My fine existence in a *golden* clime.

. . . .

For as *Apollo* each *eve* doth devise
A new appareling for *western* skies;
So every eve, nay every spendthrift hour
Shed balmy consciousness within that bower.
And I was free of haunts umbrageous;
Could wander in the mazy forest-house

. . . .

[Of] birds from coverts innermost and drear
Warbling for very joy mellifluous sorrow—
          (*Endymion*, III, 454-55, 463-68, 470-71)[27]

Wind, evening, west, sunset, gold, Apollo, some aspect
of the familiar complex occurs with every appearance of
the nightingale. It might be expected, of course, that sunset and evening would occur, since the bird traditionally
is a night warbler, beginning its song with the onset of
dusk. The fact is, however, that this is solely a matter of
poetic tradition, for nightingales sing day and night; and
it is hardly to be supposed that so keen an observer as
Keats, resident in that part of England where nightingales are to be found, could have been ignorant of it.[28]
The inescapable inference is that Keats *chose* to accept
the poetic tradition, because it suited his purposes to

[27] My italics in all above examples. In the last citation, the traditional sorrowful song identifies the warblers as nightingales.
[28] H. W. Garrod, "The Nightingale in Poetry," p. 142, certifies
this fact, little known beyond the "Nightingale Line." Keats's
friend Charles Brown attests [*Keats Circle*, II, 65] that the poet's
famous nightingale ode, inspired by the singing of a nightingale
that had built a nest close to the house they were sharing, was
composed in the morning. He does not state that the bird was
singing at the time, though the immediacy of the poem's opening
lines powerfully conveys that impression.

do so. Then, having once firmly accepted the nightingale into the complex of symbols attending his central conception, its appearance among other symbols of the same complex, however far removed from superficial relevance, became an ordinary matter of simple, perhaps subconscious, association. Certainly the example from *Endymion*, above, links together a chain of associated images in its description of love's spell which is anything but inevitable; yet, given the elements with which Keats habitually worked, and the appearance of one of them at the beginning of the passage, one can almost anticipate the clicking into place of the other pieces.

But one might note more particularly, in the examples above, the singers' relation to the listener. In the first, the bird sings from a "far bower"; in the second, it is apprehended only by means of the notes that strike the ear; in the third, its nest is given as an extreme example of secret seclusion; in the fourth, its song comes from "coverts innermost" of the forest. This situation obtains in references to the nightingale elsewhere in the poetry, in the epistle "To George Felton Mathew" (45-46), where the nightingales sing from among "covert branches," and in the first book of *Endymion* (828-29), where the bird sings "upperched high, / And cloister'd" among the leaves. It is, in fact, virtually a condition of the nightingale's occurrence in Keats's poetry that it be not seen. When it is considered cumulatively that, *un*like the wind and sea, the bird is a living creature and therefore a conscious and purposeful singer, and that, again *un*like the wind and sea, its song is naturally heard as musical, and that, *un*like the other birds in Keats's poetry but *like* Apollo, it is never seen but has its presence attested by the effect of its song, the nightingale is readily conceived as what in fact it seems to have become for Keats, a local manifestation of the god himself—not merely a medium for his voice, but an earthly surrogate.[29]

An extension of this conceit, at one farther remove, is found in a poem which mentions neither Apollo nor the nightingale, the sonnet "On the Grasshopper and Cricket." Like Apollo, and like the nightingale, the grasshopper and cricket of the sonnet are living creatures whose songs are heard by men, though the singers are not seen. The poem's intention, stated in the words that open both oc-

[29] H. W. Garrod, "The Nightingale in Poetry," pp. 136-37, cites a passage from Aristophanes' *The Birds* which he translates as follows:

> Nightingale, awake,
> Bride of my soul, and shake
> Slumber off; and once more ringing
> The never-enough-rung dirge of Itys,
> Pour from lips whose grief delight is
> The unmatched magic of thy singing.
>   Hark! from those dim bowers of bryony
> Pure it issues: hark! on high, on high,
> Surging. Golden-haired Apollo
> Hears and starts and, fain to follow,
> Wakes on his ivory-pointed lyre
> Strains responsive; while the Choir
> Immortal rise; whose feet divine
> Move in music one with thine;
> And humbly heavenly lips prolong,
> Nightingale, *thy* diviner song!

Although the "Golden-haired Apollo" is a familiar Keatsian figure, and the line "Pour from lips whose grief delight is" resembles closely Keats's "Warbling for very joy mellifluous sorrow" (*Endymion*, iii, 471), both are classical commonplaces. Rather more noteworthy is the almost diametric reversal of the situation of Keats's Apollo ode, the natural music here tuning the heavenly harmony. And it is of special interest, of course, to find in so prominent a classical source a specific identification between the songs of Apollo and those of the nightingale. Again there is no evidence of Keats's acquaintance with the passage, but if he had none, it is the more remarkable that he captured with such fidelity not only the spirit but the method and the precise equivalents of classical mythology.

tave and sestet, is to assert "The poetry of earth," which is represented by the summer song of the grasshopper and the winter song of the cricket. Since Keats habitually thought of the audible poetry of earth as the song of the god, this concentration of the whole of that poetry in the individual songs of the grasshopper and cricket places them, with respect to inspirational function, in a position approximating that of the god. It would be quibbling, I think, to object to the vehicles' being mere insects, or to question whether, technically, Apollo sings through them or has created them to sing on his behalf, since the clear intention of the whole poem is simply to assert that the natural music of earth, whatever its local source, is always available to those who will listen for it.

It is not irrelevant, incidentally, that the sonnet was written to time, in friendly competition with Leigh Hunt, and that the subject was not arbitrarily chosen by Keats but by Hunt. In both structure and clarity the sonnet is one of Keats's best; yet, although Hunt had great facility in composition, Keats was the first to finish the contest.[30] One infers that, though the given subject was not an accustomed one, it was so readily adaptable to Keats's operative poetic philosophy that by a simple transposition of subject identities he could rapidly write off a nearly perfect poem. What the grasshopper and cricket are in this sonnet is what the nightingales are in Keats's more habitual thought, the unseen singers of that poetry of earth which is the song of its god.

Up to this point we have been concerned chiefly with specific details of the Apollo ode and its "gloss," the sonnet "How many bards," and with the immediate impli-

[30] The account of the contest may be found in Charles and Mary Cowden Clarke, *Recollections of Writers* (New York, [1878]), p. 135.

cations and extensions of the symbolic complex which they reveal. Necessarily, the discussion of one set of occurrences creates an imbalance of attention and tends to suggest the poet's strict fidelity to a narrow set of terms and concepts which are, in fact, not so much exclusive symbols as symbolic norms. If we emphasize evening, the west, and sunset, it is not because they have a unique virtue for Keats but because they occur in the context in which Keats most explicitly reveals the bridge between the natural and the ideal in his aesthetic, and because their frequent recurrence in contexts overtly concerned with the practice of poetry suggests the persistence in his consciousness of a particular set of relationships which were to him the basic building blocks of his whole conceptual structure. He seems certainly to have recognized, however, the insecurity of a theory whose validity depended upon its restriction to a single hour of the day, and incidentally, the limitations of a god with powers so restricted. And while he may, himself, have found the sunset hour most conducive to poetic composition, he had no difficulty, with a god of song who was also god of the sun, in allusively extending the god's range of diurnal efficacy. Thus we have, concurrent with the elements already cited, such "daytime" lines as:

Fresh *morning* gusts have blown away all fear
    From my glad bosom,—now from gloominess
    I mount for ever—not an atom less
Than the proud laurel shall content my bier.
No! by the eternal stars! or why sit here
    In the Sun's eye, and 'gainst my temples press
    Apollo's very leaves . . .
("To a Young Lady Who Sent Me a Laurel Crown")

Too partial friend! fain would I follow thee
Past each horizon of fine poesy;

. . . .

But 'tis impossible; far different cares
Beckon me sternly from soft "Lydian airs",
And hold my faculties so long in thrall,
That *I am oft in doubt whether at all*
I shall again see Phoebus in the morning:
  ("To George Felton Mathew," 11-12, 17-21)

O Poesy! for thee I grasp my pen
That am not yet a glorious denizen
Of thy wide heaven; yet, to my ardent prayer,
Yield from thy sanctuary some clear air,

. . . .
            . . . that I may die a death
Of luxury, and *my young spirit follow*
The morning sun-beams to the great Apollo
Like a fresh sacrifice. . . .
    ("Sleep and Poetry," 53-56, 58-61)[31]

Similarly, if we have been preoccupied with the sounds
of sea, wind, and bird-song, it is not because only these
evoked a response from the poet but because he happened to specify them in an important passage relating
to his central conception and continued to use them as
representative of nature's harmony. But he could also
speak of such functionally affective sounds as these, for
example:

            . . . seasons when I've thought
No spherey strains by me could e'er be caught

. . . .
That the still murmur of the honey bee
Would never teach a rural song to me:
    (Epistle: "To My Brother George," 3-4, 13-14)

Small, busy flames play through the fresh laid coals,
And their faint cracklings o'er our silence creep

[31] My italics in all above citations.

Like whispers of the household gods. . . .
("To My Brothers")[32]

It will be noted in the five passages cited above, however, that although the poet moves from the end of the day to its beginning, and includes sounds which do not occur in the two poems we have taken as normative, each excerpt has one or more points of contact with the conceptual framework we have been exploring. Obviously, each has been included here for that reason. But the point to be inferred is not that Keats always included some external identifying mark of his theoretical construction; it is, rather, that he refused to be bound by the strict letter of his own "law," preferring instead to use it as a nucleus for the accretion of conformable particles of experience. He did not turn the theory on and off but rather made it accommodate as many things as possible.

The greatest virtue of Keats's system may have been, indeed, the extent of its accommodation. Though it established tests for itself (nature against myth, and the reverse), these tests operated to include, rather than exclude, the great variety of normal experience. For the poet's attempt, at all times, seems to have been to establish the relevance of every experience to a comprehensive, meaningful pattern in which the physical and spiritual aspects of life might be seen as coadunate members of

[32] E. C. Pettet comments on the extent to which the very naming of sounds occurs: " 'Rustle', 'murmur', 'hum', 'whisper' (and their derivatives) are significantly prominent in Keats's vocabulary." He also observes, simply as a matter of record and without reference to anything but the fact, that "Where sounds are described in Keats's poetry they are usually soft and delicate ones—the 'rustle of the reaped corn', the whisper of leaves, the murmuring of breezes, fountains and streams, the humming of bees . . ." [*On the Poetry of Keats* (Cambridge, 1957), p. 73 and note]. All the sounds that he names as typical, it will be observed, are voices of the natural world.

one comprehensive whole. Myth provided a symbolic medium for expressing this unity; and observation of his own experience in the worlds of nature, intellect, and art provided him with natural loci for the extension and material verification of myth itself. Sometimes, as in the examples above, evidence of the adaptation process clings to the finished work. But where there is no such evidence, we cannot safely conclude that the poet was creating his effects at random, for some of his transmutations are extremely subtle and must be pieced together from hints in a variety of contexts. We cannot consider all of these, for they would take us into an unprofitable investigation of minutiae, but a few of them, by virtue of their recurrence, constitute significant extensions of the symbolism attached to Keats's central hypothesis and should therefore be noted.

One of these, which occurs frequently in Keats's poetry, is wine. The poet's delight in good claret is a matter of record,[33] and many of the references to wine in his poetry simply communicate the pleasure of drinking it. But there is also an occasional note of its utility as an intoxicant, an available Lethe, for the banishment of insistent memory. Such is its use in one of the earliest poems, "Fill for me a brimming bowl," in which the poet calls for it as an aid (which proves to be ineffectual) in the eradication of desire for a beautiful woman whom he affects to have seen. In one of his last poems, "What can I do to drive away / Remembrance from my eyes?" which reflects his feelings about Fanny Brawne and strikingly resembles in development the earlier poem, he

---

[33] *Letters*, II, 56, 64, 90, *passim*. Most people, however, find it hard to believe Haydon's story that Keats's self-indulgence extended to the sprinkling of his tongue with cayenne pepper in order to increase his pleasure in the coolness of the wine [*The Autobiography and Memoirs of Benjamin Robert Haydon*, ed. Tom Taylor, 2 vols. (London, [1926]), I, 302].

again meditates this easy way out, but rejects it as "vulgarism." In both cases the wine is literally intended, its function is negative, and it is rejected, in the former case as impractical, in the latter as improper.

But in the period between these poems, development in another direction, less literal and more positive, may be discerned. In the epistle to Clarke, wine becomes a metaphor for poetry:

> By this, friend Charles, you may full plainly see
> Why I have never penn'd a line to thee:
>
> . . . .
>
> Because my wine was of too poor a savour
> For one whose palate gladdens in the flavour
> Of sparkling Helicon:
>   ("To Charles Cowden Clarke," 21-22, 25-27)

Despite the poet's confusion of the mountain with its spring (Helicon for Hippocrene), it is clear that his poetry is represented as a draught comparable, though not equal, to one from the sacred fountain of the Muses, i.e. classic poetry. A hint of the associational process by means of which wine becomes a metaphor for poetry may be seen in the adjective "sparkling," here applied to the waters of the fountain. In other contexts it is a quality of wine. In the epistle to George, where the poet represents the ability of imagination to people the air with ideal visions, one pleasure of his ethereal revellers is in

> Their rich brimm'd goblets, that incessant run
> Like the bright spots that move about the sun;
> And, when upheld, the wine from each bright jar
> Pours with the lustre of a falling star.
>   (Epistle: "To My Brother George," 39-42)

In his occasional poem "On Receiving a Curious Shell," he inquires, "Hast thou a goblet for dark sparkling wine?"[34] And in *Endymion* (I, 154) a priest carries a sacramental urn of "mingled wine, out-sparkling generous light."

One may be justified by these hints in an attempt to supply the analogical process that Keats has not given us. Wine is identified in one place with poetry; in several others, with light. In the normal course of Keats's thinking, poetry itself is sufficiently identified with light by having its source and sanction in the god of light. Thus, it is rhetorically asserted in "I stood tip-toe" (125-26), "what has made the sage or poet write / But the fair paradise of Nature's light?" the myth here being accommodated to the language of natural perception. As for wine, it is the concentrated essence of a fruit that has grown to ripeness through absorption of the sun's rays. It is, in fact, precisely the same thing in the physical sphere that poetry is in the intellectual, for poetry is the

---

[34] I do not recall anyone's having noticed that the literal wine of this passage and the metaphors of poetic wine and water, in the epistle to Clarke, are linked by association with the poet Tasso. The full stanza in which the line above occurs is as follows:

> Hast thou a goblet for dark sparkling wine?
>   That goblet right heavy, and massy, and gold?
> And splendidly mark'd with the story divine
>   Of Armida the fair, and Rinaldo the bold?

The epistle to Clarke continues from the point at which it is terminated above (27-31):

>   . . . small good it were
> To take him to a desert rude, and bare,
> Who had on Baiae's shore reclin'd at ease,
> While Tasso's page was floating in a breeze
> That gave soft music from Armida's bowers. . . .

For our present purposes, it is enough to note the complex imaginative linking of poetry and the "breeze" in the concluding lines of the latter quotation.

concentrated essence of human experience, nurtured, in another capacity, by the same god who ripens the fruit. And finally, wine and poetry, these twin essences of Apollo's grace and power, may be equated in their effects. The exaltation which results from the drinking of wine is frequently matched, in Keats's verse, by the effects of poetry or song. For example, when the poet, in "Sleep and Poetry," asks to breathe the pure air of poetry's "heaven," he pleads that it be "Smoothed for intoxication by the breath / Of flowering bays" (57-58). And when Peona sings to Endymion, accompanying herself on the lute:

> Surely some influence rare
> Went, spiritual, through the damsel's hand;
> For still, with Delphic emphasis, she spann'd
> The quick invisible strings, even though she saw
> Endymion's spirit melt away and thaw
> Before the deep intoxication.
>
> (*Endymion*, I, 497-502)

Given such compact association, one may come to expect that Keats's wine will properly sparkle with the light that is the life of poetry.

But for the wine that *is* poetry, let us look at several different passages. The first provides the setting for the description, in *Endymion*, of a Latmian priest carrying sacramental wine. The priest is part of a ceremonial procession headed by young damsels and

> A crowd of shepherds with as sunburnt looks
> As may be read of in Arcadian books;
> Such as sat listening round Apollo's pipe,
> When the great deity, for earth too ripe,
> Let his divinity o'er-flowing die
> In music, through the vales of Thessaly.
>
> (*Endymion*, I, 139-44)

Note that when Apollo's divinity overflows it takes the form of music, presumably, in this case, pastoral poetry. I think this is more than verbal synaesthesia, that it is a typical Keatsian compression of imagery, in which the god is conceived as his essence of light, in himself and in the effects of that essence on the world of organic nature, and that the processes between the ripening of grapes under this influence and the overflowing of the wine goblet are allusively implicit in lines 142-43. I freely admit that this is a far fetch, and that Keats may simply be inventing a likely episode in Apollo's nine-year superintendence of Admetus' flocks. But the temptation to see it as a direct "historical" explanation of poetry's origins, consistent with the notion of a god who makes exemplary music for man, and amenable to treatment in metaphors already habitual with the poet, is so strong for me that I like to believe it was so for Keats too. In any case, I put the reading forward as a reasonable explanation of a poetic language that is otherwise dizzyingly inconceivable. For another, and unambiguous, overflowing or overbrimming of the god:

> Hence Burgundy, Claret, and Port,
>   Away with old Hock and Madeira,
> Too earthly ye are for my sport;
>   There's a beverage brighter and clearer.
> Instead of a pitiful rummer,
> My wine overbrims a whole summer;
>   My bowl is the sky,
>   And I drink at my eye,
>   Till I feel in the brain
>   A Delphian pain—
> Then follow, my Caius! then follow:
>   On the green of the hill
>   We will drink our fill

Of golden sunshine
Till our brains intertwine
With the glory and grace of Apollo!

What is music in the previous passage, in this is light,
metaphorically represented as wine. And in the overflowing of Apollo's glory and grace in the spiritually intoxicating golden sunshine that is drunk in at the eye, we
have, transferred to another physical sense, the familiar
poetry of earth that is conventionally heard as a natural
music which eventuates in the echo that is human song.
And all together, source, natural medium, and literary
end-product, are constituents of that beauty which the
proem of *Endymion* assures us can lighten our spirits.
Among the elements there mentioned are the sun and
moon, various details of terrestrial nature (I, 13-19), "the
dooms / We have imagined for the mighty dead" (I, 20-
21), and finally, "All lovely tales that we have heard or
read: / An endless fountain of immortal drink, / Pouring
unto us from the heaven's brink." (I, 22-24) Even in
casual prose the terminology persists. In November 1817,
distinguishing for his friend Bailey what he takes to be
the characteristic activities of a complex mind, and the
materials proper to the operation of each, Keats mentions
thought, which depends upon "increase in knowledge,"
and *imagination*, to which is necessary the "Wine of
Heaven," which he defines as "the redigestion of our most
ethereal Musings on Earth."[35] It is such a definition as,
with equal ease, he might at any time have given to
poetry.[36]

[35] *Letters*, I, 186.
[36] David Perkins, *The Quest for Permanence*, pp. 248-49, not
only observes that wine has metaphorical implications in Keats's
poetry but reflects that it "was at one time or another explicitly
linked with poetry, with imagination, with happiness, with 'heaven,'
in short with all that the nightingale represents." Happily for the

Another extension of Keats's basic construction, or a sort of grounding of it in first principles, is the view of human life as a process comparable to one revolution of the seasons in external nature. This is, to be sure, an archetypal conception so ancient as to be the virtual earth-mother of all analogy. The distinctive feature in Keats's use of it is his focus on the growth of the mind, rather than on the mere facts of physical vigor and decay. For this, the basic text is the following sonnet:

Four seasons fill the measure of the year;
  There are four seasons in the mind of man:
He has his lusty Spring, when fancy clear
  Takes in all beauty with an easy span:
He has his Summer, when luxuriously
  Spring's honied cud of youthful thought he loves
To ruminate, and by such dreaming nigh
  His nearest unto heaven: quiet coves
His soul has in its Autumn, when his wings
  He furleth close; contented so to look
On mists in idleness—to let fair things
  Pass by unheeded as a threshold brook.
He has his Winter too of pale misfeature,
Or else he would forego his mortal nature.

The process relates to the mind, but mind in the sense of imagination. In Spring and Summer, the active periods of growth and consolidation, it is "fancy" that does the ingathering for the substantial work of "dreaming." The fancy is fed by "beauty" (natural, one concludes), and the dreaming process thus sustained opens visions of immortal truth, i.e. of "heaven." Up to this point, the poem is a compendium of Keats's aesthetic. Since he is

---

fruit of my laborious years, Mr. Perkins has negative capability and did not develop at any length the implications of his casual discovery.

writing not about the poet but about man in general, Autumn is characterized simply by a spiritual condition of serenity and contentment. For the poet, one may suppose, there is a reaping time to come.

Indeed, the idea of poetry as an intellectual harvest is, in all probability, the point from which Keats began composition. The central idea of the sonnet, adapted to the vocation of poetry, with all its essential elements in the same relationship to each other but carried to a more explicit conclusion, is expressed by the poet in a letter to his brother Tom. Commenting on the magnificence of the scenery he was encountering on his walking-tour in the north, he concluded, "I shall learn poetry here and shall henceforth write more than ever, for the abstract endeavor of being able to add a mite to that mass of *beauty which is harvested from these grand materials, by the finest spirits, and put into etherial existence for the relish of one's fellows*."[37] The idea of poetry as a harvest of the mind is perhaps best remembered in the opening quatrain of the sonnet, "When I have fears," where the poet meditates the possibility of being cut off by untimely death from the fulfillment of his artistic purposes:

> When I have fears that I may cease to be
>> Before my pen has glean'd my teeming brain,
> Before high-piled books, in charact'ry,
>> Hold like rich garners the full-ripen'd grain. . . .

The metaphor of poetry as harvested grain, but a harvest that depends upon the grain's being "full-ripen'd" in the course of the poet's sufficiently long life, completes the analogy of the mind's growth with the seasons of the year and consolidates the two spheres of Apollo's "ripening" influence.

It might be observed, of course, that the metaphor,

[37] *Letters*, I, 301, italics mine.

however ingenious, is perfectly appropriate and comprehensible in its particular context and requires no external intellectual support. Since it is quite clear, however, that Keats did abstract and intellectualize his perceptions, the fitness of the metaphor for its subject must be less a ground for reproach than a compliment to the poet's ability to mediate with perfect clarity between the private world of his abstractions and the public world of generalized experience. In any case, the harvest symbol is central in Keats's thought and, in one form or another, recurs repeatedly throughout his work. We have already noted its relation to Apollo in the area of external nature, and the simple analogy by which means the god's ripening influence on the fruits of earth is made comparable to the maturing of the human mind, over which he also presides. In terms of Keats's habitual symbols, the representation of both poetry and Autumn's harvest in consistent association with the image of gold confirms the identical nature, in his mind, of the Apollinian influence on both spheres.

Moreover, probably because of its happy implication of inevitable fulfillment, Keats was accustomed to associate the seasonal cycle of nature with his own heavenward-aspiring intellection. In a heavenly vision, Endymion blows a note on Diana's horn and is rewarded with a Spenserian procession of the four seasons (*Endymion*, IV, 420-24). Again, the poet verifies his "vast idea" of the "end and aim of Poesy" by referring it to elemental certainty: " 'Tis clear / As any thing most true; as that the year / Is made of the four seasons—" ("Sleep and Poetry," 293-95). Had he conceived this certainty as mere change, simple mutability, the whole tenor of his poetry would have been different. What he did conceive of, throughout his poetic life, though with varying degrees of hope for its spiritual extension, was not merely change but process, the basic life cycle as a pregnant ripening toward fulfillment: "green fruit would swell / To melting pulp" (*Endymion*, I, 836-37); "fruit ripening in stillness" (Sonnet: "After dark vapours"); Autumn and the sun conspiring to "fill all fruit with ripeness to the core; / To swell the gourd, and plump the hazel shells" (Ode: "To Autumn").

The distinction between change and process is important, for the view that is held governs the way in which facts will be observed and interpreted. As one writer has put it: "Change merely abstracts the contingent differences and stresses their relation, without taking the substantial ground of necessity into account. . . . Nature in its concrete reality is not merely changing, but 'becoming,' and in the movement of becoming, as in all movement, is a necessity of direction . . . and it is the idea of force with which we grasp this necessity of direction."[38] Keats saw necessity of direction, inferred from it the idea of force, and from force the idea of purpose—all of which he summed up in the concept of Apollo. When in the "Four seasons" sonnet he analogized the growth of the human mind to the process of growth in nature, he simply made explicit in a relatively conventional form the view he had long held of an essential relationship between them. Apollo hovers unseen.

The exercise of influence upon the linked realms of external nature and human spirit, with more explicit emphasis on spiritual influence, is related in *Endymion* (III, 30-31, 34-40):

A thousand Powers keep religious state,
In water, fiery realm, and airy bourne;

. . . .

[38] Martin Foss, *Symbol and Metaphor in Human Experience* (Princeton, 1949), p. 28.

Yet few of these far majesties, ah, few!
Have bared their operations to this globe—
Few, who with gorgeous pageantry enrobe
Our piece of heaven—whose benevolence
Shakes hand with our own Ceres; every sense
Filling with spiritual sweets to plentitude,
As bees gorge full their cells.

The passage is interesting for its suggestion that there are more things in heaven, at least, than are dreamt of in our philosophy,[39] but it serves our immediate purpose merely to note that the origin in divine influence of both our physical and our spiritual nourishment is here directly affirmed. And the operation of the related processes is peculiarly Keatsian: the divine purpose is manifested in external nature, which affects our human senses and, through them, confers the reward of spiritual understanding. The cooperating natural process is subsumed in the spiritual, being its agent in function and its microcosm in character. Thus the lesser, more tangible, process can be separated from that greater one, of which it is the constituent, and serve as a metaphor of purely human processes and values. In the section of the poem from which the lines above are taken, Keats does just that. He speaks of the human tyrants who blast the felicity of divine benevolence to mankind as creatures who "browse away / The comfortable green and juicy hay / From human pastures" and "sear up and singe / Our gold and ripe-ear'd hopes" (*Endymion*, III, 3-5, 7-8). Though the framework here is political rather than aesthetic, the metaphor of organic process remains constant.

[39] While I am by no means persuaded that Keats had anything like the knowledge or interest in those Hermetic systems derived from the *Timaeus* which are attributed to him by Bernard Blackstone [*The Consecrated Urn*, (London, 1959) pp. 77, 150, *passim*], he does seem to be hinting at them in the first few lines of this passage.

The metaphor appears again in a political context in the sonnet "To Kosciusko," where it introduces the most subtle and elaborate development of all the attendant extensions of Keats's mythologized poetic. Keats's political liberalism found something to admire, without distinction as to nationality or specific circumstance, in all who had ever risen grandly to the challenge of tyranny. His liberalism was a strong factor in his early admiration of Leigh Hunt (as attested by the sonnet "Written on the Day That Mr. Leigh Hunt Left Prison"), and, for the same reason, such names as Brutus, Wallace, Tell, and Kosciusko are significantly prominent in his early poetry. Here is the sonnet "To Kosciusko":

> Good Kosciusko, thy great name alone
> > Is a full harvest whence to reap high feeling;
> > It comes upon us like the glorious pealing
> Of the wide spheres—an everlasting tone.
> And now it tells me, that in worlds unknown,
> > The names of heroes, burst from clouds concealing,
> > Are changed to harmonies, for ever stealing
> Through cloudless blue, and round each silver throne.
> It tells me too, that on a happy day,
> > When some good spirit walks upon the earth,
> > Thy name with Alfred's, and the great of yore
> Gently commingling, gives tremendous birth
> To a loud hymn, that sounds far, far away
> > To where the great God lives for evermore.

It will be noticed immediately that the "harvest" is again one of mental attitude or spiritual state, in this case a "high feeling" which is identified in the ensuing lines with harmony. One may take it as the sonnet's essential statement that the harmony is between earth and heaven, resulting from the existence of an earthly being who fulfills the heavenly ideal and is, therefore, not only *persona grata* in both spheres but a link between them. It is in the lives of such heroes that men see through the discord of discrete events to the comprehensive harmony of being that is possible in the human condition. Kosciusko's function for the generality of men thus corresponds in the sphere of action to that of the poet in the sphere of contemplation. But to the poet, one may infer, men like Kosciusko stand in a special relationship, much like that between poet and nature. Clearly perceived through the discordant elements which constitute the life of each (i.e. nature and hero) is an essential harmony which reflects the harmony of heaven and serves as inspiration to the poet, to whom the hero's very name comes like music. But Kosciusko is not a passive instrument, like the wind or sea; he is a man who has made choices, has consciously *willed* the pattern of his life. His role, like the nightingale's but in greater degree, is therefore Apollinian, for he is not only the agent but also the creator of harmony. The sonnet's representation of this harmony in terms of the music of the spheres forms another link with Apollo, who, by the analogy of harmonious celestial movement with the harmony of music, was also the classical presider over astronomical order.

Given Keats's working fiction of a poet's Elysium, and his innocently violent political idealism, one might reasonably expect to find some place in his system for humanity's heroes. An Elysium for heroes has, after all, a far more ancient and widespread sanction in the literature of antiquity than an Elysium for poets.[40] But there appears to have been a more cogent reason for the inclusion of patriots with poets in Keats's Apollinian scheme. It will be noted that Kosciusko's name is paired with Alfred's, in the eleventh line of the sonnet above; and

[40] For the literary history of both, see G. Giovannini, "Keats' Elysium of Poets," *MLN*, LXIII (1948), 19-25.

the two occur together again as champions of "the goaded
world" in "Sleep and Poetry" (385-88), where their por-
traits are catalogued with the rest of the art objects in
Leigh Hunt's study. It *could* have been from the circumstance of their being represented together there that
Keats chanced to associate them when he was writing
the sonnet. But Alfred's name seems consistently to have
been a touchstone for Keats and occurs oftener in Keats's
poetry than that of any other patriot-hero.[41] He is also
mentioned twice in the letters, and on both occasions as
a paragon.[42] Of the others whose names occur more than
once in the poems, none but Sidney is ever mentioned
in the letters. Such evidence suggests that Alfred was the
symbol of an ideal that could be locally represented by
any one of a number of other heroes; just as, say, Apollo
is the symbol of an ideal that can be locally represented
by a nightingale or a grasshopper. The question is, how
did Alfred attain to such eminence in Keats's esteem?

It appears that more than the inevitable schoolboy
knowledge was at work here, and that Alfred's name

[41] Alfred is referred to in four poems: in the sonnet to Kosciusko,
in the epistles to Mathew and Clarke, and in "Sleep and Poetry."
Kosciusko appears twice, in the sonnet addressed to him and in
"Sleep and Poetry," in both places associated with Alfred. William Tell appears twice, in the epistles to Mathew and Clarke,
and is associated in both with Alfred. Sidney [undoubtedly Alger-
non, not Sir Philip, though Keats speaks in one of his letters of
"the two Sydneys" as great men of former times (*Letters*, I, 397)]
is twice mentioned, in the sonnet "Oh! how I love" and in the
lines beginning "Infatuate Britons," written on the anniversary of
Charles II's restoration. Brutus, Wallace, Russell, and Vane appear
once each.

[42] Keats says his own temperament is such that he could "be as
proud of being the lowest of the human race as Alfred could be
in being of the highest" [*Letters*, I, 142]. In another place he remarks, "I like, I love England, I like its strong Men. . . . Give me
a barren mould so I may meet with some shadowing of Alfred in
the shape of a Gipsey, a Huntsman or as [*for* a] Shepherd" [*Letters*, I, 242].

was elevated for Keats by an outside association. The nexus is to be found, I believe, in Leigh Hunt's poem, "The Feast of the Poets," a satirical survey of contemporary British letters, in which Apollo descends to earth and passes judgment on the practising poets of the age. At Apollo's entrance, Hunt affects inability to describe his magnificence and concludes the attempt by confessing,

> No,—nobody's likeness will help me, I see,
> To afford you a notion of what he could be,
> Not though I collected one pattern victorious
> Of all that was good, and accomplish'd, and glorious,
> From deeds in the daylight, or books on the shelf,
> And call'd up the shape of young Alfred himself.[43]

Hunt appended to these lines a lengthy note, clearly aimed at the Prince-Regent, the general tenor of which may be gathered from this excerpt: "A note upon Alfred might be indulged me, on the strength of his having been reckoned the 'Prince of the Saxon Poets'; but the name of that truly great man is not to be mentioned without enthusiasm by any constitutional Englishman,— that is to say, by any Englishman, who truckling to no sort of licentiousness, either of prince or people, would see the manliest freedom of a republic, adorned by the graces and quickened by the unity of a monarchy.—But to whom indeed, that has an admiration for any great or good quality, is not the memory of Alfred a dear one? —a man, beloved in his home, feared by his enemies, venerated by his friends,—accomplished in a day of barbarism,—anticipating the wisdom of ages,—self-taught,

[43] Leigh Hunt, *The Feast of the Poets, with Other Pieces in Verse*, Second Edition (London, 1815), p. 3. In the first and second editions the passages cited are identical, except for slight variants of punctuation. I cite the second merely because it has been more continuously accessible to me.

and what is more, self-corrected,—a *Prince* too, who sub-
dued the love of pleasure,—a Monarch, who with power
to enslave, delighted to make free,—a Conqueror, who
could stop short of the love of conquest . . . a Sage, in
short, who . . . practised every art of peace as well as
war, of leisure as well as activity . . . cleared his country
from its invaders, and . . . established the foundation of
those liberties, upon which we are at this moment enjoying our every-day comforts."[44] Keats almost certainly
knew the work, for it went through several editions in
the years when he was most impressed with Hunt, and
there is a probable allusion to it in the epistle to Clarke
(44-45), where Hunt is mentioned as one "who has told
you stories / Of laurel chaplets, and Apollo's glories."[45]
Given Hunt's identification in it of Apollo with Alfred,
and of Alfred as the allusive antitype of the modern
figure for opposition to whom Keats most admired Hunt,
the special prominence of Alfred in Keats's mind is readily understandable. Nor is it difficult to see how the very
name of the patriot-hero Kosciusko, a later creation on
this prototype, could set the spherey strains of heaven
ringing.

That men could themselves so participate in the orchestration of universal harmony is a significant fact of
Keats's organizing conception, and one that has not been
adequately recognized. Critical tradition has it that Keats
came late to an awareness of humanity and contented
himself in his early verse with sensuous responses to suburban prettiness.[46] Such traditions die hard, even in the

[44] *Ibid.*, pp. 41-42.
[45] Colvin says the allusion is "of course" to Hunt's *Feast of the
Poets* [*John Keats*, p. 113]; Lowell says Keats "had probably read
and admired" the poem [*John Keats*, I, 119]; Finney believes
Keats had "very probably" read both the first edition of 1814 and
the second edition of 1815 [*Evolution of Keats's Poetry*, I, 72].
[46] For example, Joseph Warren Beach, *The Concept of Nature*

face of the poet's repeated affirmation that he wrote poetry "To sooth [*sic*] the cares, and lift the thoughts of man" ("Sleep and Poetry," 247), and (granting the prettiness) they fail to note the extent to which man is a part of the spiritual scenery of the early poetry. There were limitations to his view, as Keats discovered, and to some extent they were the limitations imposed by the felt necessity of relating all things to a single unifying conception. But if the conception proved finally to be inadequate, it was not because humanity was left out of it. Rather, it was because Keats's humanitarianism was too intellectual, too idealistic, too abstract. Like many another Romantic, he oversimplified the problems of human existence and, as a consequence, tended to think of men as of merely two kinds—those whose lives *were* poetry and those whose lives *needed* poetry. The men whose soothed cares and lifted thoughts were to testify to the ameliorative power of poetry were perhaps seen as more inert, depressed, and spiritually enslaved than, for the most part, they had any reason to think themselves, while those rare spirits who lent their lives to the physical and spiritual liberation of their fellows were perhaps seen as possessing more truth than in fact proved negotiable in the world of common circumstance. Cer-

---

in Nineteenth-Century English Poetry (New York, 1936), p. 32: "In its humblest and commonest sense, nature refers to the 'beauteous forms' of the external world, as distinguished from man and his works. . . . Among the romantic poets, none represents better this phase of nature-poetry than Keats, in such pieces as 'Sleep and Poetry' or in the famous opening lines of 'Endymion.' No one is happier than he in his review of 'Nature's gentle doings'; no one brings such nosegays of charming and variegated items, crushing together into one fistful so many samples of 'the poetry of earth.' And we know from Keats the simple and all-sufficient justification of nature in this sense—'A thing of beauty is a joy forever.' In this sense nature means flowers, birds, brooks, breezes and moonlit glades."

[83]

tainly the power of poetry to effect such a reorientation of first principles as would then readjust automatically the perspective of lesser, practical dilemmas was vastly overrated. Yet the idealism of conception and application which produced the distortion was certainly in essence humane. It was simply not close enough to home.

The human figures who people Keats's intellectual landscape include the patriots of every land and era, and, of course, the poets. Both are saints in Keats's cosmos, but the poets are especially dear to the god, whom they continue to serve after death as they served him in life; both are accessible, in their mortal works and in the memory of their prototypal persons, as guides to the living men who come after them. What they guide men toward is a perception of the elemental harmony in which, as creatures of the cosmos, all men are necessarily participants. Their instrumentality, as it is the nearest human approximation of the cosmic harmony, and the most acceptable evidence of reverence for the presiding god of harmony, is song. The poets in Elysium sing to the god, in the Apollo ode. The lives of the heroes *are* song, in the Kosciusko sonnet, where the presence of a good spirit on earth strikes a chord that vibrates sympathetically in Elysium and blends the disparate heroes' names into a harmonious hymn "that sounds far, far away / To where the great God lives for evermore." Note here that music, even as it comes from the god, is what man at his best renders back to the god. Just so, the poet, in "Sleep and Poetry" (27-40), responsive to the whispering hymn of nature which "gives a glory to the voice," replies with "Sounds which will reach the Framer of all things." The human perception of universal harmony engenders a reverence for its Author which is expressed in the homage of imitative repetition. Whatever the form of this hymnic worship, its mode is to "echo back the

voice of thine own tongue" ("Sleep and Poetry," 52).
Thus, in the terms that Keats chose for their representation, the life of heroic action may be considered to be,
and the life of poetic contemplation *is*, an affirmative
dedication to the *imitatio Apollinis*.[47]

[47] This imitative ideal is what Keats was attempting to embody
in some lines from "Sleep and Poetry" (162-66) which have proved
troublesome:

> Is there so small a range
> In the present strength of manhood, that the high
> Imagination cannot freely fly
> As she was wont of old? prepare her steeds,
> Paw up against the light. . . .

Sidney Colvin, while admiring the passage of which they are a
part, grants that "a prosaic and rational" fault-finder might well
ask, "What is it . . . that the imagination is asked to do? Fly, or
drive? Is it she, or her steeds, that are to paw up against the
light? And why paw?" [*John Keats*, p. 119]. While a certain
awkwardness of language must be acknowledged, there is really
no mystery about the passage's meaning. Clarification is to be
found in the little song, "Apollo to the Graces," which Colvin
himself first published. In its third line, Apollo announces his readiness to begin his daily task of driving the sun's chariot in these
words: "My Steeds are all pawing on the thresholds of Morn."
Against this background, the lines in question from "Sleep and
Poetry" are interpretable only as a metaphor for imagination's
necessarily imitative Apollinian activity. The idea probably fails
to be conveyed because the image seems to have no reference
point in the poem other than the image of the charioteer who is
seen in the poet's vision (125-56), and who is not Apollo but the
imaginative type of the poet. (Descending from the heavenly plane
to which he is not native, hence must travel with "glorious fear,"
but to which his powers give him virtually unlimited access in
the Apollinian mode, he communes with natural forms until their
imaginative or spiritual essences yield up to him a language which,
with "hurrying glow," he tries to capture in his writing; and then,
his task successfully completed, he reascends to his proper sphere,
i.e. "Into the light of heaven. . . .") Here, as occasionally elsewhere, Keats dipped casually into his reservoir of private symbol
without sufficient attention to the reader's capacity for recognition.
If C. L. Finney's dating is correct [*Evolution of Keats's Poetry*, I,
230], the clarification of the "pawing" image in "Apollo to the
Graces" was not written until about a year after the completion

In the course of this introductory exposition we have
had occasion to examine passages from nearly forty of
Keats's poems, all but a half-dozen or so antedating his
brief period of mature greatness. The number is significant, for it reveals the extent of the poet's early preoccupation with the intellectual structure that clarified
for him the relations of the inner and outer worlds of experience, and it illustrates the degree to which the symbols of that structure had become the habitual expressive
medium of his thought.

At the center of that thought, inferable from the uni-
formity of its relations to a variety of symbolic images
and mythological constructions, is an aesthetic theory in
which the poetic imagination is seen as the mediating
agency between the worlds of substance and idea. Influenced by physical sensations of pleasure and by intellectual perceptions of complementary relationships between the worlds of mind and natural form, the poet is
induced to hypothesize an unseen energizing force, con-
terminous with the universe itself, in which both physical and intellectual effects have their source and in the
context of which they coexist in harmonious fusion and
balanced intensity. Sense and intellect, responding to
stimuli from the natural world, thus lead to the threshold
of a truth that activates and transcends that world. However, since the human faculties of sense and intellect are
restricted in their operations to the world of sensible
forms and separable conceptual entities, exploration of a
plane to which sense and intellect have no direct access
must be accomplished by the faculty of imagination.
Since the imagination need not contend solely with rela-

of "Sleep and Poetry," an interval during which the superficially
inexplicable image remained fixed, vivid, and precise in the poet's
mind.

tions among the discrete effects observable in the natural
world, it suffers none of the logical limitations imposed
upon consecutive reason and can therefore explore directly the world of ideal harmony in which the effects
are known ultimately to be comprised. And from this
world of the *super*natural, the imagination returns with
perceptions of absolute truth which it then casts in terms
drawn from experience of the natural world, and so en-
riches the understanding of all mankind.

Although Keats's conceptual emphasis ultimately falls
on the nature and agency of the poetic imagination, the
process, leading from sensory perception to spiritualized
conception, is essentially that which Donne represented
as the necessary avenue to love:

> So must pure lovers' souls descend
>   T'affections, and to faculties,
> Which sense may reach and apprehend,
>
>   . . . .
> Love's mysteries in souls do grow,
>   But yet the body is his book
>   ("The Ecstasy," 65-67, 71-72)

and which led Milton to apprehension of an un-Keatsian,
far more orthodox empyrean:

> There let the pealing organ blow
> To the full-voiced choir below,
> In service high and anthems clear,
> As may with sweetness, through mine ear,
> Dissolve me into ecstasies,
> And bring all Heaven before mine eyes.
>   (*Il Penseroso*, 161-66)

TWO

Endymion

AN APPROACH

CONDESCENSION is the attitude that predominates in critical assessment of Keats's early poetry, and in many ways this is just. Measured by any standard, including that of his own later achievement, the pre-*Endymion* poetry is frequently sentimental and often less exuberant than luxuriant in its verbal excesses. If it was conceived on the highest principles, the poet had yet not matured in his own idiom, and, indeed, the principles themselves were conducive to variously amorphous and fanciful expression. If readers condescend to such poetry, it is not because it is absolutely bad (or they would not read it at all) but because they recognize it as the imperfect apprentice work—frequently occasional, often dashed off in the haste of momentary inspiration, and sometimes imitative—of a poet whose later greatness justifies the uneven experience of examining his earlier works.

When we approach *Endymion*, however, the critical attitude is necessarily more complicated. *Endymion* is a sustained work, of obviously serious intention, to which the poet devoted the major part of his energy during approximately one-quarter of his active writing-life.[1] On such grounds, it claims our sober attention. There are many evidences within it, however, that Keats had not yet entirely emerged from his apprenticeship, and his own preface acknowledges the poem's imperfection. We

[1] I include the extended period of its correction, copying, and proofreading.

may thus be tempted to see it as merely an extended exercise of a kind already familiar and judged to be negligible. In fact, the critical tendency has been to adopt one view or the other, and to represent the poem as either a giant step toward conceptual and architectonic maturity or a puerile ramble through an unweeded and unconscionably vast garden of immature themes and forms.

My own view moderates these extremes but abides in respect for the poet. Many vices of diction that had characterized Keats's previous poetry are still apparent, but in proportion to the poem's length they are, I think, scarcely cause for more than an admirer's occasional regret. Some passages seem overrich in imagery, and to the extent that one feels himself, at these points, eddying in the poem's main current, this is a defect. Yet I hope to be able to demonstrate that many of these passages are not mere self-indulgence in poetic fancy but integrally related elements in the poem's thematic progress. I do believe that, although there are digressions, the poem shows considerable architectural skill once its thematic core is discovered. But I cannot conclude that the poem's theme represents any sort of advance in Keats's thinking. It is, rather, at once the major poetic representation and the swan song of the aesthetic that had sustained the poet up to this point in his career, but which he was soon to find no longer tenable.

My discussion, then, will support the view that the Endymion story, as treated by Keats, is basically that of a young man who has become disaffected with the ordinary physical world, and with his own mortal relationship to it, because he has had a vision of a higher mode of existence. What he must learn, and does, in the course of his experiences, is that the higher level to which he aspires is not to be achieved by abandonment of the limited powers with which he has been endowed as a human being, or by disparagement of the physical world which serves as the arena of human activity, but that these are indeed the only possible avenues to the fulfillment of his ideal vision.[2] This narrative and thematic program therefore embodies and illustrates the theory of poetic imagination discussed in the previous chapter, in which the imagination was seen to draw its strength from the natural world and to proceed by that means to comprehension of the ideal. Endymion's adventures thus represent successive stages in the poetic imagination's growth to full maturity.

The Endymion myth was perfectly adapted to the representation of such a process of development, for it represented in the persons of Endymion and Cynthia the union of mortal and divine, of mundane and celestial. Keats was not here obliged to make his own myth, as to a certain extent he had had to build up his Apollo myth out of bits and pieces of received lore, and he was therefore not initially hampered by the difficulties of communication which attend the use of a relatively private context of allusion. It is true that the Endymion of classical antiquity was not all of a piece; he had figured in several related legends, from which he emerged variously as the ideal of manly beauty, the type of serene indifference to worldly ambition, and the inheritor of eternal youth. But in the long history of English literary allusion and adaptation he is almost exclusively cast in the narrative role used by Keats, that of the moon god-

[2] I am aware, of course, that I "support," and do not originate, this view of the poem. See, for example, Douglas Bush, *Mythology and the Romantic Tradition in English Poetry*, p. 95. What I have to contribute to the continuing dialogue on *Endymion* is not radical novelty but coherent specificity, a demonstration of the multitudinous ways in which Keats said what he meant, throughout the poem, and of the consistency of this with what he had been saying all along.

dess's mortal lover.[3] It is also true, however, that union between a mortal and a deity is a staple, indeed almost the *sine qua non*, of classical story, and it is relevant to ask why, from all the available possibilities, Keats chose this particular legend as the vehicle of his poem.

It is easy enough to say, and to demonstrate, that Keats was particularly susceptible to the beauty of the moon. Lunar references and encomia are abundant in his pre-*Endymion* poetry, and, as one might expect from a person of Keats's sensibility, he was moved not only by the variousness of the moon's appearances but also by the appearances of other objects touched with its light. His close observation of its merely visual effects is seen in such early poems as the sonnet "To Lord Byron":

> . . . when a cloud the golden moon doth veil,
> Its sides are ting'd with a resplendent glow,
> Through the dark robe oft amber rays prevail,
> And like fair veins in sable marble flow;[4]

and "To Hope," in which the title's abstraction is adjured "Where woven boughs shut out the moon's bright ray," to "Peep with the moon-beams through the leafy roof." But among these graphic notations of visual experience one also finds the subjective aesthetic judgment, as in "Calidore" (157), "Lovely the moon in ether, all alone" and a shading of the visual effect toward mythological personification, as in the sonnet "To My Brother

[3] The fullest single treatment of the Endymion legend in classical story and English literary history is Edward S. LeComte, *Endymion in England: The Literary History of a Greek Myth* (New York, 1944).

[4] There is a possible literary influence on even such descriptions, however. The image of sun or moon obscured by clouds is a favorite with Spenser (e.g. *Faerie Queene* I, vii, 34; II, vii, 29; II, ix, 16; III, iii, 19), who occasionally gives it as detailed a treatment as Keats does here (e.g. *Faerie Queene*, III, i, 43).

George": "Cynthia is from her silken curtains peeping /
So scantly, that it seems her bridal night, / And she her
half-discover'd revels keeping." The full significance of
this mythological drift, which is manifested with increasing frequency as we approach the time of *Endymion's*
composition, emerges in the following lines of "I stood
tip-toe":

> . . . the moon lifting her silver rim
> Above a cloud, and with a gradual swim
> Coming into the blue with all her light.
> O Maker of sweet poets, dear delight
> Of this fair world, and all its gentle livers;
> Spangler of clouds, halo of crystal rivers,
> Mingler with leaves, and dew and tumbling streams,
> Closer of lovely eyes to lovely dreams,
> Lover of loneliness, and wandering,
> Of upcast eye, and tender pondering!
> Thee must I praise above all other glories
> That smile us on to tell delightful stories.
> For what has made the sage or poet write
> But the fair paradise of Nature's light?
>
> (113-26)

The movement of the passage is from simple visual effect
to personification of its source as an agent of beauty
throughout the natural world, and an agent of sufficient
power to bring poets into being because its basic quality
is the conveniently ambivalent essence of *light*. Indeed,
the specific object of the poet's apostrophe virtually disappears in the last couplet as the essential quality is suddenly precipitated from the poetic solution.

Although Keats has not left us any other record of his
mental processes at this point, one cannot fail to observe
that Cynthia here receives the sort of paean elsewhere
reserved for Apollo, that she assumes his function of in-

spiring poets, that the inspiration she furnishes is manifested, like Apollo's, in the natural world, and that she
shares with him, indeed is reduced in essence to, his distinguishing quality (as sun-god) of light. She has, in
other words, for all practical poetic purposes become
identical with him.

When it is recalled that, by virtue of their sharing the
task of illuminating the earth, Apollo and Artemis (or
Phoebus and Phoebe, or Cynthius and Cynthia) were
classically represented as twins of a single birth, one can
readily divine the reason for Keats's merely apparent
transfer of affection and can reasonably postulate that
the same motives which no doubt led him to extend the
effective time-span of Apollinian inspiration from the
sunset hour to the whole period of the god's diurnal
presence also operated toward the inclusion of the moon
in his mythopoeic poetic. With the twins Apollo and
Cynthia providing day and night illumination of the
arena of human experience, there remained no time when
the world was without that visible enlightenment of
which, for Keats, the intellectual corollary was poetic inspiration. The inclusion of Cynthia in his scheme therefore constituted the systematic fulfillment of his working
hypothesis that "The poetry of earth is never dead."[5] And,

[5] Additional incentive toward the identification of Cynthia with
Apollo, if more were needed, might have been given Keats by his
reading of Drayton's "Man in the Moone," which we know Keats
owned in one of John Smethwick's editions of Drayton's poems
[Keats Circle, I, 254] and which has been called "one of the chief
sources of Endymion" [C. L. Finney, Evolution of Keats's Poetry,
I, 177]. In Drayton's poem there is not only the traditional account of twin birth (279-82) but a comparison between the four
quarters of the moon's cycle and "the Foure Seasons of my Brothers Yeere" (391-92), and, ideally adapted to the strengthening of
Keats's own conception, the following:

> . . . wise Apollo, that doth franckly lend
> Her his pure beames, with them doth likewise send
> His wondrous knowledge, for that God most bright,

obviously, the choice of Cynthia's pursuit as the subject of a narrative romance necessarily acquires, from this understanding of her identity, a pointed conceptual significance.

Still, however reasonable the assimilation of Cynthia to Keats's overarching scheme, and the writing of a verse romance around her, may seem in retrospect, the indications are that the poet came haltingly and by indirection to these consummations. We know that Keats had for some time wished to try his hand at a metrical romance. It is generally supposed that Leigh Hunt's publication in February 1816 of "The Story of Rimini" provoked a desire for emulation which culminated, that spring, in Keats's writing of the "Specimen of an Induction to a Poem" and "Calidore." Though he subsequently published them in the 1817 volume, neither can have given him much joy. The "Induction" is sweetly and tritely Spenserian, and its agglomeration of tenuously related stereotypes of nature and chivalry perfectly reflects its argument, i.e. that the poet wishes to write a romance and doesn't quite know how to begin. "Calidore," however, the poem for which presumably the "Induction" was written, is replete with the elements (evening, west, sun, gold, nature sounds, nightingale) which Keats habitually associated with both Apollo and poetic composition. One might infer, then, that Keats felt his romance narrative capable of embodying a more intellectually significant truth than is normally associated with such compo-

---

King of the Planets, Fountaine of the Light:
That seeth all things, will have her to see,
So Farre as where the sacred Angels bee.

(479-84)

My citations and line numbering are taken from the second volume of *The Works of Michael Drayton*, ed. J. William Hebel, 4 vols. (Oxford, 1931-35).

sition. Unfortunately for this ambition, his *theory* of imagination seems to have been more inventive than his actual *narrative* imagination. After a long prologue filled with natural description that incorporates many of Keats's personally significant symbols, at the point where actual storytelling could no longer be reasonably delayed, the poem abruptly breaks off.

Frustrated thus in his attempt to write a metrical romance, and in his attempt to draw meaningfully upon his small store of potent symbols, Keats fell into relative inactivity for several months. As he was obliged to take his final medical examinations late in July, it is not surprising to find this interval lean in poetic composition. While his main effort probably went into his medical studies during the summer, he kept his hand in at poetry, and no doubt regained the confidence he had lost in the ill-fated "Calidore," by occasionally composing things that he knew he could do well without too much effort—sonnets and, I believe, much of the loco-descriptive nature verse that constitutes the bulk of "I stood tip-toe." As more urgent matters crowded in upon him, however, it would have been natural to let this busy-work slide. But in August, having passed his examinations and thus been confronted with the necessity finally to make a choice between the careers of medicine and poetry, Keats removed himself to Margate for a period of solitary reflection, writing, and self-assessment. After some vacillation, he began to produce poems almost continuously, and the principal extensions of his orienting aesthetic and its attendant symbolism, as reviewed in the previous chapter, date from this time.

At the risk of seeming to press a point, I cannot forbear the suggestion that at this crisis in his life the poet might well have been struck by a curious coincidence, namely that his choice lay between two modes of service

to the same god. That Apollo was anciently the god of
healing, Keats would have known from Spenser and the
classical dictionaries, as well as from the Hippocratic
Oath (beginning, "By Apollo Physician . . ."), with
which he must surely have become acquainted during his
just-completed medical studies, though he probably did
not have to swear it.[6] Given his conceptual orientation,
it is certainly not impossible, therefore, that Keats was
influenced in his decision for poetry by the reflection
that whatever service he might render in the medical
profession would be limited and local in time and place,
while the profession of poetry, with its capability of conferring benefit upon all posterity, was an infinitely higher
form of service. That he was thinking of his choice of
careers in terms of humanitarian service is clear from the
epistle "To My Brother George" (especially lines 67-
112), which was composed during the period of decision.
Very soon afterwards, he was to conclude "I stood tip-
toe" with a paean to the healing power of poetry, or the
healing effects of an incident in the creation of a particular poetic myth (see the fuller discussion below). And
much later, though the idea may have been with him
for years, he was to state the case directly, in *The Fall of
Hyperion* (189-90): "sure a poet is . . . Physician to all
men."

In any case, among the first fruits of Keats's renewed
poetic activity was the sonnet "To My Brother George"
(cited above), where suddenly, in an enlarged catalogue
of natural effects which are wondrous to the poet (the
sun in morning as well as evening, the voice of the sea,

---

[6] I have been unable to learn whether the oath was being ad-
ministered in Keats's time, but, as he was under legal age, his
licensing was probably deferred, and so must have been whatever
other commitments attended the beginning of practice. See William Hale-White, *Keats as Doctor and Patient* (Oxford, 1938),
p. 32.

the moon), Cynthia appears in the role of Endymion's bride. Here, though perhaps the thought did not occur immediately, was an authentic subject for a romantic verse tale. In the following month, September, came the verse epistle "To Charles Cowden Clarke," which contains a similar catalogue of natural effects (sunrise, breezes, golden corn), these being represented as directly conducive to poetry, and here Cynthia appears in the climactic position (93-96). By her inclusion in such a list, she begins unmistakably to enter the Apollinian preserve. In all "innocence" perhaps, Keats had by now alluded to Cynthia as a romance figure in one poem and as an exemplar of nature's poetry-making power in another. It was almost inevitable that, if they had not already done so, the ideas must soon coalesce.

And at this crucial point the firm lines of the development blur. By early October Keats was back in London. During that fall and winter his circle of friends was widening, his social life was increasingly active and exciting, and this excitement found expression in the poems he was writing. Most of these poems have to do directly with the subject of poetry itself, or of its creators, and they reflect, if not a settled mind, at least increasingly firm commitment. There is still a great deal of questioning in them of the road to take, but there is no longer the question of whether the journey ought to be made.

The chief of these poems, in dedication and firmness, is "Sleep and Poetry." The precise time of its composition is not known, but there is general agreement that it falls somewhere in, or perhaps was a continuing project throughout, November and December of 1816.[7] Keats

---

[7] Amy Lowell, *John Keats*, I, 215-16, and C. L. Finney, *Evolution of Keats's Poetry*, I, 136, arrive at the same conclusion for entirely different reasons, and Hyder Rollins, *Letters*, I, 32, implies his concurrence with both. W. J. Bate, *John Keats*, pp. 122-

has a great deal to say about the poetic calling in this work, and it is here that one finds the famous lines (96-125) in which his anticipated progress is charted, from wandering in the realm of Flora and Pan, through periods of dalliance with the nymphs of classic imagination and delighted perusal of lovely tales of human life, to culmination in the nobler recording of the agony and strife of human hearts. The general movement of the passage is from lyric to romance to heroic poetry, and while the focus of description is on the gentler aspects of human experience, there is no question whatever of where the poet expected his apprenticeship in delight to lead him. The idea of an heroic poem was already with him as an ultimate goal, but it is clear that the poet did not yet feel himself ready for it. Indeed, in terms of his own prospectus and his achieved body of work, he had not yet left the realm of Flora and old Pan. It remained to him first, before moving on to heroic poetry, to tarry with white-handed nymphs and lovely tales of human life.

Meanwhile, elsewhere in "Sleep and Poetry," he was defining the nature and function of poetry. Apollo is clearly the presiding deity of all this disquisition; he is alluded to directly three times (60, 183, 202) and indirectly almost as often as one is willing to countenance his identification with those symbolic equivalents discussed in the previous chapter. And not surprisingly, the twin essences of this sun- and poetry-god are ultimately abstracted for the quintessential definition, "A drainless shower / Of light is poesy" (235-36). It is at this point that "Sleep and Poetry," the concluding work in Keats's first published volume, most nearly touches the developmentally significant "I stood tip-toe," the poem with

---

23, and Aileen Ward, *John Keats: The Making of a Poet*, p. 88, agree as to general period.

which that volume begins and which Keats had been refurbishing while he wrote "Sleep and Poetry." In "I stood tip-toe," the corresponding statement is, "For what has made the sage or poet write / But the fair paradise of Nature's light?" (125-26) And there the referent is Cynthia. The two poems overlap and join in thematic import at these points, where the aesthetic theory, hitherto embodied in a variety of Apollinian images, is abstracted and stated in terms of the single image most readily identifiable with both Apollo and Cynthia, that of light.

I think we can trace the probable source of this concatenation if we remember that Keats had failed, earlier in the year, to complete a poetic project that was important to him, the composition of a verse romance. The failure in this single kind implied some lack of ability to sustain poetic composition, no matter how pretty was the talent that so employed itself, and as a consequence, Keats for perhaps the first time began to doubt his poetic calling. The time from the retreat to Margate to the completion of "Sleep and Poetry" was one of indecision, as reflected in the preoccupation of the poetry of that period with the subject of poetry itself and with the increasingly comprehensive extension of the epistemological and aesthetic system upon which Keats justified to himself a commitment to poetry. The remarkably full, though variously stated, "essay on criticism" that is embedded in "Sleep and Poetry" summarized the thinking of this interval and signaled an end to indecision.

Before the self-doubt could be considered effectively overcome, one gap remained to be filled—the production of a verse romance. This would simultaneously cancel the failure of the previous spring, demonstrate to the poet the strength and competence of his imagination, and constitute the forward step toward a poetry of high serious-

ness which the program outlined in "Sleep and Poetry"
implicitly prescribed. "Sleep and Poetry" itself, in its abstraction of light, as an essential quality, from both the
deity and the natural effects in which Keats had been
accustomed to embody it, provided the key. Apollo's
natural and metaphorical essence could be abstracted
and its qualities attributed to his mythological twin sister,
the moon, for whom the poet more or less fortuitously
had already found uses in his writing. Since a romantic
legend already accompanied her name, the poet's invention would not be strained, and since she lent herself so
readily to the adaptation of those symbols customarily
identified with Apollo, he could the more readily infuse
his romance with the more-than-ordinary significance
with which he so evidently had tried to invest "Calidore."
And, happily, he already had a substantial set of verses
written, onto which the romance elements might easily
be grafted. These were, of course, the descriptive lines
beginning, "I stood tip-toe upon a little hill," which had
too many nice touches to be thrown away, yet had been
untouched since summer for lack of a direction in which
to carry them on. They could now assimilate the romance
element and go out into the world under the title of
Endymion.

That the present version of "I stood tip-toe" came
into being on something like this principle and this time-
table I infer from two facts, one quite simple to describe
and the other somewhat complex. For the first, Keats referred to the poem by the name of *Endymion* only once,
and that was in a letter of December 17th in which he
indicated that he was then at work on it.[8] The second
fact has to do with the state of Keats's working draft.

Owing to the disappearance of some of the draft's manuscript pages, and owing further to Keats's having re-

[8] *Letters,* I, 121.

distributed some of the original passages in the poem's final form, and added others, the successive stages of the work's composition are very hard to ascertain.[9] What can be said, however, is that the poem shows signs of uncertain intention. As an example of altered intention, there is the fact, first noted by Amy Lowell and later confirmed in fuller discussion by Professor Garrod, that Keats's numbering of lines in the original draft indicates that the matter subsequently included in lines 61-106 did not at first have any place in the poem.[10] I find this appearance of altered intention the more interesting because I believe the draft manuscript also shows that the lines most significant in the development we are tracing, those which include the identification of Cynthia with light and with poetic inspiration (123-50), and those celebrating the union of Cynthia and Endymion (196-214), were originally composed as separate units and were subsequently fitted into a poem which had not at first been intended to accommodate them.

The first of these passages (123-50) appears on one side of a single sheet of paper and is not continuous, at either end, with the lines written on the other side of the sheet. Moreover, these lines (123-50) replace four others, or perhaps eight, that had originally followed line 122 but were subsequently canceled.[11] And not only is this passage unrelated to the matter on the reverse side of the sheet, but the lines on the reverse side (87-106) are a portion of those which Lowell and Garrod agreed were not a part of the original composition. That is, the sheet apparently was employed for the composition of differ-

[9] For a discussion of the materials and problems, see H. W. Garrod (ed.), *Poetical Works*, pp. lxxxiv-lxxxviii, whose description I rely upon, though our hypotheses differ.

[10] Amy Lowell, *John Keats*, I, 151; H. W. Garrod (ed.), *Poetical Works*, p. lxxxvi.

[11] *Poetical Works*, p. 7n.

ent kinds of addenda. The second set of lines (196-214) is missing, as a unit, from the manuscript. While there are any number of possible explanations for their disappearance, at least one of these is that they did not constitute part of the original composition, and hence did not find their way into the small bundle of draft sheets that was preserved. This manuscript separateness of the passages specifically devoted to Cynthia, as both inspirer of poets and bride of Endymion, strongly encourages the inference of their being, in fact, interpolated matter.

As it happens, the only other place in the manuscript where Cynthia is named is at line 239, where her name is substituted for the original word "Alas." The lines between 214, which concludes the missing manuscript introduction of the topic of Cynthia's romance with Endymion, and 239, where Cynthia is again named, are purportedly in celebration of the wonderful effects on the world of her bridal consummation. Taken by themselves, however, they could be about almost any regenerative influence on the world, and they sound suspiciously (with their allusions to Apollo and healing breezes) like a subjectively idealized description of poetry's power in the world as Keats was inclined to conceptualize that power and as he had recently described it in the verse epistle to his brother George.

Now, it also happens that, where the missing manuscript portion (196-214) begins, our attention has just been called to a poet on the top of Mount Latmus who is about to be inspired, by the natural beauty around him, to invent the myth of Endymion and Cynthia. The function is, clearly, to illustrate a prior argument that such natural inspiration was the ancient source of poetic myth. But the lines in the missing draft section suddenly and illogically shift the emphasis from the illustrative example of the poet creating his myth to the substance of the myth itself. What seems to have happened is that Keats, for late-developing reasons of his own, decided to claim for the Endymion-Cynthia myth certain values which he had originally intended to claim for poetry in general, and that what had at first been conceived as an illustrative example of imagination's sources in the natural world was at some later time seen by the poet to be a possible symbolic formula for it.

With this emphasis, the poem went all awry, but it scarcely mattered. It was already doomed as a verse romance, chiefly because of the nature and stages of its genesis. For one thing, Keats, in continuing the orientation of Cynthia's introduction into the sonnet to George, where the "revels" of the wedding night provide the basis of the allusion, had started his romance at the point where it should logically have ended. For another, he had so far subordinated his romance to his aesthetic theory that his heroine's personality disappeared in the metaphorical light of the lunar orb. There is no reason, of course, for Keats to have rested content with failure, the actual number of lines devoted to Cynthia and Endymion being so few and so obviously interpolated as not to preclude reorientation of the whole, unless he had glimpsed a more fruitful way of organizing his creative activity. The radical redirection in the lines with which "I stood tip-toe" came to an end suggests that he had. And so he abandoned the artificially spliced-together romance, permitted the poem to be published in the 1817 volume, without title, as pleasantly versified natural description with highlights of historical fancy and poetic theory, and soon afterwards plunged into the task that all this temporizing had finally brought into focus for him. In early spring he again separated himself from the pleasures of society, withdrew to the Isle of Wight, and began the *Endymion* that the theory of "Sleep and Poetry" and its crude objectification in "I stood tip-toe" had progressively revealed to him.

But one may wonder, if Keats's verse romance were to be centrally concerned with the pursuit of those qualities which the poet habitually associated with Apollo, why the god himself should not have been the focus of attention. To this there are several possible answers. Simply in terms of literary tact, the narrative action of a love pursuit lends itself to the pursuit of a woman by a man. Had Apollo been the object of pursuit in any received legend, Keats might conceivably have taken it for his framework. It is at least equally possible, however, that he would not have, for the program he had outlined in "Sleep and Poetry" gave him good reason to hold his presiding deity in reserve for a more suitably august role in a heroic poem. It is impossible to know at exactly what point he fixed on the story of Hyperion for this purpose, but before he had finished *Endymion*, Keats knew that it was to be his next major project.[12] As "Sleep and Poetry" makes clear, however, heroic poetry was a goal which he consciously deferred to a later stage in his poetic maturity. With such humility as this implies, it is at least reasonable, and I am willing to leave it at this conjectural level, that he did not yet feel equal to risking the grandeur of his Apollo figure either in the verse romance that he was working himself up to write or in a premature heroic poem. No such objection could be raised to the use of Apollo's twin sister, however, in a poem whose

[12] The very choice of Hyperion as title-character, the Titan who was to be succeeded by Apollo, indicates the conceptual influence of Keats's Apollinian orientation on even his subject matter. Discussion of *Hyperion*'s genesis in the poet's mind can be deferred until we consider that poem itself, but it has seemed relevant here to introduce it as at least a negative factor in Keats's substitution of one deity for another at a crucial point in the development and exposition of his deity-centered aesthetic.

kind precluded the necessary austerity and control of heroic story. In any case, it is as well to remember that at no time, from the emergence of Cynthia in Keats's continuous consciousness through "I stood tip-toe," does she actually displace Apollo—she simply merges with him, becomes his alter ego. Having firmly arrived at this conceptual understanding, Keats could let Apollo himself, the origin of that light which Cynthia perfectly reflected, await the more finished poetical treatment which the experience of a long narrative poem would make possible. When the poet felt himself worthy of the task, he could then let his beneficent male deity shoulder the burden of amelioration in that more austere poetry of the agony and strife of human hearts which "Sleep and Poetry" projected as the high consequence of apprenticeship in the gentler forms of composition.

One cannot be certain of the precise order in which all these ideas occurred to Keats, or of the clarity with which he first conceived them; but close attention to his actual poetic progress during the fourteen months between his first desire to emulate Hunt's verse romance and the beginning of composition on his own *Endymion* reveals a progression of essentially the kind sketched here. Keats's immediate ambitions in poetry, and the systematic development of his chief intellectual concerns, with their concomitant objectification in an enlarging frame of symbolic reference, brought him to the point where, in the writing of "I stood tip-toe" and "Sleep and Poetry," their juncture promised a rich and cogently organized program of composition, the first fruit of which was to be *Endymion*. For reasons that Keats could not yet imagine, it was also to be the last.

It is enough for our present purposes, however, to recognize that, in Keats's initial conception of the poem as a whole, Endymion's pursuit of Cynthia was seen as

[105]

ENDYMION

the romance equivalent of the poet's pursuit of poetry.
In this consists the whole basis of the poem's allegory.[13]
As an anticipatory specimen of *Endymion*'s allegorical
method, nothing is of more interest than the way in
which Keats manages, within the poem itself, the transfer of power from Apollo to Cynthia, taking the shepherd
prince over the same ground that he had himself traveled in the enlargement of his poetic vision. Keeping in
mind Keats's initial devotion to Apollo, the special efficacy of the sunset hour, and finally, the sharing of Apollo's
power with Cynthia and her ability to serve in his stead
as inspirer of poetic vision, let us look at Endymion's first
revelation of the dream that is to compel his actions
throughout the remainder of the poem.

[13] That the poem *is* an allegory is a position to which I am so
persuasively led by the evidence that it becomes almost a matter
of definition rather than of argument. If Cynthia stands for Apollo,
and Apollo represents the source and ideal essence of poetry, then
Cynthia is a symbol. And if allegory is the narrative form of symbolic representation, then *Endymion* is allegory.

The most recent anti-allegorist is E. C. Pettet [*On the Poetry of
Keats*, pp. 127-29], who argues, on the apostrophe to the moon in
"I stood tip-toe," that "there is nothing to suggest that Keats at
this time attached any important symbolical significance to the
moon: it is merely what it had always been from his earliest
poems, a central image of luxurious delight . . ." and that the references to the Endymion-Cynthia romance in the sonnet to George
and in "I stood tip-toe" reflect the poet's attraction to "the erotic
quality of the legend." Professor Pettet further maintains that the
program of development that Keats envisaged for himself in "Sleep
and Poetry" indicated, for the immediate future, "a kind of poetry
that expresses, and in poet and reader stimulates, sensuous and
erotic pleasure . . . poetry of the sort that he had been steadily
composing for a year or more," and that it precluded, in the imminent *Endymion*, "the elaborate metaphysical allegory with which
he is now commonly credited." Though I cannot offhandedly en-
dorse whichever of the "elaborate metaphysical" interpretations
Professor Pettet had in mind at the moment of writing, I believe
his preliminary argument to have been met by the points so far
considered in this chapter, and I can only hope that the discussion
to follow will be found persuasive.

[106]

Endymion first represents himself as having been drawn to a particular spot at the edge of a wood where he could with special advantage see the full power of the sun-god in his setting:

> ... in that nook, the very pride of June,
> Had I been used to pass my weary eves;
> The rather for the sun unwilling leaves
> So dear a picture of his sovereign power,
> And I could witness his most kingly hour,
> When he doth tighten up the golden reins,
> And paces leisurely down amber plains
> His snorting four.
>
> (I, 545-52)

By the light of the sun's last rays Endymion suddenly sees a bed of flowers which had never been there before, and, speculating on the significance of their appearance, sits down beside them:

> Now when his chariot last
> Its beams against the zodiac-lion cast,
> There blossom'd suddenly a magic bed
> Of sacred ditamy, and poppies red:
> At which I wondered greatly, knowing well
> That but one night had wrought this flowery spell;
> And, sitting down close by, began to muse
> What it might mean.
>
> (I, 552-59)

The magic bed of flowers that is revealed to the lover of sunset is composed, significantly, of "sacred ditamy and poppies red," the two flowers given in Lemprière (Keats's favorite classical dictionary) as sacred to Diana, or, which is the same thing, Cynthia.[14] Overwhelmed by the

---

[14] From the essay on "Diana" in John Lemprière, *Bibliotheca Classica*, Revised Edition (London, 1804). The influence of

difficulty of assigning a reason for the sudden appearance of the flowers, and lulled by the scent of the poppies, Endymion drifts into sleep.

The dream that follows is too long for convenient citation in full. In summary, Endymion dreams that he is gazing at the stars when suddenly the doors of heaven are opened to his gaze. But as he tries to penetrate the mysteries thus made accessible to him, they begin to fade from sight. Reluctantly lowering his eyes from the zenith to the horizon, he is rewarded by the appearance through the clouds of the loveliest moon he has ever seen. Dazzled by its beauty, his spirit goes out to it, but he is disappointed again when it disappears behind an even darker cloud. Raising his eyes to the zenith again, Endymion is startled to see a radiant goddess approaching from on high. Her physical description, which follows immediately, is disappointingly that of a Regency coquette, with one interesting exception echoing the preoccupation of several past years: "Speak, stubborn earth, and tell me where, O where / Hast thou a symbol of her golden hair? / Not oat-sheaves drooping in the western sun" (I, 608-10). The silver moon-goddess is here en-

---

Lemprière on the poet was first documented by Charles Cowden Clarke, who recalled that during Keats's schooldays, "his constantly recurrent sources of attraction were Tooke's 'Pantheon,' Lemprière's 'Classical Dictionary,' which he appeared to *learn*, and Spence's 'Polymetis'" [Charles and Mary Cowden Clarke, *Recollections of Writers*, p. 124]. The italics, which place the emphasis on Lemprière, are Clarke's. Aileen Ward [*John Keats: The Making of a Poet*, p. 421] argues that Keats had no particular interest in mythology until late in 1816, and that Clarke was therefore either mistaken altogether in his recollection of Keats's interest in Lemprière [p. 417] or mistaken in the motive for Keats's youthful fascination with the volume—which she thinks may have been merely one of prurient interest in the illustrations of the goddesses [p. 19]. I will not vouch for anyone's memory, including my own; but I have seen several contemporary editions of Lemprière, and none of them has had any illustrations.

hanced by the adornment which had hitherto been used to identify the god "of the golden hair," and the point of comparison in describing its glory is the customary harvest gold of Apollo's making, seen in the western light of Apollo's setting.

The remainder of the dream is given to the first love-encounter of Endymion and the moon-goddess and is of no special moment here. The immediate point is that Endymion, a lover of the sun (and especially of its evening glory), has been made subject, by that means within himself, to the influence of the moon, whose equal beauty he perceives in his dream. Had he not been devoted to the sun's beauty, he would not have been a regular visitant of that place where the grandeur of its setting was most advantageously seen. Had he not been a regular visitant to that place, he would not have seen, in the sun's last rays, the sacred flowers of Diana, whose scent lulls him into that dream in which he perceives the moon's full beauty and is rewarded with the reciprocal love of the moon-goddess herself (though he does not yet know her identity). For Endymion, as for Keats, a special devotion to natural beauty has earned a special revelation; and for Endymion, as for Keats, this revelation includes both a more extensive perception of natural beauty and a closer communion with the divine presence than are granted to less devoted mortals. And finally, Endymion is virtually handed over by his presiding deity to another of equal virtue, just as Keats was led by his concept of Apollo to a recognition of Cynthia's value in the total scheme of his aesthetic understanding. All of this is implicit in the episode Endymion describes, and a knowledge of the significance for Keats of the details included in the account reveals its meanings with perfect clarity. Without such knowledge, of course, it all seems mere random fancy.

Insofar, then, as Cynthia is to be looked upon allegorically as the representative of Apollo, the question arises as to how the kind of authority she is permitted to wield in Keats's poetic theory is adaptable to the framework of romance. The narrative basis of the poem is the love quest of Endymion for Cynthia. Since this same quest is, on the thematic level, the poet's search for authentic imaginative experience such as can lead him to the intuition of truths beyond the normal limitations of human perception, it is appropriate to inquire about the mutual relevance of narrative and theme. Are we simply to suppose that the poet's quest of authentic inspiration is, in its difficulty, comparable to the lover's pursuit of his beloved? Or is there a closer link, a more organic relationship between the two, within the poem itself?

I believe there are several perceptible links. The action of the poem, for instance, takes place in four areas: on the earth, in the underworld, in the sea, and in the air, successively through the four books. Colvin rejects the supposition of Bridges and de Selincourt that Keats thus intended his hero to explore the four elements of earth, fire, water, and air, on the sufficient ground that fire is not even implied, much less stated.[15] Colvin does not, however, provide any other hypothesis for the multiple scenes of action, and only Dorothy Hewlett, among subsequent scholars, has offered an alternative reference point, i.e. the travels through earth, water and air in Southey's "The Curse of Kehama."[16] While Southey's poem may, of course, have had a suggestive influence, it would not explain the relevance of the poem's backgrounds to its purposes. The real link is to be found, I believe, in Keats's favorite classical dictionary.

[15] Sidney Colvin, *John Keats*, pp. 173-75.
[16] Dorothy Hewlett, *A Life of John Keats*, Second Edition, Revised and Enlarged (New York, 1950), p. 170.

The classical minutiae that Keats evidently gleaned from the pages of Lemprière, such as the sacredness of the ditamy and poppy to Diana and of swans to Apollo, suggest great care in its perusal. It seems most likely, then, that he would have read carefully each article given to the various classical identities of his poem's heroine, and, considering the significance given to love in the poem, that he would have studied attentively the articles on the classical love deities. In such a perusal he would have found that the power of his poem's goddess "was extended over heaven, the earth, the sea, and hell. . . ."[17] He was, of course, familiar with her threefold influence over heaven, earth, and hell, as his sonnet "To Homer" illustrates, and the association of moon and tides could have provided the area of the sea. But here, without the necessity of intellectual carpentry, is a concrete statement that her influence was reckoned in antiquity to extend to every possible sphere of the physical world. For the full understanding of her nature, then, nothing could be more appropriate than to have Endymion explore every natural area of her influence, especially in a poem designed to explain the essential relevance of natural perception to the contemplation of that ideality which we associate with the divine. And how much more appropriate such a plan would be to his purposes one discovers in Lemprière's article on Cupid, where it is stated that "as his influence extended over the heavens, the sea, and the earth, and even the empire of the dead, his divinity was universally acknowledged. . . ."[18] The god of love and the goddess of light are thus given, uniquely in Lemprière, so far as I have been able to ascertain, comprehensive influence over the same four spheres of nature;

[17] *Bibliotheca Classica*, article on "Hecate."
[18] *Ibid.*, article on "Cupido."

ENDYMION

and these, by no coincidence, become the areas through which Endymion pursues in love the queen of light.

Indeed, such overlapping of divine functions to the point of a conceptual merging of identities is powerfully rendered in the image chosen by Keats to represent the chief intensity of the kind of experience discussed in the "fellowship with essence" lines,[19] ". . . at the tip-top / There hangs by unseen film, an orbed drop / Of light, and that is love" (I, 805-7). In this most concentrated expression of the values upon which both narratively and thematically the poem is constructed, love is expressed as the distillation of light. And light, as we know from Keats's practice up to this point, is the symbol-essence of human understanding carried to the threshold of divine intuition, to the point at which, and only at which, true poetry becomes possible. The pursuit of light, in a spirit of love, through a natural universe whose every region is jointly governed by the deities of light and love, is therefore by no means an idle poetic fancy but rather an almost irreducible allegorical substratum upon which to construct a poetic romance illustrative of the epistemological assumptions that currently underlay the poet's understanding of the creative mind and its characteristic activity.

If I do not misread his awkward syntax, it would seem that no less a reader than Shelley understood the poem to be concerned with the poetic mind. Though not overfond of *Endymion* as a whole, in his general characterization of the poem he said that "everything seems to be viewed by the mind of a poet which is described in it."[20] It is especially interesting that Shelley should consider

[19] To be more fully discussed below, in the detailed analysis of the poem.
[20] *The Letters of Percy Bysshe Shelley*, ed. by Roger Ingpen (London, 1909), II, 716.

[112]

Keats's love story to be descriptive of the mind of a poet, as I believe he means to suggest here, for he was, himself, soon to make an explicit equation of imagination and love essentially identical with that which is implicit in *Endymion*. In his *Defence of Poetry*, addressing himself to the moral function of poetry, Shelley speaks of the "Elysian light" in which poetry clothes its impersonations of life, and follows immediately with this formulation: "The great secret of morals is love; or a going out of our own nature, and an identification of ourselves with the beautiful which exists in thought, action, or person, not our own. A man, to be greatly good, must imagine intensely and comprehensively; he must put himself in the place of another and of many others; the pains and pleasures of his species must become his own. The great instrument of moral good is the imagination; and poetry administers to the effect by acting upon the cause."[21] That is, the highest agency of moral good is love, and poetry conduces to love because its own essential quality, imagination, is operatively identical with love. Both love and imagination consist in a going out of our natures in sympathetic identification with natures other than our own. Each is the effective analogue of the other and operates toward the same end. Both are, to return again to Keats's language in *Endymion*, "self-destroying" (I, 799). This is the expression Keats uses to describe the achievement of the "chief intensity" of love as the climax of imaginative self-projection (I, 795-807). Who influenced whom in the formulation of this view is unimportant for our present purposes.[22] What does strike one most forci-

[21] Percy Bysshe Shelley, "A Defence of Poetry," in *The Selected Poetry and Prose of Percy Bysshe Shelley*, ed. by Carlos Baker (New York [Modern Library], 1951), p. 502.

[22] Priority is less important than the fact of social intercourse; and, by the time he began to work on *Endymion*, Keats was at the peak (if he had not already just passed it) of his personal ac-

bly is that Shelley should have recognized the poem as a description of the poetic mind, and that he should have expressed his own view of the poetic imagination in terms of the love principle which provides the basis for the action of *Endymion*. I consider these facts not as primary evidence but certainly as confirmatory indications of likelihood that the pursuit of love, in the poem,

---

quaintance with Shelley. While it has been neither proved nor disproved, there is Medwin's story that "Shelley told me that he and Keats had mutually agreed, in the same given time (six months each), to write a long poem, and that the Endymion, and Revolt of Islam were the fruits of this rivalry" [Thomas Medwin, *The Life of Percy Bysshe Shelley*, 2 vols. (London, 1847), I, 298]. Considering Keats's rather combative attitude toward Shelley [attested to in *The Autobiography of Leigh Hunt*, ed. J. E. Morpurgo (London, 1949), pp. 273-74], it is at least no more unlikely that *Endymion* was conceived as a corrective of Shelley's recently published *Alastor*, as one critic has suggested [Leonard Brown, "The Genesis, Growth, and Meaning of *Endymion*," *SP*, xxx (1933), 618-53]. But one can probably get closer to the atmosphere of the relationship in the contemporary remarks of Keats's friend Benjamin Bailey, in a letter of August 29, 1818, to John Taylor, on what he takes to be a major flaw in *Endymion*, "The approaching inclination it has to that abominable principle of *Shelley's*—that *Sensual Love* is the principle of *things*." Of which, Bailey adds, "I believe him to be unconscious . . ." [*Keats Circle*, I, 34-35]. Everything we know about Bailey suggests that he habitually stopped lending out his mind at the first hint of pernicious doctrine, so we need not take seriously his interpretation of *Endymion*'s actuating principle, especially since his disclaimer of Keats's intentions assures us that Keats had not expressed such an idea to him as his purpose. But his instinct to see Shelleyan doctrine in the poem reflects his fear of Shelley's influence over Keats at this time, and one would be at a loss to account for this fear on any grounds but his knowledge of their intimacy. Keats himself, for other reasons, appears to have feared an excess of Shelleyan influence, for during the latter stages of *Endymion*'s composition (October 8, 1817) he wrote to Bailey, "You see Bailey how independant my writing has been . . . I refused to visit Shelley [at Great Marlow, on Shelley's invitation], that I might have my own unfettrd scope—" [*Letters*, I, 170], and the following January he complained to his brothers that Hunt and Shelley were being over-

is intended to signify not so much the externally systematized Platonic world view that many critics have inferred (nor the idealized eroticism inferred by others) as the romance equivalent of the imagination's search for "light," in the sense in which it had been habitually understood in Keats's mythologized poetic.

THE POEM

The majority of critics have seen some sort of allegory or submerged pattern of meaning in *Endymion*, but the difficulty of assimilating its diverse elements has precluded anything more than general agreement about the poem's over-all implications.[23] By all odds the most fre-

---

critical of *Endymion* because he had avoided consultation with them during its composition [*Letters*, I, 214]. C. L. Finney [*Evolution of Keats's Poetry*, I, 295] adduces evidence of Shelley's suasive conversational influence on philosophic discussions within the Hunt circle in the months just prior to the beginning of *Endymion*, though Finney's purpose is to support his neo-Platonic interpretation of the poem. We are left, then, with a variety of suppositions about the nature of Shelley's influence but no doubt at all that it existed, and so much so that Keats feared to be intellectually compromised by it. His fear might have been at least partly generated by an embarrassed awareness that he already owed Shelley more than he wished to owe to any immediate contemporary: the opening lines of *Queen Mab*'s second section contain images that Keats had turned into symbols, a phrase or two that he had taken into his own poetry intact, and a central statement that describes the method and end of most of Keats's poetry through *Endymion*. While Keats cannot have done anything more than adapt these felicities to an already-established rationale, they nevertheless suggest at least one reason for Keats's desire to avoid so ready an influence. Still, it is altogether likely that they discussed poetic theory, at one time or another, and that the close correspondence of their views and of the terms in which they are expressed, as noted in the text, above, was therefore not merely fortuitous.

[23] I have been granted no exemption from the difficulties encountered by all other commentators, for they are inherent in the poem as written. As examples of the general problem, and as

quent interpretive rationale put forward is the Platonic—
which I think radically mistaken. If in a mood of piety
toward historical precedence we choose to call Platonic
any bias of mind favoring ideal experience, we are on
safe enough ground with Keats (though in trouble on

---

anticipatory of questions that may be raised about my own subsequent reading, consider the following aspects of only the first book:

(1) The "fellowship with essence" passage (I, 777 *et seq.*) has
been almost universally taken, on Keats's implied authority (i.e.
that "when I wrote it, it was a regular stepping of the Imagination towards a Truth" [*Letters*, I, 218]), as the key to the poem.
It must certainly be taken into account, but it is difficult to rest
easy with any interpretive reading of a continuous narrative which
is based upon a single statement of intention the truth of which
the poet had not himself arrived at until three-quarters of the first
book, including the whole basic narrative situation, had already
been written. And further, I do not recall that any commentator
has observed the inappropriateness of placing this thematic statement in the mouth of Endymion, whose sole function throughout
the poem's narrative action, however that may be interpreted, is
to learn experientially much of the truth of what he here so confidently asserts as his life's credo.

(2) Endymion describes to his sister Peona, at considerable
length (I, 572-681), his first vision of the dream-maiden. Then,
in reply to Peona's scoffing at his faith in dreams (I, 739-60), and
in support of his "fellowship with essence" theory, he claims to
have seen his beloved twice more (I, 918), once mirrored in the
bottom of a well (I, 895-96), and again, presumably in full flesh,
within a woodland cave (I, 965-71). The last of these meetings is
strongly sensual in implication but shadowy in narrative substance.
From the description given, it could be inferred either that Endymion enjoyed full physical union with his beloved in the cave, or
that he merely heard her voice there and glimpsed her form.
Whatever is decided here makes some difference to one's interpretation of their love meeting in Book II, yet neither view can be
absolutely proved or disproved. Despite the suggestive wording of
the passage, I incline to the belief that it was not Keats's original
intention to imply more than a glimpse of the dream-maiden at
this point, for the whole section is introduced by Endymion's hesitant speculation that there *must* be grounds, behind his original
vision, for "A hope beyond the shadow of a dream" (I, 857), for
his subsequent experiences have made him "scruple whether that

a hundred other fronts). But if we say that Platonism, in any of its *systematic* formulations, governed the events and argument of Keats's poem, we must prepare ourselves to ignore significant elements in either our definition or the poem, or both. In what follows, simply because it is a conscientiously developed example of one

---

same night / Was pass'd in dreaming" (i, 860-61). Now, surely, if he had met his dream-maiden incarnate in the cave, and dallied in love with her there, he could no longer harbor any "scruple" about the existence "beyond the shadow of a dream" of the maiden in his original vision, and could confidently assert to Peona that his faith was not in the dream but in the reality which the dream had merely prefigured. It would seem that the tactic of introducing the second and third appearances of the dream-maiden was intended to make Endymion look not quite the fool that Peona's natural skepticism about the dream would make him (since her view is clearly that of the practical-minded person whom the average reader might be supposed to be), but that, perhaps because of an interruption in composition, the poet forgot his secondary intention by the time he wrote about the third encounter. In this belief, I read the meeting in Book ii as only the second love-making occasion.

(3) As will be seen in its place, I interpret most of Book ii as corrective of a revulsion from the world of nature suffered by Endymion after his first dream-vision. That this revulsion takes place is unambiguously demonstrable, but there are several passages (i, 884-87, 898-905, 951-57) which show him *after* his dream, if not in quite the same sort of harmony with nature as before, not revolted by it either—and one of these nature experiences confers a balm upon his spirit. However, this one restorative experience with nature can be plausibly argued, I think, to be not so much natural as a part of the supernatural experience in which Endymion is again vouchsafed a vision of his beloved. Of the others I can only say that I take as indicative of Endymion's general response to external nature, from the time of his original dream, the implication of his promise to Peona that he will reform himself and return to those habits of life which characterized his normal existence before the dream—including just such a lingering contemplation of nature (i, 483-86) as he later says (i, 545-52) was his custom until the time of the first dream. When he says that he will resume the former customs and attitudes, then I can only suppose that he has meanwhile left them off. For the further plausibility of this argu-

kind of Platonic argument, and the one perhaps best known to American students, and because, without being conspicuously better or worse than others of its kind, it reveals the difficulties inevitably encountered in such a reading, I should like to refer occasionally to C. L. Finney's interpretation of *Endymion* as a poem grounded in Renaissance neo-Platonism.[24]

Finney argues that the four major episodes of the poem, embodied successively in its four books, represent stages in a neo-Platonic ascent from substantial to essential beauty, and that these are, in order, (1) appreciation of the beauty of nature, (2) appreciation of the beauty of art, (3) friendship, and (4) love.[25] The justification for this ladder-like scheme Finney locates in the famous poetic statement:

> Wherein lies happiness? In that which becks
> Our ready minds to fellowship divine,
> A fellowship with essence; till we shine,
> Full alchemiz'd, and free of space. Behold
> The clear religion of heaven! Fold
> A rose leaf round thy finger's taperness,
> And soothe thy lips: hist, when the airy stress

---

ment I must rely upon one's judgment of my whole reading of the poem.

These are merely a few examples of the inconsistencies and contradictions with which the interpreter of the poem must contend. As the poet's two prefaces to the work, and his famous letter to Shelley, of August 1820, indicate, he was himself fully aware of its deficiencies. Still, it is equally clear that the poem was a major undertaking, of earnest intent, and where inconsistencies exist the critic must not abandon the attempt at criticism but must weigh the contradictions as scrupulously as he can in terms of the most comprehensive conceptual framework that the whole progress of the poem, and his own understanding of the poet's mental and artistic processes, suggest to him.

[24] *Evolution of Keats's Poetry*, I, 291-319.
[25] *Ibid.*, I, 298-99.

Of music's kiss impregnates the free winds,
And with a sympathetic touch unbinds
Eolian magic from their lucid wombs:
Then old songs waken from enclouded tombs;
Old ditties sigh above their father's grave;
Ghosts of melodious prophecyings rave
Round every spot where trod Apollo's foot;
Bronze clarions awake, and faintly bruit,
Where long ago a Giant Battle was;
And, from the turf, a lullaby doth pass
In every place where infant Orpheus slept.
Feel we these things?—that moment have we stept
Into a sort of oneness, and our state
Is like a floating spirit's. But there are
Richer entanglements, enthralments far
More self-destroying, leading, by degrees,
To the chief intensity: the crown of these
Is made of love and friendship, and sits high
Upon the forehead of humanity.
All its more ponderous and bulky worth
Is friendship, whence there ever issues forth
A steady splendour; but at the tip-top,
There hangs by unseen film, an orbed drop
Of light, and that is love. . . .

(I, 777-807)

Unfortunately, the passage presents more difficulties than supports for Finney's analysis. One of them, which he recognizes immediately, is that Keats is "unorthodox" in placing love higher than friendship in his value system. On this he can only comment that, while Spenser and Shakespeare consider friendship more elevated, because free from sexual attraction, in most of the Elizabethan sonnet sequences "friendship is ignored and love is the sole theme."[26] It might properly be pointed out, of course,

26 *Ibid.*, i, 299.

[119]

that it is one thing to discuss both love and friendship, and to assign them relative values, and quite another thing to celebrate love without reference to friendship.[27] To say that Keats is "unorthodox" is, further, to imply either that he did not fully understand or that he chose to distort the basic value scheme of his poem. Neither alternative conduces to confidence in the proposed value scheme as a foundation for a critical reading of the poem.

Another problem posed for Finney by the "fellowship with essence" lines is that the second stage of his ladder, appreciation of the beauty of art, is left out of them. There are "old songs," "ditties," and hints of heroic story, but these are not presented as objects for contemplation, or indeed as having any substantial existence outside the creative consciousness of the human subject. They are part of nature's "Eolian magic" and represent the imaginative activity of the person inspired to creative dreaming by the sound of nature's voices. This is, of course, simply the process discussed at length in our previous chapter.

Most serious of the objections to Finney's reading of these lines, however, is the fact that the steps in the "ladder" do not exist in any necessary relationship. Keats does not, in good neo-Platonic style, assert that each stage in the process prepares one for experience of the next and higher stage. On the contrary, there are various essences to be in fellowship with, and, while liberation from the world of brute sense is most intensely enjoyed at the level

[27] Elsewhere Finney says that "The neo-Platonic philosophy of beauty was the basic philosophy of the erotic literature of the Renaissance," and cites Petrarch's sonnets to Laura as an example [*ibid.*, I, 292]. To the extent that this is true, the problem remains the same, for love is not overtly *preferred* to friendship, it is simply represented as a manifestation on the human level of the divine power that binds the universe together. In other words, it is another aspect of neo-Platonism altogether.

of love, it appears to be absolute at any level of responsive experience. Even those whose simple pleasure in
nature leads them to imaginative dreaming "have . . .
stept / Into a sort of oneness, and [their] state / Is like
a floating spirit's."[28] Nowhere does Keats say that it is
necessary to experience this *before* one can participate
in the progressively more rarefied essences of friendship
and love, as the ordinary neo-Platonic ladder would require. Each experience is complete, though some are
more intense than others. Again, this is less consistent
with the idea of a Platonic hierarchy than with the theory
discussed in the previous chapter, in which we saw that
nature, *or* art, *or* the memory of great men is, each in its
own way, capable of moving the percipient to direct con-

[28] Newell F. Ford, *The Prefigurative Imagination of John Keats*
[Stanford University Publications, University Series, Language and
Literature, Vol. IX, No. 2] (Stanford, 1951), pp. 14-15, wishing to
deny that "essence" should be understood in a "transcendental
sense," says that Keats uses the word as a synonym for "thing of
beauty" or "shape of beauty," i.e. that "essence" lacks its usual
philosophic meaning and refers simply to objects or concepts capable of stimulating imaginative activity. In support of his view, he
cites the line, "Feel we these things? . . ." and affirms that " 'these
things' refers unmistakably to rose leaves and the various manifestations of music." He is right in general about the "things"
(though the rose leaves are objective entities, while the various
manifestations of music are subjective responses to the objective
sound of the wind), but he entirely misplaces his emphasis, for the
process is valuable less for the "things" than for the *feelings* engendered by them. The "things" exist, willy-nilly, but they have
no significance for us until we "feel" them; and that is where
Keats places his emphasis, for it is at the moment of feeling, he
says, that we participate in oneness with the "things," i.e. with
their essences, and become like floating spirits in our freedom from
objective limitation. Their substance, like ours, has spatial and
temporal existence, but substantial identity is the precondition, not
the culmination, of the process. The rose leaf is therefore not the
essence but the object which operates upon our senses so as to
generate an inner feeling of transcendence over both the object and
the means by which we perceive it, leading us to a fellowship of
our essence with its own.

templation of ideality. The "degrees" of which the poet speaks are levels of experiential intensity, not prerequisites to be first achieved and then abandoned as the subject spirit becomes progressively more refined. We may, however, take the "fellowship with essence" lines as signifying merely the general idea of degree in attainment of supernal vision, and, accepting that as closer to neo-Platonic intention than to any other historically articulated system, inquire whether the four stages through which Finney says Endymion passes are, in fact, demonstrable in the poem.

The first one, appreciation of the beauty of nature, supposedly manifested in the action of Book I, clearly is not. The closest Finney comes to defining Endymion's appreciation of natural beauty is in his representation of a two-stage exposition of its general desirability. This is based, first, on the same "fellowship with essence" lines that he had previously acknowledged to be not a part of the action but a statement of the poem's theme, and, secondly, on an apostrophe to the moon in the *third* book (142-44, 162-69), which he says represents "the worship of a particular thing . . . as a symbol of natural beauty."[29] Further, he confuses here, as in his former discussion,[30] the "clear religion of heaven" with nature—which Keats quite clearly represents as the means to attainment of that clear religion, and not the religion itself.

So far as the action of Book I is concerned, the truth is that not only does Endymion not achieve the limited state of ascent and grace to which a neo-Platonic appreciation of the beauty of nature might entitle him, but he forsakes the world of nature altogether, as loathsome to him in comparison with the vision of divine beauty

[29] *Evolution of Keats's Poetry*, I, 303.
[30] *Ibid.*, I, 299.

presented by his dream.[31] In explaining to his sister Peona the cause of his melancholy, Endymion recounts his vision of the dream-maiden and confesses that, after her disappearance,

>   all the pleasant hues
> Of heaven and earth had faded: deepest shades
> Were deepest dungeons; heaths and sunny glades
> Were full of pestilent light; our taintless rills
> Seem'd sooty, and o'er-spread with upturn'd gills
> Of dying fish; the vermeil rose had blown
> In frightful scarlet, and its thorns out-grown
> Like spiked aloe. If an innocent bird
> Before my heedless footsteps stirr'd, and stirr'd
> In little journeys, I beheld in it
> A disguis'd demon, missioned to knit
> My soul with under darkness; to entice
> My stumblings down some monstrous precipice:
> Therefore I eager followed, and did curse
> The disappointment.
>
> (I, 691-705)

That is, nature not only has lost its beauty for him, but has taken on a sinister aspect of purposive contrariety to his divine aspirations, such as to leave him in mortal despair. It is precisely this condition that the poem exists to explore. Endymion has not taken the first step upward but has slipped down into a frightful intellectual and emotional abyss. As a mortal, he cannot participate immediately in the immortal world of his visioning, but, having had a glimpse of that immortal perfection, neither can he any longer find beauty or fulfillment in the world

---

[31] An alert reader will see Finney guardedly acknowledge this, just before directing attention to a variety of other matters [I, 303], but he will not find an explanation of how, in Book I, Endymion redeems this flaw and qualifies himself for the second stage of ascent.

provided for our mortality. The reconciliation of these apparent opposites of real and ideal must be the end of the process which begins with this dilemma.

The second stage that Finney sees Endymion passing through, comprising the action of Book II, is appreciation of the beauty of art. The underworld entered by Endymion, Finney says, "symbolizes the imaginative world of art—in particular, the world of poetry—into which man is led in pursuit of ideal beauty. Endymion's cult of natural beauty in the first book was a necessary preparation for his cult of artistic beauty in the second book."[32] There are several things wrong with this assessment. As we have seen, in the first book Endymion was so far from having a "cult" of natural beauty as to reject such beauty altogether. In the second book this process of rejection is continued, though with a different object and a different significance. And further, the underworld of the poem is hardly, in its descriptive details, representative of the world of art.[33] Art exists in it, i.e. in a "mimic temple" (II, 256) and a statue of Diana (II, 262),

[32] *Evolution of Keats's Poetry*, I, 306-307.
[33] Finney says [*ibid.*, I, 307] that his interpretation of the underworld as the world of art "is supported by the nature of the marvels which Endymion experiences there" and quotes the lines (II, 249 *et seq.*):

> . . . wonders—past the wit
> Of any spirit to tell, but one of those
> Who, when this planet's sphering time doth close,
> Will be its high remembrancers: who they?
> The mighty ones who have made eternal day
> For Greece and England.

Finney confuses the raw materials and the finished product. Keats does not say that what Endymion sees is art but that great poets have made works of art out of such materials. The lines strike me, in their context, as no more than the conventional poetic apology for not carrying on, because unable to do it justice, a descriptive catalogue which the poet is wearying of and which he fears his readers may find equally tedious.

[124]

but for the most part, what Endymion sees "With all its lines abrupt and angular" (II, 228) is mineral beauty in its natural state, marble, sapphire, diamond, gold, "One faint eternal eventide of gems" (II, 225). The distinguishing characteristic of all this magnificence, whether of art or nature, is that it is inorganic, nonliving, matter. However dazzling to the eye, it is "a gleaming melancholy" (II, 223), "monstrous" (II, 231), "fantastic" (II, 238), "where sameness breeds / Vexing conceptions of some sudden change" (II, 235-36).

Endymion passes through all this, "where silence dead / Rous'd by his whispering footsteps murmured faint" (II, 267-68), "Till, weary, he sat down before the maw / Of a wide outlet, fathomless and dim, / To wild uncertainty and shadows grim" (II, 271-73). There he falls prey to

> The deadly feel of solitude: for lo!
> He cannot see the heavens, nor the flow
> Of rivers, nor hill-flowers running wild
> In pink and purple chequer, nor, up-pil'd,
> The cloudy rack slow journeying in the west,
> Like herded elephants; nor felt, nor prest
> Cool grass, nor tasted the fresh slumberous air;
> But far from such companionship to wear
> An unknown time, surcharg'd with grief, away,
> Was now his lot. And must he patient stay,
> Tracing fantastic figures with his spear?
> 'No!' exclaimed he, 'why should I tarry here?'[34]
>   (II, 284-95)

[34] Although Endymion is undoubtedly representative, throughout the poem, of the poetic intelligence, he is nowhere presented in the act of artistic creation for its own sake, so I would not wish to make too much of a point which I cannot avoid noting nonetheless: that in this world of fantastic shapes, the images he traces with his spear's point are also fantastic. It is a small and subtle

In this resolve, nourished by a sudden yearning for the rejected world of natural process, he hurries back to the statue of Diana, to whom he prays:

>   'O Haunter chaste
> Of river sides, and woods, and heathy waste,
> Where with thy silver bow and arrows keen
> Art thou now forested? . . .
> . . . .
>   . . . Wheresoe'er it be,
> 'Tis in the breath of heaven: thou dost taste
> Freedom as none can taste it, nor dost waste
> Thy loveliness in dismal elements;
> But, finding in our green earth sweet contents,
> There livest blissfully. Ah, if to thee
> It feels Elysian, how rich to me,
> An exil'd mortal, sounds its pleasant name!
> Within my breast there lives a choking flame—
> O let me cool it the zephyr-boughs among!
> A homeward fever parches up my tongue—
> O let me slake it at the running springs!
> Upon my ear a noisy nothing rings—
> O let me once more hear the linnet's note!
> Before mine eyes thick films and shadows float—
> O let me 'noint them with the heaven's light!
> . . . .
> Oh think how I should love a bed of flowers!—
> Young goddess! let me see my native bowers!
> Deliver me from this rapacious deep!'
>   (II, 302-5, 309-24, 330-32)

Since Endymion does not know the identity of his

---

touch but wholly consistent with what I take to be an underlying aesthetic assumption of the poem, i.e. that the quality of a work of art is determined by the quality of the perceptual experience out of which it is made.

THE POEM

dream-maiden, he is unaware of the irony, apparent to
the reader, of his acknowledgment that Diana (or Cynthia), who is to him representative of escape from the
world of nature, finds her own Elysian felicity in that
very world. Far from coming to an appreciation of inorganic immutability, in art or otherwise, he has begun
properly to appreciate the world of living nature from
which, for his own good, he has been temporarily exiled.
Having rejected that world in Book I, its reacceptance
is the first step in his lessoning of how the divine is
truly to be apprehended.

This rationale has already been hinted by, presumably,
the moon-goddess of his dreams, whose voice first sent
him into the underworld with these words:

> 'Descend,
> Young mountaineer! descend where alleys bend
> Into the sparry hollows of the world!
> Oft hast thou seen bolts of the thunder hurl'd
> As from thy threshold; day by day hast been
> A little lower than the chilly sheen
> Of icy pinnacles, and dipp'dst thine arms
> Into the deadening ether that still charms
> Their marble being: now, as deep profound
> As those are high, descend! He ne'er is crown'd
> With immortality, who fears to follow
> Where airy voices lead: so through the hollow,
> The silent mysteries of earth, descend!'
>
> (II, 202-14)

While the passage has the narrative function of getting
Endymion to where he has to go, that could have been
done more easily in other ways. Its chief function is to
guide not so much Endymion as the reader, who sees
that the shepherd prince who scorns the earth and yearns
for heaven has sought his immortality too precipitately.

ENDYMION

He must learn that it is to be achieved not by direct assault on heaven, from the upper reaches of human experience, but by submission and descent. He must give up the heights and savor the "hollows" of the world. The movement is from aspirant being to humble nothingness. If the underworld reveals the barrenness of beauty divorced from common life, the submission to experience of it represents spiritual descent. Until he has gone such steps, Endymion will not understand the first principles of that nature in which his mortality participates and through which alone he may perceive authentic intuitions of more exalted being. In its frequently reiterated command to "descend," the ethereal guide thus provides the moral and epistemological imperative that governs the whole action of the poem.

Book II proceeds, from this point, in the two-steps-forward, one-step-backward narrative pattern that characterizes most of the poem. Endymion's prayer to be delivered from that "rapacious deep" is not immediately granted, because fulfillment of his quest for ideality requires his continued submission to this discipline.[35] However, having requested the sight of living nature, he is rewarded with a magical flowering of his grotto, which is accompanied by a sweet and subtle music (II, 339ff.). Pursuing the verdurous path toward the music's source, he arrives in a chamber where sleeps Adonis (II, 387ff.), whose cycles of sleep and waking are identified, as in classic lore, with the seasonal cycles of winter and summer (II, 477-80). Endymion is informed by an attendant cupid that, by special favor, he is being permitted to view an immortal scene not often vouchsafed to mortal eyes (II, 433-39).

[35] Venus tells Endymion that she would deliver him to the upper air immediately were she not certain that his present circumstances destined him for ultimate blessedness (II, 573-78).

It is, frankly, difficult to accommodate all the strands of compositional recitative and aria in this section—and in much of the remainder of the second book—to any single pattern. Keats seems here to have been experiencing more than ordinary difficulty in filling his 4,000 lines with Poetry,[36] and the progress of the narrative is frequently interrupted by digressive comment. Still, the outline of this action shows it to be clearly relevant to the poet's encompassing idea. Renewed sympathy with the natural world brings Endymion a soul-gladdening return of its effects, by which he is led to an authentic vision of that immortal world toward which he aspires. Since Adonis is a mortal who achieved immortality as the beloved of a goddess, he is an appropriately encouraging sign to Endymion at this point in his trial; and since his immortality is identified with the life of nature, he is a fitting sign of the necessary link between the natural and the divine. I think it no accident, either, that Endymion is given, for refreshment in the bower of Adonis, not ambrosia and nectar but "wine, / Alive with sparkles," rich cream, and a selection of choice fruits (II, 441-55), i.e. not essences but substances, rare enough, as their description attests, for the delectation of gods, but the produce of that very nature which Endymion had come mistakenly to despise.

After observing the summer awakening of Adonis and his departure with Venus, Endymion is left alone again, in glooming light, with all the verdure gone. Here the first cycle of his subterranean experience is repeated (II, 588-626), with the difference that, heartened by the Adonis episode and by Venus' promise of ultimate felicity, he is able to take greater pleasure in the fantastic beauty

[36] It will be recalled that the problem of invention in a long poem is thus baldly expressed in one of his comments on *Endymion*, in *Letters*, i, 169-70.

of the underworld. Soon, however, it palls again, seems "griesly" (II, 629), "Blackening" (II, 630), "strange" (II, 632), "dreary" (II, 634), and he feels lost once more (II, 649-56).

Bowing to Jove, without giving voice to any desire, he is immediately sent a huge eagle, whose back he mounts, "Committed to the darkness and the gloom" (II, 660). No longer opposing his will to his experience, but thus blindly and passively submitting himself to circumstance, he is carried "Down, down" (II, 661)—again the image of descent—to a paradise of natural beauty (II, 663-79), where all his senses become "Ethereal for pleasure" (II, 672). The sequence of events here should be carefully noted, for the pattern is significant. Overwhelmed in all his senses by the stimuli of natural beauty, Endymion experiences an exaltation of mood so ethereal that his mind turns again, by natural association, to his queen of beauty, the dream-maiden (II, 686-700), and, reclining himself on a bed of moss, he suddenly finds her there (II, 707-14). This second meeting is possible only because certain necessary conditions have been met. So long as his aspiration scorned the earth, he was frustrated in his search for immortal beauty. But his two-stage descent into the depths of the world, in the process of which he has learned the coldness of unliving beauty, has yearned once more for the life of nature, has followed where it led, and finally has experienced on his senses the full intoxication of its beauty, has prepared his spirit, in the only proper Keatsian way, for apprehension of the divine.[37]

With this understanding, I must believe that the scene of love-making which follows (II, 715-827) has been

[37] Endymion's first vision of the dream-maiden, it will be recalled, resulted from his devotion to the natural beauty of the sunset (I, 540 *et seq.*).

variously misinterpreted. It is certainly sensual, and from the standpoint of good taste it deserves E. C. Pettet's characterization as "unabashed eroticism, vulgar and sickly-sentimental by turns."[38] Yet I think Pettet mistaken when he says that its appropriateness lies in its harmony with the whole "tale of sensuous human passion" that he takes *Endymion* to be;[39] and I think Finney mistaken when he says that Keats here "confused a nympholeptic dream with a vision of ideal beauty";[40] and I think Thorpe mistaken when he says that Endymion has here "experienced sensual love to the full" in order to be made ready for growth toward humanitarian sympathy,[41] a cause-and-effect relationship difficult to verify either in or out of the poem. Granted that Keats here reveals more of his own imaginative life than perhaps he knows, we might yet suppose that, with Milton's Raphael, he is "lik'ning spiritual to corporal forms." And we might suppose so not only in charity but because the whole rationale of the poem so indicates, and because Keats in effect tells us that that is how he wishes us to understand the encounter. As to rationale, the dream-maiden, here and throughout the poem, obviously represents an ideal, as opposed to the "real," i.e. she is an essence (of the moon) with which the receptive soul might properly wish to be in fellowship. As long as this relationship is presented to us in the framework of a narrative romance, there is scarcely any conceivable way in which the mingling of essences could be represented but by the union of bodies —always allowing that there could be better taste in some of the descriptions. As for Keats's own estimate of the

[38] *On the Poetry of Keats*, p. 171.

[39] *Ibid.*, p. 171.

[40] *Evolution of Keats's Poetry*, i, 296, repeated in slightly different language at i, 309.

[41] C. D. Thorpe (ed.), *John Keats: Complete Poems and Selected Letters* (New York, 1935), p. 140n.

scene, Endymion's comments after Cynthia's departure are explicit enough to unriddle the question. Though we have seen him enjoying her body, he says that he has "tasted her *sweet soul* to the core" (II, 904, my italics), and he laments that, having risen thus high in the rarefaction of experience, lesser "spiritual" stimuli must inevitably have a diminished effect on him in future (II, 904-12). The *intention*, therefore, is not erotic, however ambiguous may be its representation.[42]

How wrongly Endymion estimates the effect of his experience is revealed partly in the language of his lament and partly in the immediately ensuing action. In the lament itself, he repines that,

> Now I have tasted her sweet soul to the core
> All other depths are shallow: essences,
> Once spiritual, are like muddy lees,
> Meant but to fertilize my earthly root,
> And make my branches lift a golden fruit
> Into the bloom of heaven:
>
> (II, 904-9)

The reaction is similar to that experienced after the first visit of Cynthia, comprising unfavorable comparison of lower experience with higher. The principal difference is in what constitutes the lower level of experience, and this, in turn, depends upon the kinds of meetings with Cynthia. On the first occasion, she was met only in a dream, and Endymion was then convinced of the superiority of visionary experience to that of organic life, with the consequence that he rejected the life of nature alto-

[42] It should not be necessary to quibble about the "intentional fallacy" in this case, since the differences among critics are wholly on the question of intention—whether Keats intended a celebration of erotic love or the elaboration of an allegory, and whether his imagery therefore is intended to be primarily affective or symbolic.

gether. But with the discipline of his wanderings in the second book, he has come to renewed appreciation of the physical and has had opportunity to discover though his understanding of it is yet imperfect) that the physical and essential exist in close interrelationship. Cynthia now visits him, not in a dream but in her own ethereal person, and this verification of her existence is Endymion's reward for both his persistence and his readjusted natural sympathies. Upon her departure this time, having experienced the highest possible spiritual exaltation through immediate fellowship with her tangible essence, he does not reject the physical, as he had done when he believed in the absolute disjunction of physical and spiritual, but fears that other physical objects, which he now recognizes as agencies of essence, will have comparatively less power to elevate his spirit. When we consider the terms of his complaint, however, recalling the complex of associated ideas and images discussed in the last chapter, we see that he is again lamenting something which, better understood, is precisely the right thing for him. That the essences of lower objects should so stimulate his natural growth, as an earthly, mortal man, as to make his "branches lift a golden fruit / Into the bloom of heaven" is to realize in his works the proper dynamic relationship between man and his natural environment. Endymion's momentary disappointment thus wrings from him an unconscious formulation of the lesson that he is well on the way to learning but has not yet fully grasped.

The action that follows immediately upon this lament illustrates the process which Endymion has just enunciated, and further, it reveals to us, if not to him, how wrong he was in estimating the aftereffect of his union with highest essence. Most of the critical commentary on the Alpheus and Arethusa episode has been oriented toward the growth of human sympathy in Endymion.

While this is certainly an important element in it, I believe that its immediate function is its illustration of an aesthetic rather than a humanitarian truth. For the process undergone by Endymion here is precisely that discussed at length in our previous chapter, presented, of course, in the framework of Endymion's present growth situation. Most critics, while necessarily aware of the narrative details, discuss the passage as if Alpheus and Arethusa were actually present, and as if Endymion's prayer for fulfillment of their love were a reaction to a scene of passion as vividly concrete as, say, the Venus and Adonis episode. In fact, however, Endymion is simply interpreting a nature phenomenon imaginatively, under the influence of the love experience, or fellowship with essence, that he has just gone through.

What really happens is that Endymion has no sooner finished his complaint about the muddy lees of experience remaining to him than he hears a faint humming sound which rapidly increases in intensity. Suddenly, twin fountains burst from the earth on either side of him, both of which, without pause, then course wildly through his grotto (II, 912-26). They are, and they remain, merely streams of water. As Endymion watches the progress of their uneven courses it strikes him that they are *like* pursued and pursuer (II, 927-28), and in this conceit he watches them until he tires of speculation on "the mystery" (II, 929-30). But the speculative activity has brought him round again to reflection on his just-vanished bliss (II, 931-32), and in that mood, or train of thought, he becomes conscious of a sound like "the whispering of trees" (II, 934), presumably, since it ceases when the two streams finally plunge over a far-off subterranean cliff (II, 1008-9), the now-distant sound of the rushing waters. The wooing dialogue that follows, in which the twin streams are represented in the classical roles of Alpheus and Arethusa (II, 936-1008), is *never* said to be articulated any more clearly than this. What is happening is that, under the influence of his fellowship with the highest essence, Endymion is entering sympathetically into fellowship with a lower one, terrestrial rather than celestial nature, and is interpreting the natural sound in the light of his own governing preoccupation. The result is the lifting of "a golden fruit / Into the bloom of heaven," or the creation, from natural sound, of a humanly articulated poetic myth.

This process of translating natural sound into human song is the same as that which Keats, as narrator, described more fancifully and elaborately, a few hundred lines earlier, as governing his own creative activity through the course of the whole poem. *Endymion*, he said there, is a "ditty"

> Not of these days, but long ago 'twas told
> By a cavern wind unto a forest old;
> And then the forest told it in a dream
> To a sleeping lake, whose cool and level gleam
> A poet caught as he was journeying
> To Phoebus' shrine; and in it he did fling
> His weary limbs, bathing an hour's space,
> And, after straight, in that inspired place
> He sang the story up into the air,
> Giving it universal freedom. There
> Has it been ever sounding for those ears
> Whose tips are glowing hot. . . .
>
> . . . .
>
> For quenchless burnings come upon the heart,
> Made fiercer by a fear lest any part
> Should be engulphed in the eddying wind.
> As much as here is penn'd doth always find
> A resting place, thus much comes clear and plain;

> Anon the strange voice is upon the wane—
> And 'tis but echo'd from departing sound. . . .
>
> (II, 830-41, 844-50)

Such stories are latent in the world of nature, requiring only a sensitive human intelligence for translation into human song. This translation, it will be recalled, is the most acceptable worship of the god whose overseeing brings to ripeness the beauty of both object and subject, external nature and the perceiving mind—a god whose alter-ego is the object of pursuit in the present narrative. It is the process described at greater length in "I stood tip-toe" (125-210), where Keats first essayed, abortively, the Endymion story. It is the process which, without the poet's final recording activity, is described in *Endymion*'s "fellowship with essence" passage (I, 783-94):

> hist, when the airy stress
> Of music's kiss impregnates the free winds,
> And with a sympathetic touch unbinds
> Eolian magic from their lucid wombs:
> Then old songs waken from enclouded tombs;
> Old ditties sigh. . . .

Now, like the poet who has recreated him, Endymion lifts the golden fruit of his imaginative response to natural sound into the bloom of heaven, and, from the perspective of his own love longing, blesses with a prayer for their union (II, 1013-17) the archetypal lovers he has conceived in his fellowship with the essence of their natural force.

And so Endymion begins the redemption of his fall from nature in Book I. He has come, first, to a renewed appreciation of its beauty (prayer after first exposure to inorganic beauty, culminating in the Venus and Adonis episode); then, to a total sensuous response which car-

ries his consciousness beyond the level of sense altogether (descent to verdant grotto, culminating in union
with Cynthia); and finally, to imaginative penetration
into, and sympathetic identification with, the elemental
activity of natural objects and forces (interpretation of
sound of waters, culminating in prayer for Alpheus and
Arethusa). Far from having his count of magic objects
reduced by the intensity of his experience with Cynthia,
he has gained from it an intuitive insight hitherto lacking
in his responses to nature. He is now ready to enter sympathetically into that larger sphere of nature which embraces his own kind, the sphere of mortal humanity.

The passage from one set of relationships to another
is signalized by a change of scene, as Endymion finds
himself moved from underground to undersea. The usual
view of commentators on the new set of relationships is
that, from the Alpheus and Arethusa episode on, through
Book III, Endymion is learning friendship, or humanitarian sympathy.[43] In a general way this is true, so long
as we do not suppose that it is something Endymion is
learning for the first time, as a further stage in some sort
of neo-Platonic growth. For this is simply another instance of his *re*learning something lost after his original
vision of ideality in the person of the dream-maiden. Just
as he lost sympathy with external nature and had to be
brought back into sympathy with it by the experiences
detailed in Book II, he also fell out of communion with

[43] Finney complicates it by clinging, despite the cumulative
weight of his own evidence, to the neo-Platonic view, maintaining
that Keats began with the neo-Platonic conception of personal
friendship, but was influenced by Bailey's and Wordsworth's Christian humanitarianism to a generic universalizing of Endymion's
human sympathies [*Evolution of Keats's Poetry*, I, 310]. This is
the second major point at which Finney sees Keats subverting the
neo-Platonic doctrine, which he yet maintains is basic to the poem's
conceptual scheme.

his own kind, after the initial vision, and in Book III must be brought back into sympathy with man.

That he has fallen away from human relationships is made quite explicit in Book I. Man is included in the totality of nature's life at the summary conclusion of the description which introduces and sets the scene for the human action of the whole poem:

> . . . cold springs had run
> To warm their chilliest bubbles in the grass;
> Man's voice was on the mountains; and the mass
> Of nature's lives and wonders puls'd tenfold. . . .
>
> (I, 102-5)

The springs, the grass, the mountains, man, all are part of a complex and dynamic whole. Into the natural scene come the Latmians, to do honor to the nature-god Pan, and our first sight of Endymion is in the opening procession of the festival to Pan, where, as Prince, he would have to join in his people's communal worship. However, even on this high ceremonial occasion, when the inferiority to the god which he shares with his subjects would most publicly link his identity with theirs, he seems aloof and abstracted, "like one who dream'd" (I, 176), and frequently his chariot reins "would slip / Through his forgotten hands" (I, 180-81). During the service of worship, he stands in the assembly "wan, and pale" (I, 191). Afterwards, when various festive activities are initiated, Endymion avoids the groups engaged in dancing and athletic games and joins the soberer circle discussing philosophic matters. As the conversation turns to the afterlife, each one looks forward to his own future bliss—and, significantly, the bliss that each envisions is a resumption of some human association previously interrupted by death. One hopes to rejoin "His quick gone love" (I, 375), another "his rosy child" (I, 379), others "Their fellow

huntsmen o'er the wide champaign / In times long past"
(I, 386-87).

> Thus all out-told
> Their fond imaginations,—saving him
> Whose eyelids curtain'd up their jewels dim,
> Endymion.
> > (I, 392-95)

Endymion not only does not envision a future bliss of
eternal human fellowship, but does not even participate
in the human society of which he is now a member, for

> His senses had swoon'd off: he did not heed
> The sudden silence, or the whispers low,
> Or the old eyes dissolving at his woe,
> Or anxious calls, or close of trembling palms,
> Or maiden's sigh, that grief itself embalms:
> But in the self-same fixed trance he kept,
> *Like one who on the earth had never stept.*
> > (I, 398-404, italics mine)

That this condition of spiritual separateness is neither
enviable in itself nor a mark of Endymion's superior sensitivity we learn from the narrator, who repeatedly tells
us, in his own voice, that Endymion is under a "curse"
(I, 412), that he must be won back to "a healthier brain"
(I, 465), for he is indeed "Brain-sick" (II, 43). The cause
of his brain-sickness, as Endymion tells his sister Peona,
is the vision he has had of his dream-maiden, whose ideal
perfection is such "That, when I think thereon, my spirit
clings / And plays about its fancy, till the stings / Of
human neighbourhood envenom all" (I, 620-22, italics
mine). Quite clearly, then, the rejection of humanity is,
equally with the rejection of external nature, a part of
Endymion's mistaken response to his ideal vision and
must be corrected before he can arrive at a true perspec-

tive. When we recall how, in Keats's earlier poems, the heroes of humanity were adapted to his scheme of universal harmony, the linked emphases on nature and humanity in this allegory on the making of a poet are wholly predictable.

Endymion's return to human sympathy proceeds by means of the concrete illustrative precept embodied in the figure and story of the ancient Glaucus, whom Endymion meets almost immediately in the undersea world, and with whose fate he is ultimately obliged to join his own. The orientation in which we are to evaluate the Glaucus parable is provided by the proem, or introductory exposition, to Book III. Thinking for a moment of the kings of the earth, the poet begins:

> There are who lord it o'er their fellow-men
> With most prevailing tinsel: who unpen
> Their baaing vanities, to browse away
> The comfortable green and juicy hay
> From human pastures; or, O torturing fact!
> Who, through an idiot blink, will see unpack'd
> Fire-branded foxes to sear up and singe
> Our gold and ripe-ear'd hopes. With not one tinge
> Of sanctuary splendour, not a sight
> Able to face an owl's, they still are dight
> By the blear-eyed nations in empurpled vests,
> And crowns, and turbans. With unladen breasts,
> Save of blown self-applause, they proudly mount
> To their spirit's perch, their being's high account,
> Their tiptop nothings, their dull skies, their thrones.
>
> (III, 1-15)

The distinguishing characteristic here is the inward-turning of self-love. Those whose high positions lay upon them the obligation of service to their fellow men too often gratify their own desires through exploitation of their fellows. The standard by which we are to judge such actions follows immediately, in the comparison of these corrupt earthly rulers with the rulers of the universe, the "thousand Powers" who "keep religious state, / In water, fiery realm, and airy bourne" (III, 30-31). The operations of most of these are hidden from us, but there are a few whose works have effects clearly discernible to us, a few "whose benevolence / Shakes hand with our own Ceres; every sense / Filling with spiritual sweets to plenitude" (III, 37-39). The first of these, since it is a fructifying generative force, is probably intended to suggest the sun-god Apollo; the second, who fills us with "spiritual" sweets, is the moon-goddess Cynthia, as the passage which follows (III, 40-71) specifies in considerable detail. Her "benediction [of beauty] passeth not / One obscure hiding-place, one little spot / Where pleasure may be sent" (III, 61-63). Life-giving food and spirit-nourishing beauty are the benedictions of benevolent deity. Those mortals who eschew the giving role of godhead, and live only to and for themselves, are clearly living contrary to the first principles of universal power. And, since the goddess cited at greatest length in illustration of this point is Endymion's beloved, there can be no doubt about the lesson he will have to learn in order to achieve immortal union with her.

Endymion is put to the test with the first person he meets on the ocean floor, and he almost fails. Coming unexpectedly upon old Glaucus, who greets him with a glad heart, his first thought is for himself, his fear of a death which is never threatened and his grief over permanent loss of his love thereby (III, 255-77). Ironically, calling upon the name of his unknown beloved, he cries, "I care not for this old mysterious man" (III, 277-80). In this "blindly contumelious" attitude (III, 285), he glares "high defiance" at the poor old man (III, 281-82), only to discover that "the grey-hair'd creature wept" (III, 283). Shocked at his own heartlessness, he kneels in penitence before the aged figure (another small visual image of descent), thus passing his first test (III, 284-90). As we later learn that his own fate has predestinately been made dependent upon his relationship with Glaucus, this submissive acknowledgment of a claim upon his human sympathy is no small matter.

Having established satisfactory acquaintance, the two set out to perform a task the purpose of which Glaucus clarifies by means of autobiography. While the details naturally differ, the pattern of his story, up to a point, is quite similar to that of Endymion's own. In his youth, Glaucus was a fisherman, who took the same sort of pleasure in nature (III, 319-24, 340-67) as Endymion had formerly done. But this eventually proved insufficient gratification, and, like Endymion, he foolishly desired more than the simple bounty of nature—he desired to "interknit [his] senses" with the element that stirred him most profoundly, and so "plung'd for life or death" into the sea (III, 372-84).[44] There he saw and fell in love with Scylla, whose timidity, however, caused her constantly to flee from him (III, 398-410). As impatient as Endymion, he found himself unable to bear the agony of his unfulfilled desire and so sought out the enchantress Circe, in the hope of finding a shortcut to happiness.

[44] Glaucus' love of the sea, objectified in his love of the elusive nymph Scylla, corresponds to Endymion's love of the moon, objectified in his love of the elusive Cynthia. I strongly suspect that Endymion's long and ardent apostrophe to the moon, which is inserted (belatedly and not very appropriately, since the sea bottom is a poor vantage point for seeing moonlight) at the beginning of the action in the present book (III, 142-87), was intended to supply a necessary link in our understanding of the relationship among nature, love, and ideality which impels the unwitting Endymion on his narrative course, and to do so in time for our perception of the parallels between Glaucus' and Endymion's differing quests.

It should not escape notice that it is his own happiness he has in mind, and not Scylla's, for his subjective movement has been in an inward-turning spiral. As a fisherman, happy in the blessings of the natural world, it had been one of his pleasures to leave anonymous daily gifts of fish for the poor who lived along the seashore (III, 368-71). This benevolent link with humanity was of course broken when, consulting his own desires, he abandoned the human world for the interknitting of his senses with the very element of the sea. In his subsequent pursuit of Scylla, he does not once speak of the happiness he can bring to her, who obviously fears him, but only of the growth of his own passion. (In this he is more culpable than Endymion, who has ample reason to believe that he is as much beloved as loving.) It is not surprising, then, to find that, when he arrives at Circe's realm, the gratifications offered to his self-indulgence readily make him a "tranced vassal" to this "arbitrary queen of sense" (III, 459-60).[45]

The passage descriptive of Glaucus' thralldom to Circe (III, 412-76) is rich in uses of the image complex discussed in the previous chapter. Keats goes out of his way, for instance, to mention that Circe is "Phoebus' daughter" (III, 414). And Glaucus awakens on Circe's isle, after drifting to it in a swoon, in the "light of morn" (III, 419), hearing the natural "hum of bees" (III, 419) and the human music of the lyre (III, 421). Circe's speech comes to him like music (III, 444-45) and puts him in mind of

[45] Keats's unmistakable intention to show Glaucus' passion for Circe as in itself wrong might reasonably have led Newell F. Ford to doubt his view of the whole poem as a celebration of erotic love, for that sort of love is nowhere more gloriously fulfilled than in Circe's kingdom. Ford's contention [*Prefigurative Imagination of John Keats*, pp. 62-64] that the sin of Glaucus here is not sensuality but infidelity does not persuade. Have we been given *any* reason, up to this point, to suppose that Scylla cares?

Elysium (III, 428). Circe inquires of his readiness for love in terms of ripeness (III, 440) and offers herself as a tempting fruit ready to be plucked (III, 441-43). Her seductive charm immerses his existence in a "golden clime" (III, 455). The varieties of pleasure Glaucus experiences there he likens to the variety with which "Apollo each eve doth devise / A new appareling for western skies" (III, 463-64), and the chief image in a brief catalogue of such delights is of the invisible nightingale singing in the depths of the forest (III, 470-71).

Since we must assume that this extraordinary cluster of vitally related and normally exalted images is not accidental, while it is quite clear that the beauty it projects is meretricious, a real problem in interpretation must be acknowledged. I think it safe to assume, considering the whole drift of the poem, that Keats is not here suggesting the spuriousness of either poetry or his favorite conception of its inspiration. Of the remaining possibilities, then, one (for which there is warrant in the text, at III, 449-53) is that Keats drew upon the most potent images in his arsenal in order to represent the enormous power of a temptation sufficient to make Glaucus forget his passion for Scylla. There is additional support for this view in Glaucus' characterization of Circe's world as a "specious heaven" (III, 476), where, if it is specious, it also has all the attributes and attractions of the highest conceivable human goal. Another possibility is that Keats is counterpointing the elevated implications of his imagery to the debased and selfish response of Glaucus, in order to imply a comparison between right and wrong responses to sensation. The implication of the tacit comparison is that pleasures of this kind which *end in themselves*, and do not impel the spirit to a quest for fellowship with essence, or participation in the ideality of which they are merely the substantial projection, are not only valueless to the receiver but pernicious. This possibility, which admittedly would be more evident to Keats than to the average reader, is suggested in the reference to Circe as an "*arbitrary* queen of sense" (III, 459, italics mine), i.e. a purposeless stimulator of sensation, leading it nowhere. I think either, or both, of these interpretations amenable, on different levels, to the poem's over-all conception.

However that may be, Glaucus' adventure in sensual self-gratification completes his removal from human good. Awakening one morning to find Circe gone, he seeks her through the forest, only to discover her tormenting former lovers whose bestiality of passion has culminated in their metamorphoses into animals. One of these, in the shape of an elephant, pleads with the enchantress:

> I sue not for my happy crown again;
> I sue not for my phalanx on the plain;
> I sue not for my lone, my widow'd wife;
> I sue not for my ruddy drops of life,
> My children fair, my lovely girls and boys!
> I will forget them; I will pass these joys;
> Ask nought so heavenward, so too—too high:
> Only I pray, as fairest boon, to die. . . .
>
> (III, 543-50)[46]

All the "heavenward" joys that have been forfeited in this land of merely sensuous intensity are the pleasures of ordinary human association: earthly rule, fellowship in arms, the domestic affection of wife and children. Perceiving how grossly he has been deluded, Glaucus flees, only to be caught by Circe and cursed to a thousand years of senility, and ultimate death, in the undersea kingdom to which he had aspired. Even so, the full force of his penalty does not show itself until he returns to the

---

[46] There being no evident reason or authority for the change in line 547, I retain here the punctuation of Garrod's first edition.

sea, where he discovers his innocent beloved, Scylla, slain by the vengeful Circe (III, 615-23), and subsequently finds himself, because of the weakness of his curse-aged limbs, unable to save a drowning shipload of fellow human creatures (III, 645-65).[47] His self-absorbed abandonment of human values thus culminates not only in enforced isolation from his own kind but in his becoming both a direct and an indirect destructive agent of those creatures to whom he is in natural feeling most closely bound.[48]

But perhaps because Glaucus had *desired* to help the drowning mortals—in any case, immediately after their tragedy—a hand appears before him with a scroll which tells him how the curse under which he exists can be mitigated. Two activities are prescribed: Glaucus must explore "The meanings of all motions, shapes, and sounds; / . . . all forms and substances / Straight homeward to their symbol-essences" (III, 698-700); and "in chief" he

[47] There is no reason to believe, as some readers do (presumably in an attempt to assimilate every detail to a dominant love theme), that this is a shipload of lovers and that the lovers later restored by Glaucus and Endymion are the passengers from this ship. The lovers who are restored are all those who have drowned during the term of Glaucus' bondage, not simply those on this ship (III, 721-23). The point of this episode, therefore, is not that Glaucus has failed other *lovers* but that he has failed other *people*. The agony of his frustration is part of his punishment for a sin against humanity, not against love.

[48] Lest there be an objection that Glaucus is "Immortal . . . of heavenly race" (III, 589) and therefore, by definition, not human, one might point out two facts: (1) Though sired by Neptune, in the classical story which Keats adapted, Glaucus neither manifests godlike powers nor shows himself aware, in Keats's story, of any difference between himself and ordinary mortals, hence is as effectively human, for narrative purposes, as Achilles, Aeneas, or any other divinely descended hero of classical story; and (2) the fact of Glaucus' immortal parentage, hitherto of no moment, is introduced only as a qualifying factor in Circe's curse, no doubt to explain why Glaucus is not subjected to the usual curse of transformation into animal form.

must salvage the bodies of all lovers who have perished in the sea, preserving them till such time as a youth (Endymion), "by heavenly power lov'd and led," shall come to assist him in a ritual which, we subsequently learn, will bring about the lost lovers' resurrection (III, 701-10).

Every aspect of this injunction speaks to Glaucus' fallen condition. The world of universal nature, which he had first abandoned and had later (on Circe's isle) blindly enjoyed as a mere instrument of his own sensuous pleasure, must now become the subject-means of a search for essential truth. Humanity, which had ceased to be meaningful for him when he abandoned human society for immersion in the ocean element, he must now labor to preserve—and, significantly, those mortals are given to his preservation who have, through love, established voluntary bonds between themselves and others of their own kind. Of final significance is the fact that he cannot work out his salvation alone but must join with another human creature, Endymion, in the last phase of his redemptive process. Endymion, of course, concludes his own restoration to human sympathy in the same act of humane collaboration with Glaucus.

As the two go about their pious tasks of revivification, the third book of the poem builds toward its close in a rising crescendo of music and an increasing intensity of light, with the interspersion of other image-elements from Keats's familiar complex. Obedient to his instructions, Endymion breaks a wand against a lyre, ". . . and straight with sudden swell and fall / Sweet music breath'd her soul away, and sigh'd / A lullaby to silence" (III, 766-68). Ordered to scatter fragments of the torn scroll on Glaucus,

> 'Mid the sound
> Of flutes and viols, ravishing his heart,
> Endymion from Glaucus stood apart,

And scatter'd in his face some fragments light.
How lightning-swift the change! a youthful wight
Smiling beneath a coral diadem,
Out-sparkling sudden like an upturn'd gem,
Appear'd. . . .

(III, 771-78)

Showering the remaining fragments on the many rows of
dead lovers, Endymion watches as

each lifted up its head,
As doth a flower at Apollo's touch.
. . . .
All were re-animated. There arose
A noise of harmony, pulses and throes
Of gladness in the air . . .
. . . .
They gaz'd upon Endymion. Enchantment
Grew drunken, and would have its head and bent.
Delicious symphonies, like airy flowers,
Budded and swell'd, and, full-blown, shed full showers
Of light, soft, unseen leaves of sounds divine.
The two deliverers tasted a pure wine
Of happiness. . . .

(III, 785-86, 790-92, 796-802)

The legions of restored lovers, including Glaucus,
whose worthiness has finally won him his Scylla, swarm
toward the palace of Neptune to offer up prayers of
thanksgiving. But when its golden gate is opened for
them, its brightness "made those dazzled thousands veil
their eyes / Like callow eagles at the first sunrise" (III,
858-59). Within, they find Neptune enthroned, with Cupid at his right hand and Venus at his left (III, 864-65),
and overhead,

> there did spring
> From natural west, and east, and south, and north,
> A light as of four sunsets, blazing forth
> A gold-green zenith 'bove the Sea-God's head.
>
> (III, 875-78)

As the horn of Triton rings through the glowing palace, and the Syrens begin to sing (III, 888-89), Venus draws Endymion to her and renews her promise that his love will be fulfilled (III, 903-21). Then all join in a hymn to the three presiding deities, to Neptune, of whom it is affirmed, rather gratuitously, that

> Thy bright team
> Gulphs in the morning light, and scuds along
> To bring thee nearer to that golden song
> Apollo singeth, while his chariot
> Waits at the doors of heaven
>
> (III, 955-59)

to Venus, whose whole tribute is cast in terms of gentle music, including that of nature,

> 'Breathe softly, flutes;
> Be tender of your strings, ye soothing lutes;
> Nor be the trumpet heard! O vain, O vain;
> Not flowers budding in an April rain,
> Nor breath of sleeping dove, nor river's flow,—
> No, nor the Eolian twang of Love's own bow,
> Can mingle music fit for the soft ear
> Of goddess Cytherea!
>
> (III, 968-75)

and to Cupid, who is the "Dear unseen light in darkness! eclipser / Of light in light!" (III, 986-87).

The hymn is ended by a brief mythological pageant, in the midst of which Endymion is overcome by the exalta-

[149]

tion of the moment and, swooning away, is carried to the surface of the earth. As he goes, he hears in his inner consciousness the voice of his beloved, promising an early consummation, for "Immortal bliss for me too hast thou won" (III, 1024). One would hesitate to say that more is intended by this than the expression of a goddess's happiness over her impending fulfillment in love. And yet, the climactic announcement that a goddess has won immortal bliss through the actions of a mortal strongly implies a conception of reciprocal action and complementary relationship between heaven and earth, each being distinct in kind but bound to and in some measure dependent upon the other. To the extent that this inference has validity, it imposes upon mankind the necessity of acting *as* man, and this is what Endymion has done. For the act of piety by means of which Endymion won eternal felicity for the goddess was not a ritual act of devotion performed on direct behalf of the Olympian gods, but the cooperative joining with another mortal in humane alleviation of the last evil of mortality, so as to make possible for many other mortals the extended enjoyment of that affection with which they had bound themselves to one another. In this way Endymion has been brought back to the healthy normal condition in which he had existed before his first vision of the moon-maiden. He has now only to readjust his conception of what constitutes ideal love, and this the fourth book of the poem provides.

Book IV is needlessly complicated, as the poet, in his desperation to fill out 4,000 lines, virtually admits at one point (IV, 770-73). The danger to criticism is in getting lost in the maze of will-he-won't-he narrative turns, much of which I am convinced is mere poetic filling.[49] By this

[49] Such is the conviction, too, of those who read the poem differently than I. Cf. Newell F. Ford, *Prefigurative Imagination of John*

I do not mean that the stages of Endymion's experience cannot be reconciled to one another, but rather that there are more stages than the apparent plan of the whole poem required.

Before considering the effects of individual episodes in it, it is as well to have an over-all view of this book's total action, which is as follows: Awakening on the surface of the earth once more, Endymion sets about making a sacrifice to the gods, when suddenly he is interrupted by the sound of a lament. Following in the direction of the sound, he comes upon an Indian Maid, whose beauty is such that he thrice declares his love for her. After the third declaration, Mercury appears briefly and provides them with two winged horses. Mounting the horses, they are carried aloft until both horses and riders, having entered the zone of the god Sleep, drift into unconsciousness. Endymion then dreams that he is on heaven's pavement, where he fraternizes familiarly with the gods until Cynthia appears, whom he at last recognizes as his dream-maiden. Assuming that this is to be (as it might well be) the end of his long quest, he springs toward her, only to awaken from the dream. Fully awake, he finds the scene unchanged; he is indeed in heaven with Cynthia and the other gods, but so, he discovers, is the Indian Maid. Perplexed whom to choose, he kisses the Indian Maid, at which Cynthia, weeping, vanishes. Bitterly disappointed, he yet renews his commitment to the Indian Maid, and they continue their flight through the regions of the air. As the moon slowly rises, however, Endymion is horrified to see the Indian Maid fading away,

---

Keats, pp. 69, 71, 77, 81, 83. And E. C. Pettet [*On the Poetry of Keats*, pp. 191-92] seems to be persuaded that the elements have no organic inevitability when he says that Endymion's "union with Cynthia must always strike us as a purely mechanical narrative contrivance for bringing the poem to some sort of conclusion."

and he is left alone. Having now lost both objects of his love, he sinks into a despairing neutrality of emotion, a "Cave of Quietude" within the soul, which lies deeper even than the despair which provoked it. At this point, unknown to him, the heavenly powers begin to assemble for his forthcoming marriage to Cynthia. Meanwhile, borne back to earth, Endymion discovers his Indian Maid awaiting him there, and, renouncing forever his heavenly aspirations, swears eternal love to her, of such kind as can only exist in, and be nourished by, the world of mortality and natural beauty. To his bewilderment and sorrow, she then tells him that such a love as he has described can never be theirs, though she cannot explain why. As he broods dejectedly on this fresh disappointment, his sister Peona suddenly appears, and, with many expressions of delight in the discovery that he, who had been given up for lost, still lives, she urges him to bring the Indian Maid home with him, marry her, and resume his proper role as governor of his people. Tormented beyond endurance by the complexity of his situation, Endymion vows to eschew all alliances, live the life of a hermit, and see no other person than Peona, through whom he will govern his people and with whom he urges the Indian Maid to live, bound for his sake by vows of chastity. All agreeing to this scheme, they are in the act of parting when Endymion calls them back and requests one final meeting with the Indian Maid, to take place at Diana's (Cynthia's) temple, at the sunset hour that evening. When the appointed hour arrives, he makes his way to the rendezvous in great bitterness of heart, which is expressed in terms of ironic self-pity and self-contempt. Arriving at the temple, he is amazed to see his Indian Maid transformed before his very eyes into Cynthia, who offers a rather brief and inadequate apology for the long delay in their union, after which they vanish together into an immortality of bliss. Peona, who has been promised the freedom of the forest and the opportunity to meet them there often in the future, turns homeward in great and understandable wonderment at what she has seen.

Despite all the turns and counter-turns of narrative action, it is quite clear that the most significant fact of the fourth book is not any particular episode in it but the introduction of the Indian Maid, who provides, through almost the entire action, an alternative and therefore contradictory object for Endymion's love, and who is finally revealed to be merely an embodiment of Cynthia herself. The crucial problem of accounting for her has brought forth a variety of hypotheses, to which I should like to add my own.[50]

[50] Sidney Colvin [*John Keats*, p. 197] sees her as simply one evidence of the great lesson Endymion must learn, that "all transient and secondary loves, which may seem to come between him and his great ideal . . . are really, when the truth is known, but encouragements . . . visitations and condescensions to him of his celestial love. . . ." E. de Selincourt [(ed.), *John Keats: The Poems*, Seventh Edition ⟨second reprinting of the fifth edition, of 1926⟩ (London, 1951), p. 443] believes that the Indian Maid "typifies intense human love, which is keenest when brought into being in sorrow," though he does not indicate how this identity is related to the other Cynthia-identity. C. D. Thorpe [*Mind of John Keats*, pp. 60-61] identifies her with "the spirit of sorrow and suffering in the world," for Keats believed that "the poet must find in the tragedy of the world his poetic salvation. . . ." C. L. Finney [*Evolution of Keats's Poetry*, I, 319], sliding well down the scale of his neo-Platonic ladder, to a position which would normally be the first or second stage of ascent, says, "The beauty of a particular woman is a manifestation of ideal or essential beauty, Keats meant, and the love of a particular woman is the highest means by which man can attain a fellowship with essence." Newell F. Ford [*Prefigurative Imagination of John Keats*, pp. 70-72] regards the Indian-Maid disguise as just that, a means for Cynthia to visit her earthly lover without the embarrassment of detection in heaven, where she is inconveniently identified as the goddess of chastity. However, presumably in order to sustain his earlier point that Glaucus' sojourn with Circe represents the sin of infidelity in love,

The whole tendency of the poem up to this point has been toward the realignment of Endymion with all the values of the phenomenal world which he had rejected as a consequence of his original love dream. There has been no suggestion that the quest of ideal and immortal truth and beauty is itself reprehensible—indeed, there have been several indications (e.g. the promises of Venus and the assurances of Cynthia) that the quest will be rewarded if Endymion persists in it. However, since Endymion is not immediately granted fulfillment of the love that he and Cynthia both desire, and is obliged to undergo the prolonged and often unhappy process of the quest, the very difficulty of the quest clearly has some necessary purpose. Endymion must qualify for, show himself worthy of, access to that immortal world toward which he aspires. As we have seen, however, the process of qualification has not been one of refining earthly characteristics out of his nature, but of bringing him into acute awareness of and participation in the values of purely human existence. In Book I, after his dream of perfection, Endymion had eschewed external nature; in Book II he was redeemed from this fault. In Book I, after

---

and thus to protect his position that the whole poem celebrates sensual love, Ford complicates the disguise motif by giving as a further reason for it Cynthia's desire to test Endymion's constancy. If this is so, Endymion fails the test throughout the fourth book and should certainly not be rewarded at its end by union with Cynthia. E. C. Pettet [*On the Poetry of Keats*, pp. 192-200], in an argument drawn from general experience, suggests that the Cynthia/Indian Maid figure is simply the erotic ideal of adolescent daydreaming; as Cynthia, the gloriously imagined love partner, and, as Indian Maid, the alluring but faintly unsatisfactory fulfillment in real life. There is no doubt much to recommend this view, but it seems to me that its truth lies in its explanation of the figure's psychological origins, which in no way explains what Keats, perhaps indeed rationalizing and self-deceived, intended us to take her for in his self-conscious and morally earnest poem.

his dream, he had removed himself from participation in human society; in Book III he was redeemed from this fault. In Book I, the cause of his other defections was the love of a goddess met in a dream. For the completion of his re-education, then, he must love another human being, not a goddess capable of conferring eternal benefit upon him, but a mortal as weak, limited, and wretched as himself, and one upon whom he can himself confer a benefit. If he would be as the gods, he must conduct himself as one, and (on the model of Apollo and Cynthia provided at the beginning of Book III), manifest toward one weaker than himself an outgoing, giving love. The opportunity to do this is provided by the Indian Maid, and the revelation that she and Cynthia are one confirms the whole point of Endymion's journeyings, the lesson that only by full sensitivity to and appreciation of the mundane can we come to apprehension of the divine, for they are inextricably mingled in human experience.

Once this orientation is grasped, the difficulty of reconciling the particular episodes in the last phase of Endymion's redemption becomes less crucial. Each of the episodes is simply a step toward Endymion's final abnegation of self and commitment to mortal beauty. The issue is clearly drawn at the moment Endymion first sees the Indian Maid. In a goading, mocking temptation he is adjured by the narrator,

> See not her charms! Is Phoebe passionless?
> Phoebe is fairer far—O gaze no more:—
> Yet if thou wilt behold all beauty's store,
> Behold her panting in the forest grass!
> Do not those curls of glossy jet surpass
> For tenderness the arms so idly lain
> Amongst them? Feelest not a kindred pain . . . ?
>
> (IV, 56-62)

[155]

Phoebe is fine, but here before him, panting and alive, is all beauty's store in a tangible form. The pang of attraction he feels for her is "kindred" not only because it is like her own just-expressed need of love, but because it is the pull of attraction to kindred, to a being of one's own kind. Torn between his commitment to the heavenly beauty of the dream-maiden and the powerful attraction of the mortal woman before him, Endymion finally yields to the superior strength of his mortal nature.

Keats's first impulse was to make the capitulation complete at this point, and he wrote, "Ye harmonies / Ye tranced visions—ye flights ideal / Nothing are ye to life so dainty real" (IV, 104ff., *Poetical Works*, p. 161n.). Then, apparently feeling that it was too soon for so drastic a change, he tempered Endymion's address to the Indian Maid so as to suggest greater emotional tension. Endymion calls the maid his "executioner," who "stolen hast away the wings wherewith / I was to top the heavens" (IV, 109-11), leaving him no recourse but to submit to oblivion in death, and he implores her to give him comfort in his last hours (IV, 111-24). In the light of our after-knowledge of the Indian Maid's true identity, we can understand why, at this point, she falls to weeping "As her heart would burst" (IV, 124), for Endymion, in believing that mortal love cuts him off from heaven, has in a single moment unlearned all that was to fit him for union with her immortality. And a knowledge of her true identity gives special force to her sharp reply,

'Why must such desolation betide
As that thou speak'st of? Are not these green nooks
Empty of all misfortune? Do the brooks
Utter a gorgon voice? Does yonder thrush,
Schooling its half-fledg'd little ones to brush
About the dewy forest, whisper tales?—

Speak not of grief, young stranger. . . .'
(IV, 126-32)

What, she demands to know, does he find so sinister in
the world of living nature? On what possible grounds
dare he reject its innocent beauty? It is a matter of some
moment to her, not as a self-justifying mortal but as an
omniscient immortal, that Endymion shake himself free
from his delusion about mortal nature's inadequacy.

Endymion thrice confesses love for the Indian Maid
before anything happens as a result of it. His statement
that the Maid has bereft him of his heavenly wings is
equivalent to a love declaration, and after her admoni-
tory speech, above, he openly declares, "I love thee" (IV,
138). Despite her speech, however, he remains persuaded
that such commitment to mortal nature must be the death
of him, and he asks her for a little song to soothe him in
his dying. She responds with the roundelay, "O Sorrow"
(IV, 146-290), the function of which is to elicit yet another declaration from Endymion, this time grounded on
the poem's previous teaching.[51]

The burden of the Indian Maid's lament is disappointment in love, which she has tried to assuage by recourse
to a life of pleasure. Finding that empty, she has fallen
away from her old companions and into the aching and
unwilling solitude in which Endymion found her. What

[51] I am persuaded, however, that this song was first composed
in an abbreviated form as an independent lyric, then expanded and
inserted here because of its utility in the narrative and thematic
situation. Keats twice excerpted the initial five stanzas of the song
in letters to friends [to Jane Reynolds, on October 31, 1817, and
to Benjamin Bailey, on November 3, 1817: *Letters*, I, 176-77,
181-82], thus indicating that he considered these stanzas as separable and complete in themselves. The story of the Indian Maid's
wanderings through the world as a member of Bacchus' company
does not begin until the sixth stanza and is in no way related to
the opening stanzas' lyric statement, except in its provision of
grounds (and any other would do) for the sorrow there expressed

she desires is not the numerous company of revellers, each bent on his own gratification, nor absolute solitude either, but a relationship of human feelings voluntarily mingled in mutual love. To this appeal Endymion responds. No particular reason is given, but Keats may have intended us to see how the feelings engendered in Book III would be called forth by this appeal, and further, how natural it would be for Endymion to react sympathetically to a lament originating in a cause not unlike that of his own suffering. In any case, if we are not given a logical reason for Endymion's renewed capitulation, we are given an associative phenomenal one. As her voice trails off, Endymion continues to listen to the autumnal wind soughing sadly through the trees, and as the human and natural songs merge with each other, he makes his decision for mortal love:

> Endymion could not speak, but gazed on her;
> And listened to the wind that now did stir
> About the crisped oaks full drearily,
> Yet with as sweet a softness as might be
> Remember'd from its velvet summer song.
> At last he said: 'Poor lady, how thus long
> Have I been able to endure that voice?
> Fair Melody! kind Syren! I've no choice;
> I must be thy sad servant evermore:
> I cannot choose but kneel here and adore.'
>
> (IV, 293-302)

Having thus committed himself, Endymion falls into an ecstatic paean of human passion:

> I'm giddy at that cheek so fair and smooth;
> O let it blush so ever! let it soothe
> My madness! let it mantle rosy-warm
> With the tinge of love, panting in safe alarm.—
> This cannot be thy hand, and yet it is;

And this is sure thine other softling—this
Thine own fair bosom, and I am so near!
Wilt fall asleep? O let me sip that tear!
And whisper one sweet word *that I may know*
This is the world.

(IV, 311-20, italics mine)

It is this decisive commitment to the substantial beauty
of the real world which brings Mercury and the feath-
ered steeds upon which the lovers are then borne into
the Empyrean.[52] The reason for the three declarations of
love is now apparent. Since the first two were fearful of
the consequences of earthly attachment, they had no efficacy and merely elicited from the disguised Cynthia
reactions of anger or sadness. The third one, however,
wholehearted in the acceptance of human love on its own
terms, immediately brings Endymion access to the immortal world of all his highest longings. The little scene
is a half-ritualized vignette of the whole poem's rationale.

The heavenly vision that follows for Endymion is best
understood in the context of the sequence of visions that
have been vouchsafed him. After the initial dream of
Cynthia, which came to him as a reward for his lifelong

[52] A few ominous lines (IV, 320-30) intervene between Endymion's declaration and the appearance of Mercury, seemingly
indicative of divine wrath over the speech just uttered. However,
these cannot refer to Endymion's supposed infidelity to Cynthia,
since she is the Indian Maid too. Should it be objected that Endymion is unaware of that fact, and is therefore just as morally
culpable as if she were not, it can only be replied that Cynthia is
the best judge of that, and we have every reason to believe, both
now and later, that she approves. In any case, the gift of the
winged horses, brought by the messenger of the gods, certainly
implies the approval of heaven. Given this approval, and the additional fact that no divine punishment of any kind is subsequently
visited upon Endymion, one can only suppose that the threat of
these lines is irrelevant to any interpretation whatever of the poem
as it now stands, and that it represents another idea that was
never developed.

devotion to the natural beauty of the heavens, every vision of the immortal gods has had to be earned by some improvement in his understanding. After the backsliding which followed upon his first vision, each stage of growth back toward spiritual health is climaxed by a revelation of deity, and each revelation is more impressive than the last. In the underworld, after desiring to see living nature again, Endymion is permitted to watch the awakening of the nature-deity Adonis. Later, after submitting his senses wholly to mastery by nature's beauty, he is visited by Cynthia herself. In the sea, having enlarged his sympathy to include human life once more, he is permitted to see Cupid and Venus, the god and goddess of love, together with Jove's own brother, Neptune, gloriously enthroned in the sea-god's palace. Now, after declaring his love for the "mortal" Indian Maid, he is carried to heaven itself, where he first dreams of the gods and then converses with them in full wakefulness (IV, 407-38). Seen in the context of this sequence, Endymion's final and most comprehensive vision of immortal life can only be understood to signalize the rightness of his decision for mortal love. Having realized the full glory of earthly and human beauty, he has become fit company for the gods.

As one last confirmatory test, now to be made in heaven itself, and with full knowledge of his dream-maiden's identity, Endymion is confronted with both Cynthia and the Indian Maid and is obliged to choose between them.[53] Without loving Cynthia less, he loves the Indian Maid more, kisses her twice, and sees the moon-goddess disappear (IV, 439-61). Though he might now reasonably

[53] I see no reason to quibble, as some have done, over Cynthia's occupancy of both bodies simultaneously. If this was a slip on Keats's part, I am nonetheless willing to suspend my disbelief, on the pious ground that freedom from the limitations of human possibility is an almost definitive prerogative of deity.

feel that he had made an unwise decision, Endymion remains emotionally committed to the Indian Maid, urges
their flight from a phantasmal world in which they have
no proper place, and fears lest the wrath of his forsaken
goddess be visited upon his innocent earthly choice (IV,
465-69). It is only when she too vanishes (IV, 503-10)
that despair momentarily seizes him and he slips into that
state of sublime indifference, beyond pleasure and pain,
which Keats calls the Cave of Quietude (IV, 512-48).

In this condition of near-trance, Endymion is oblivious
of all else in the universe, and hence does not see the
heavenly host beginning to assemble for his wedding to
Cynthia (IV, 552-62), nor hear their hymeneal song (IV,
563-611). Keats may have considered his hero's insensi-
bility as adequate pretext for continuing his poem through
another four-hundred lines, since Endymion cannot respond to what he does not know. Nonetheless, when we
see the marriage festival in preparation, *we* know that
Endymion has passed all his tests and is destined to receive his reward in the immediate future. Therefore,
while his further trials and actions will presumably be
consistent in spirit with what has gone before, we have
no reason to take them as matters of any determinative
consequence. Having overcome all the errors of his understanding manifested in Book I, and having chosen mortal
beauty before the gods in heaven, with full knowledge
of the alternative, Endymion has fulfilled every demand
that the poet planned, or in the framework of his conception and narrative situation could have planned, to
make on him. The remainder of the poem, though consonant with what has gone before, is chiefly melodra-
matic filler.

But the poem does go on, and some of its effects are
very much worth noting. Borne back to earth, where he
discovers the Indian Maid awaiting him, Endymion re-

news his vows of love and forswears immortal longing in
a catalogue of his sins which neatly summarizes those we
have been discussing:

> O I have been
> Presumptuous against love, against the sky,
> Against all elements, against the tie
> Of mortals each to each, against the blooms
> Of flowers, rush of rivers, and the tombs
> Of heroes gone! Against his proper glory
> Has my own soul conspired: so my story
> Will I to children utter, and repent.
>
> (IV, 638-45)

Indeed, he bends over too far backwards and depreciates
immortal yearning as a cheat:

> There never liv'd a mortal man, who bent
> His appetite beyond his natural sphere,
> But starv'd and died. My sweetest Indian, here,
> Here will I kneel, for thou redeemed hast
> My life from too thin breathing: gone and past
> Are cloudy phantasms. Caverns lone, farewell!
> And air of visions, and the monstrous swell
> Of visionary seas! No, never more
> Shall airy voices cheat me to the shore
> Of tangled wonder, breathless and aghast.
>
> (IV, 646-55)

While these lines may constitute a first flash of insight
into the attitude which became basic in Keats's later
poetry, they are out of keeping with the aesthetic vision
that *Endymion* exists to propagate, and the narrative
voice assures us that Endymion, "by fancies vain and
crude" (IV, 722), is rationalizing. The narrative disclaimer is necessary because Endymion is already destined for immortality, and we must not be permitted to
doubt that, in his heart, he still longs for it.

[162]

The Indian Maid's subsequent refusal of him (IV, 728-63) is difficult to see in any light but that of our later knowledge of her true identity. She is, in other words, not reacting to either the positive or the negative aspects of Endymion's last speech, but is simply informing him, in an unnecessarily cryptic and ominous way, that she, *as* Indian Maid, can never be his. The reason, of course, is that she will be his in her own person, as Cynthia. Since he cannot know this, however, he renounces earthly felicity and declares himself for a life of solitude. Acknowledging the validity of ordinary human experience, and not refusing the responsibility of governing his people, he yet chooses a life of separateness in which he may contemplate the heavenly mysteries that have been revealed to him (IV, 849-64). The poet's strategy in this is very sound: while Endymion's affection for the earthly, signified by his choice of the Indian Maid, is a necessary culmination of the poem's whole progress, it must not be achieved at the cost of heaven's rejection, for the poem's whole argument is that the ideal is perceived only through full appreciation of the real. The ultimate goal is still the ideal. Therefore, Endymion's full acceptance of responsibility in the real world, tempered by his willingness to forgo its pleasures in contemplation of the ideal, places him in a condition of what might be termed affirmative neutrality with respect to both. If it seems somewhat contrived in the narrative, it is yet a deft solution to a problem which had evidently been giving the poet some concern throughout his whole management of Book IV.

When Endymion then expresses the desire to see the Indian Maid just once more before starting his hermit's life (IV, 908-15), he is re-emphasizing his commitment to mortal beauty, lest his voluntary relinquishment of it seem prejudicial to its value, without compromising his resolution in favor of a life given to divine contemplation. Thus, while he remains perfectly poised between the extremes, he is yet sympathetically inclined in the direction proper to his mortal nature. A needless plot complication, this is still a clever trimming of the thematic balance now achieved and is perfectly expressive of the conceptual resolution toward which the poem had been directed from its very beginning.

Far from starting an ascent in Book I, Endymion had suffered a fall—an inevitable and necessary fall, perhaps, for anyone whose susceptibilities render him capable of more than ordinary human perception, but a real fall nonetheless. Reconciliation of the opposing tendencies of perception, directed toward an understanding of the dynamic fusion of substance and essence, was necessary to the redemption of Endymion, and this was achieved in the following three books. The final revelation that the Indian Maid and Cynthia, mortal and immortal beauty, are one (IV, 982-87) simply focuses the thematic light that was gathering in the whole course of Endymion's trial. By the end of the poem, Endymion ceases to have any strong, individual identity and disappears from our consciousness as effectively as he vanishes from the Latmian scene. What remains, or is intended to remain, is an understanding of the process by means of which he was spiritualized. It was chiefly for this purpose that Keats revived and adapted his story.

Throughout the narrative, in addition to those passages already cited, there are frequent recurrences of the language and symbolism in which Keats was accustomed to express the poetic conception which the whole poem is intended to embody. Following are a few of the most obvious.

THE POEM

The proem to the entire work states the lesson that Endymion will have to learn:

A thing of beauty is a joy for ever:
. . . .
Therefore, on every morrow, are we wreathing
A flowery hand *to bind us to the earth.* . . .

(I, 1, 6-7, italics mine)

While acknowledging, however, that the earth is not without its evils, the proem yet goes on:

. . . in spite of all,
Some shape of beauty moves away the pall
From our dark spirits. Such the *sun,* the *moon,*
Trees old, and young sprouting a shady boon
For simple sheep; and such are daffodils
With the green world they live in; and clear rills
That for themselves a cooling covert make
'Gainst the hot season; the mid forest brake,
Rich with a sprinkling of fair musk-rose blooms:
And such too is the grandeur of *the dooms*
We have imagined for the mighty dead;
All lovely *tales* that we have heard or read:
An endless fountain of *immortal drink,*
Pouring unto us from the heaven's brink.

(I, 11-24, italics mine)

The italicized elements specifically name certain familiar
properties, but everything in the passage is relevant to
the central concept that the natural beauty of the external world and of humanity at its best reflects the condition of, and places us in touch with, the divine.

Turning from general truths to his own compositional
program, the poet records his hopes for the growth of the
poem upon which he is now embarking in terms of a corresponding maturation and fruition in external nature,

[165]

suggesting a slow, natural, organic growth of the poem comparable to the kindred activity in the physical world, with the hope that both may come to golden-ripe fulfillment at the same time:

> I will begin
> Now while I cannot hear the city's din;
> Now while the early budders are just new,
> And run in mazes of the youngest hue
> About the old forests; while the willow trails
> Its delicate amber; and the dairy pails
> Bring home increase of milk. And, as the year
> Grows lush in juicy stalks, I'll smoothly steer
> My little boat, for many quiet hours,
> With streams that deepen freshly into bowers.
> Many and many a verse I hope to write,
> Before the daisies, vermeil rimm'd and white,
> Hide in deep herbage; and ere yet the bees
> Hum about globes of clover and sweet peas,
> I must be near the middle of my story.
> O may no wintry season, bare and hoary,
> See it half finished: but *let Autumn bold,*
> *With universal tinge of sober gold,*
> *Be all about me when I make an end.*
>   (I, 39-57, italics mine)

The narrative action of the poem begins with "Apollo's upward fire" (I, 95) lighting the scene of a woodland altar at sunrise, and the distant sound, as worshippers converge on the setting of worship, of human song blending with the voice of the sea:

> . . . a faint breath of music, which ev'n then
> Fill'd out its voice, and died away again.
> Within a little space again it gave
> Its airy swellings, with a gentle wave,

To light-hung leaves, in smoothest echoes breaking
Through copse-clad vallies,—ere their death, o'ertaking
The surgy murmurs of the lonely sea.

(I, 115-21)

The "sunburnt" shepherds who approach are

> Such as sat listening round Apollo's pipe,
> When the great deity, for earth too ripe,
> Let his divinity o'er-flowing die
> In music, through the vales of Thessaly

(I, 141-44)

and the priest, as noted earlier, carries a vase "Of mingled wine, out-sparkling generous light" (I, 154). The priest opens his charge to the shepherds by recalling the natural blessings for which they owe thanks, including a clear reference to the voice of godhead in natural sound: ". . . ocean's very marge, / Whose mellow reeds are touch'd with sounds forlorn / By the dim echoes of old Triton's horn" (I, 204-6).

After the service of worship, the people disperse into groups for the playing of games. Each game is characterized by a story from ancient myth, and, as de Selincourt noted long ago, it is "worth noticing that these stories suggested by the games of the holiday makers are all of them episodes in the life of Apollo."[54] It might be added that all of the activities, whether or not accompanied by an appropriate story, are referable to Apollo's influence. Some of the folk are dancing (I, 312-21), and their music is of course under Apollo's aegis. Some are listening to stories (I, 322-25) "potent to send / A young mind from its bodily tenement." I take for granted, given the Apollinian focus of every other element, and the ability of these stories to elevate the hearers' minds to divine contempla-

[54] E. de Selincourt (ed.), *Poems*, p. 424.

[167]

tion, that they are in verse, and therefore also in Apollo's province. Some are playing quoits, and the story of Apollo and Hyacinthus is recalled (I, 326-31). Some are engaged at archery, and the archer-god Apollo's slaying of Niobe's children is alluded to (I, 332-45). Some of them, seeing a distant archer holding his bow aloft, are reminded of Apollo's rescue of the Argonauts, when he dispersed the darkness, through which they blindly sailed, with the shining of his bow (I, 346-54).

After Peona has led the "brain-sick" Endymion away from the group, she restores him with a song "More subtle cadenced, more forest wild / Than Dryope's lone lulling of her child" (I, 494-95), a reference to Dryope's motherhood of Apollo's child.[55] And Peona's song is rendered "with Delphic emphasis" (I, 499). Peona's very name is suggestive of Apollo. De Selincourt notes that Peona's healing function may have suggested her name to Keats, since "wise Paeon" is mentioned in Spenser (*FQ*, III, iv, 41) as the son of Apollo and the healer Liagore; and Ovid (*Met.*, xv) mentions Paeon as the son of Apollo and, with Diana, a healer of Hippolytus.[56] Keats knew both these works, and the influence of both is repeatedly evident in *Endymion*. He might also have seen Paeon in Lemprière, where he is represented as the physician who healed the wounds suffered by the gods in the

---

[55] A manuscript variant of the song's quality is couched in terms not of direct allusion to Apollo but of Keats's equivalent in nature sounds, culminating in that of the nightingale's song:

> More forest-wild, more subtle-cadenced
> Than can be told by mortal: even wed
> The fainting tenors of a thousand Shells,
> To a million whisperings of Lilly bells;
> And, mingle too, the Nightingale's complain
> Caught in its hundredth echo.

(*Poetical Works*, p. 79n.)

[56] E. de Selincourt (ed.), *Poems*, pp. 424-25.

THE POEM

Trojan War.[57] Given so many healing associations with the name, Peona's healing function at her introduction into the story, the association of healing with the physician-god Apollo, and Peona's medicining with Delphic song, the intended association of her name with Apollo seems indubitable. It also seems indubitable, considering the chain of recondite allusions that occur in this section, that Keats deliberately embarked here on a virtuoso salting of his poem with nuggets of the purest ore.

After Endymion has recounted to his sister the whole cause of his discontent, and promised his reformation, Book I concludes with their departure, at the sunset hour (I, 988), in an image of autumn mists (I, 990-91).

In the second book, a golden butterfly (II, 61) guides Endymion through the evening sunset (II, 71) to the mouth of the cave he must enter. What he sees after descending to the underworld are such things as only the light-bringing poets can describe, "The mighty ones who have made eternal day / For Greece and England" (II, 253-54). The burgeoning of natural beauty brought about by Endymion's underworld prayer is accompanied by the sound of music which

> . . . came more softly than the east could blow
> Arion's magic to the Atlantic isles;
> Or than the west, made jealous by the smiles
> Of thron'd Apollo, could breathe back the lyre
> To seas Ionian and Tyrian.
> (II, 359-63)

In the chamber of light in which Endymion has the first immortal vision of his journey, Adonis' very blanket calls up the vocabulary of Apollo and autumn's ripened gold:

[57] *Bibliotheca Classica*, article on "Paeon."

[169]

> . . . coverlids gold-tinted like the peach,
> Or ripe October's faded marigolds,
> Fell sleek about him in a thousand folds—
> Not hiding up an Apollonian curve
> Of neck and shoulder. . . .
>
> (II, 396-400)

When Endymion alights in the bower where he will revel in love with his dream-maiden, he finds it strewn with "golden moss" (II, 671), and, while pacing about, ". . . his tread / Was Hesperean; to his capable ears / Silence was music from the holy spheres" (II, 673-75). "Hesperean" recalls the golden apples of the Hesperides, and in its conjunction with music and love is associated with Apollo in a speech from *Love's Labour's Lost*:

> For valor, is not Love a Hercules,
> Still climbing trees in the Hesperides?
> Subtle as Sphinx, as sweet and musical
> As bright Apollo's lute, strung with his hair.
>
> (*LLL*, IV, iii, 340-43)

In his letters, Keats quoted twice from this play during the writing of *Endymion*, once from this very speech, just two lines before the portion cited here.[58]

At the embowered union of Endymion and Cynthia, despairing of adequate descriptive powers, the poet laments the passing of authentic inspiration from the poetry of the modern world:

> Aye, the count
> Of mighty Poets is made up; the scroll
> Is folded by the Muses; the *bright roll*
> Is in *Apollo*'s hand: our dazed eyes
> Have seen a new tinge in the *western skies*:

[58] On May 10, 1817, to Haydon; *Letters*, i, 140-41. On November 22, 1817, to Reynolds; *Letters*, i, 189.

The world has done its duty. Yet, oh yet,
Although *the sun of Poesy* is set,
These lovers did embrace. . . .

(II, 723-30, italics mine)

In Book III, addressing Apollo directly, Keats altered a description of sunset from "When thy golden hair falls thick about the west"[59] to "When thy gold breath is misting in the west" (III, 44), changing the metaphor but not its essential attributes.

Endymion's apostrophe to the moon, in the third book, includes a retrospective summary of all the things in his experience which have been assimilated to it in his consciousness. The passage is an abbreviated anthology of Keatsian symbols, at the same time that it crisply recapitulates the process of natural inspiration, leading to imaginative ideality, which was expressed in so much of the previous poetry and which furnished the conceptual basis for *Endymion*:

Thou wast the mountain-top—the sage's pen—
The *poet's harp*—the voice of friends—*the sun*;
Thou wast the river—thou wast *glory won*;
Thou wast my clarion's blast—thou wast my steed—
My goblet full of wine—my topmost deed:—
Thou wast the charm of women, lovely Moon!
O what *a wild and harmonized tune*
My spirit struck from all the beautiful!
On some bright essence could I lean, and *lull
Myself to immortality.*

(III, 164-73, italics mine)

Reflecting that his transient love fulfillment in the previous book may perhaps never be repeated, Endymion

---

[59] *Poetical Works*, p. 129n. I reproduce the variant given in Garrod's revised edition, though it differs from, and is less metrically easy than, that entered in his first edition.

expresses his sense of loss: "ah, ripe sheaves / Of happiness! ye on the stubble droop, / But never may be garner'd" (III, 272-74).

Love as a harvest of ripe feeling is a reasonable image, but so saturated was Keats with his vocabulary of potent symbols that one is sometimes hard-pressed, in *Endymion* as in some of the earlier poetry, to find the relevance of his references. When Endymion penitently kneels before Glaucus, for instance, the old man tells him to arise "for sacred Phoebus' sake" (III, 292). It would require a great deal of casuistry to explain Apollo's concern, one way or the other, in such a matter. Again, when Glaucus describes his early life to Endymion, he speaks of a youth spent in hearing the "continuous roars" of the sea and the "sea-mew's plaintive cry" (III, 340-41), both natural sounds, and in hearing the blended sounds ashore of human music and animal cries, the "shepherd's pipe" and the "ceaseless bleatings of his sheep" (III, 359-60). Fish permitted him to feel their "scales of gold" (III, 344), and he watched waterspouts grow till they seemed "ripe" to burst (III, 347). He was happy on every "summer eve" (III, 357), and on summer mornings waited to see "Aethon [one of Apollo's chariot horses] snort his morning gold" (III, 364). The whole description is permeated with the sound, the color, the ripening so familiar in Keats's frame of conceptual reference. Yet, while it might be argued that they apply to a period of natural inspiration during which Glaucus was being brought toward that ill-conceived desire for absolute fellowship with essence which culminated in his plunge into the sea, one must feel that the verbal coinage is a little debased here, the words becoming signs of a ritual rather than of things in vital process, building to neither an emotional nor a perceptual climax. The most effective use of the symbol-complex is in such descriptions as those, later in Book

III, of the awakening lovers and of the meeting of lovers and gods in Neptune's palace. These, discussed above in the detailed analysis of the poem, unite the values of light and sound with intensity of human feeling and immortal vision to produce a total effect of crescendo which is far more impressive than the merely verbal heightening of Glaucus' youth.

Book IV opens with a desponding address to the Muse, whom the poet fears he has failed. Her origin is compressed into a terse statement which sums up Keats's whole aesthetic theory: "by the hues / Of heaven on the spiritual air begot" (IV, 2-3). The poet's sense of failure, and the failure of most of his generation, to respond adequately to her inspiration is expressed as a waste of the morning's light on a land where no poets are capable of being inspired by it (IV, 23-25).

When Endymion has expressed his love for the Indian Maid, and both are borne aloft by the winged steeds, their ascent is described as "Like two drops of dew / Exhal'd to Phoebus' lips" (IV, 348-49). Arrived in heaven, Endymion's dream (IV, 407-34) includes "Phoebus' golden bow," "golden apples," music, wine, and a procession of the Seasons in which is the inevitable "golden store" of Autumn. Again, returned to earth, Endymion's fantasy of domestic felicity with the Indian Maid (IV, 670-721) is replete with imagery of Phoebus, gold, music, the nightingale, Delphos, and a variety of miscellaneous natural beauties.

After his renunciation of normal human happiness and his resolution to live a hermit's existence, as Endymion approaches Diana's temple for what is to be his final meeting with the Indian Maid, he asks, with special emphasis on the generative power of Apollo in the natural world, and a strong suggestion thereby of his universal godhead,

[173]

> 'Why such a golden eve? The breeze is sent
> Careful and soft, that not a leaf may fall
> Before the serene father of them all
> Bows down his summer head below the west.
>
> (IV, 927-30)

Since in the narrative, Endymion's abandonment of his quest is the equivalent in the allegory of the poet's abandonment of poetry, there is acute point in this questioning of the utility of a "golden eve." Later in his progress toward the same meeting, in his bitterness at what he supposes to be the final frustration of his immortal longings, Endymion expresses himself in terms which, in their symbolic implication and in their reflection of the mood in which the fourth book opened, almost invite their interpretation as Keats's own bitterness over what he takes to be the failure of his poem:

> I did wed
> Myself to things of light from infancy;
> And thus to be cast out, thus lorn to die,
> Is sure enough to make a mortal man
> Grow impious.
>
> (IV, 957-61)

Whether his sense of failure was justified is an open question. Perhaps it was, for the poem he had intended to make a perfect embodiment and demonstration of his poetic first principles has in varying degrees eluded commentators ever since he wrote it.

There are several possible reasons for this failure. As we have seen, the vocabulary and imagery in which Keats habitually expressed his central conception of the imaginative process are abundantly in evidence throughout the poem, and the basic architecture of narrative action and its consequence is sound. That neither has had sufficient force to impress his governing purpose on later generations of interpreters must therefore be attributable to other factors.

Virtually all critics have noted the poem's digressiveness, both pictorially and philosophically, and this, of course, adds nothing to unity of effect. But more basic flaws can be detected in surveying the general drift of critical interpretation, for the critics, after all, do the best they can with what the poet gives them reason to believe is central. Since nearly all interpretations, whether of the "Platonic" or "erotic" schools, are based on either the thematic statement embodied in the "fellowship with essence" passage or the poem's various disquisitions on the power and universality of love, or a combination of the two, one must judge that the poet misplaced, or failed to clarify, his emphasis in direct address to the reader's intellect. He also failed to make clear the equivalence of love and light, in the special sense in which he was accustomed to conceive of light; and he failed to make explicit, in the poem, whether the thematic statement of the "fellowship with essence" lines expressed a priority of order in experience or simply a hierarchy of experiential intensity. And he left ambiguous the question whether these lines constitute a statement of his own theme or merely an hypothesis which Endymion opposes to Peona's argument on the impracticality of dreams. I suspect that they began as the latter, and, as his imagination went stepping toward a truth, became, rather late in the game, the former. In any case, it is doubtful whether they would ever have been taken as so thematically determinative had not the letter to his publisher survived in which Keats found it tactically wise to insist upon the importance of a slight verbal change for which any practical publisher might otherwise be reluctant to disturb material already set in type.

Despite these misplaced emphases, I believe that the

cumulative weight of the evidence presented in the reading here, consistent as it is with habits of mind and poetic
practice which run continuously through Keats's whole
early career, is sufficient to demonstrate a greater firmness and consistency of conceptual orientation in the
poem than it has hitherto been acknowledged to have.

THREE

Crisis

A CAREFREE tone predominates in the poetry written during the months immediately following the completion of *Endymion*. It might be variously described as light-hearted, or sociable, or frivolous, depending upon its manifestation in any one poem, but in whatever way it is felt, the tone is unmistakable and probably reflects the poet's relief over having finished his extended verse romance. *Endymion* had been completed in November 1817 after a half-year of dogged and often difficult composition, made the more difficult, no doubt, by Keats's attitude toward the task. He had seen it as a test of his powers and a measure of his fitness to claim the title of poet, an attitude which must certainly have turned the project into a prolonged emotional crisis.[1] Its completion, therefore, with the release of this long-felt pressure, might sufficiently account for the playfulness that finds expression in such *jeux d'esprit* as "Cat! who hast pass'd thy grand climacteric," "O blush not so," "For there's Bishop's teign," "Where be ye going, you Devon Maid," and "Over the hill and over the dale," and for the reflective amiability of the "Robin Hood" lines and the "Lines on the Mermaid Tavern."

In addition to their predominant lightness of tone, the poems of the immediate post-*Endymion* period are uniformly characterized by a much greater "Englishness" than the earlier verse, perhaps in reaction to the poet's

[1] Cf. *Letters*, I, 139, 141, 169-70, *passim*.

protracted immersion in classical story. Earnest promises
of poetic dedication are addressed to Spenser and Milton,
King Lear is celebrated in a sonnet, the Mermaid Tavern receives a tribute in octosyllabics, and Robin Hood
is taken to embody the hearty spirit of an English countryside and an English way of life now forever gone. "O
blush not so," "Over the hill and over the dale," and
"Where be ye going, you Devon Maid" exploit with gusto
such country matters as had traditionally found expression in the English ballad form in which they are cast;
and the English countryside itself appears in tersely vivid
images scattered throughout the poems of these few
months.

Concurrent with the exuberant native note, however,
the familiar machinery of Keats's mythologized aesthetic
system continues in use. In some cases the referents are
introduced so casually that they might appear almost
conventional, did we not stop to think that "Phoebus with
a golden quell" ("To Spenser") has no pre-Keatsian ante-
cedents as a specific image of the poetry-making power;
or that the likening of a book full of poems to a barn full
of ripened grain ("When I have fears," 3-4) is, if an
effective, hardly an inevitable comparison, outside the
conceptual rationale of a mind which habitually sees
both ripened grain and poetry as the products of a single
benevolent force.

It is, in fact, in these poems of the 1817-18 winter
months that the conceptual machinery finds its easiest,
least self-conscious expression. An excellent example may
be found in the linked poems, "Hence Burgundy, Claret,
and Port" and "God of the Meridian," both presumably
the results of impromptu composition while writing a letter to a friend. In the first, a mock-serious allusion to real
wine casually introduces its use as a metaphor for Apollinian poetic inspiration; and the second, taking a new

tone, expresses the awe Keats felt whenever he confronted this power deliberately and directly. The tonal
changes are so marked that one can follow the mental
and emotional processes of composition with virtual certainty. Having protested in the prose part of the letter
that he was in too frivolous a mood to write seriously,[2]
Keats began a parody of Milton's "Hence vain deluding
joys" with "Hence Burgundy, Claret, and Port," much in
the spirit of his student-days doggerel, "Give me women,
wine and snuff." The second line added Hock and Ma-
deira to the proscription list, but then it was time to supply a reason, and this had to be the inferiority of these
wines to something that could provide a higher exaltation. Inevitably, the alternative was given as the metaphorical wine of the poet's old conceiving. This explanation carried the poem through its sixth line, all, so far,
in trimeter. Up to this point the light tone had prevailed,
its last specific effect being the "pitiful rummer" of the
fifth line. With the introduction, however, of the old
metaphor that had for so long joined in the poet's mind
the two worlds of Apollo's power, the whole conceptual
apparatus came almost automatically into play, and, as
if the poet *could not* be frivolous with this theme, the
tone suddenly shifted, if not to high seriousness, at least
to emotional neutrality, with such tokens of seriousness
as "I drink at my eye, / Till I feel in the brain / A Del-
phian pain." The shift in tone, accompanied by allusions
to Apollo as god of the physical and intellectual (Del-
phian) worlds, is signalized by the shift to a more rapid
and excited two-stress meter, broken once with a trimeter
which adds metrical ballast to a line that introduces a
rhyme with Apollo ("Then follow, my Caius! then follow"), and concluded with another trimeter, which cli-

[2] *Ibid.*, 220.

maxes the poem in a paean to "the glory and grace of Apollo!"

Now having verbalized, and thus brought to the forefront of his mind, the power which he held most sacred in the world, the poet seems no longer to have found it emotionally possible to maintain either a light or a neutral tone. So he drew a line and went on with a direct address to the god, which is very like a prayer. In the first lines, "God of the Meridian, / And of the East and West," it is Apollo as sun-god who is addressed, referring back to the "golden sunshine" orientation of the previous lines. But he immediately becomes the awful spirit of poetic truth in the lines which follow: "To thee my soul is flown, / And my body is earthward press'd." And the poem goes on relentlessly to expose the poet's terror and awe of the power to which he had long since committed his whole moral being.

Impromptu the poem may be, but it is certainly not therefore merry. And when Keats appended "you must forgive all this ranting—but the fact is I cannot write sense this Morning,"[3] I think one must be very literal-minded indeed, and very indifferent to the tone and plain meaning of the poem, to suppose that he really believed the lines to be nonsense.[4] Having exposed his deepest

[3] *Ibid.*, 222.

[4] Even Amy Lowell, who characterized the whole extempore as "a pretty bit of rhyming," could not avoid seeing that it turned into "something like the expression of a real mood" [*John Keats*, I, 561]. Another misunderstood example of Keats's almost superstitious seriousness in this area can be seen in the earlier "God of the golden bow." Written as an apology to Apollo for playfully having donned laurel leaves to which he was not entitled by his achievements as a poet, it has customarily been dismissed as a verbal frolic in the vein of inebriated silliness that prompted the laurel incident itself [e.g. "The poem is mostly good fooling, without pretence to worth . . ." C. D. Thorpe (ed.), *Poems*, p. 49n.]. Without claiming anything for it as poetic achievement, I would yet affirm that the supposition of its playfulness finds no confirma-

feelings and beliefs, the poet was probably embarrassed, and, to forestall any subsequent discussion of matters which he did not wish to explain or defend, he pretended to dismiss them at their inception. His remark simply reflects a decent reticence about a subject which, as far as we know, he never discussed with his friends, perhaps for much the same reason as Sir Thomas Browne declined to discuss the truths of the Christian religion. Should it be objected that this is to compare small things with great, there is no possible reply but that, in matters of personal belief, the relevant question is less often "what?" than "how much?"

But the extemporaneity of the poem does reveal two things about Keats at this point in his career. One of them is the rootedness of his orienting conception, which could by this time so easily take over the superficial processes of his mind and shape even his spontaneous poetic composition. The other is the revelation, in the progress of the linked poems, of the truth, for Keats's own practice, of his theory of poetic inspiration. By his own admission, he began simply with "a sun-shiny day."[5] The conceptualizing mind of the poet traced the physical effect to its essential cause and clothed the journey of his spirit in the language of feeling and speculation. The result is poetry,

---

tion in the uniformly contrite and reverent diction of the poem, nor in Woodhouse's statement that Keats "mentioned the circumstance afterwards to some of his friends, along with his sense of the folly (and, I believe, presumption) of his conduct [and] said he was determined to record it by an apologetic ode to Apollo . . ." [quoted in Thorpe, *ibid.*, p. 48n. Cf. *Poetical Works*, pp. 430-31n., for another text]. Keats even took the trouble to quote, in one letter, his comments on the affair in another letter, i.e. "I put on no Laurels till I shall have finished Endymion, and I hope Apollo is [not] angered at my having made a Mockery at him at Hunt's" [*Letters*, i, 170].

[5] *Letters*, i, 220.

unpolished and imperfect, but genuine poetry none-theless.

The "Lines on Seeing a Lock of Milton's Hair" show evidence of greater care in composition but are also spontaneous and occasional in origin. Having been shown the lock of hair by Leigh Hunt, Keats wrote the lines "at Hunt's at his request" and felt that he might have "done something better alone and at home."[6] Again the poem reflects, as the essential part of its inner logic, Keats's accustomed view of the earthly poet's relation to the universal spirit of harmony. Indeed, it is built on the assumption of interpenetrating heavenly and earthly harmonies. The opening address introduces the two areas of Milton's activity: as "Chief of organic numbers" Milton was the greatest of practicing, earthly poets; as a "Scholar of the Spheres" he was also a seeker after the higher harmonies of heaven.[7] Now that Milton is gone, his heavenly part, his spirit, "never slumbers, / But rolls about our ears, / For ever, and for ever" here on earth. Yet that part of himself which he left behind him on earth, his poetry, "heavenward . . . soundest." And yet further, this heavenward-sounding poetry "Discord unconfoundest, / Giving Delight new joys, / And Pleasure nobler pinions!" Assuming that the meliorating of discord, the increase of delight, and the elevation of pleasure are functions of which the earth, not heaven, stands in need, the earthly poet therefore presumably incorporates in his work and brings to his readers intuitions of heavenly harmony. The

[6] *Ibid.*, 212.

[7] While Milton's poetry alone would have given ample pretext for the latter epithet, one wonders whether Keats ever read his academic "Prolusions," in the second of which Milton, striking the appropriate rhetorical pose of disputatious scholar, discusses celestial music and the principles of universal harmony in terms which, if unlikely "sources" of Keats's own conception, would certainly have given him aid and comfort.

poet's proper regions are seen to be so intertwined that Keats can now safely ask in mock despair the rhetorical question that he has already effectively answered, "O, where are thy dominions?" He then swears a "Delian" oath, by Milton's "soul" and Milton's "earthly love," that he too will celebrate "Beauty, in things on earth, and things above," that he too will "Leave to an after-time / Hymning and harmony. . . ." That is, given certain conditions, he will. These conditions we will consider a little farther on. The special interest of the present discussion, however, is not in what the poem is "about," for it is simply "about" Keats's desire to emulate Milton's poetic greatness. Rather, we are concerned to notice that the accustomed conception of the poet as the active intelligence through whose mediumship the continuous intercourse of earth and heaven is carried on is so unselfconsciously assumed that it *informs* a poem not specifically directed toward its exploitation. Whether it adequately represents Milton's own idea of what he was doing may be open to question, but it represents Keats's in something like a distilled form.

The theory of passive inspiration by the natural world, explicit and implicit in these poems, recurs as the subject of the unrhymed sonnet, "O thou whose face hath felt the Winter's wind," which was included in a letter to Reynolds written in mid-February 1818. After an extended and subjective prose disquisition on the virtues of intuitive and extra-logical response to experience (which restates essentially the briefer remarks on Negative Capability, of two months before, and runs to such formulations as, "let us open our leaves like a flower and be passive and receptive—budding patiently under the eye of Apollo"),[8] Keats presents his poem as an interpretation of what he has heard in the song of a thrush:

[8] *Letters*, I, 232.

O thou whose face hath felt the Winter's wind,
  Whose eye has seen the snow-clouds hung in mist,
  And the black elm tops 'mong the freezing stars,
  To thee the spring will be a harvest-time.
O thou, whose only book has been the light
  Of supreme darkness which thou feddest on
  Night after night when Phoebus was away,
  To thee the Spring shall be a triple morn.
O fret not after knowledge—I have none,
  And yet my song comes native with the warmth.
O fret not after knowledge—I have none,
  And yet the Evening listens. He who saddens
At thought of idleness cannot be idle,
And he's awake who thinks himself asleep.

The poem is built on a series of paradoxes, harvest in
the spring, light out of darkness, and so on, with the
dominant image of each successive statement chosen for
its ability to render inevitable the completion of the statement with one of the familiar symbol-elements. The central statement of the poem, and of the bird's utterance,
is in the eleventh and twelfth lines, "O fret not after
knowledge—I have none, / And yet the Evening listens,"
which, in the listening evening, carries us back to the
framework and assumptions of the theory in its earliest
and least complicated form, in the 1815 Apollo ode.

Still, while the poet was thus felicitously able to enun-
ciate and reaffirm the principles which had informed and
shaped his poetic practice almost from its beginnings, he
was by no means so serene in the possession of these
tenets as the thrush's song implies. Indeed, two of the
poems that we have just discussed include impassioned
lines which betray at least the beginnings of incertitude
and disenchantment. In the lines on Milton's hair, having
proclaimed his determination to achieve such "Hymning
and harmony" as Milton's own, Keats goes on:

But vain is now the burning and the strife,
Pangs are in vain, until I grow high-rife
   With old Philosophy,
And mad with glimpses of futurity!
              (29-32)

One is reminded, by "glimpses of futurity," of the prophetic powers of Apollo and his priesthood, but never before had Keats linked in his poetry the achievement of this power with the rational faculty. Again, and more strongly, in "God of the Meridian," the poet cries:

     God of Song,
   Thou bearest me along
   Through sights I scarce can bear:
   O let me, let me share
   With the hot lyre and thee,
   The staid Philosophy.
   Temper my lonely hours,
   And let me see thy bowers
   More unalarm'd!
             (17-25)

There were reasons enough, in the world of his ordinary experience, for Keats to feel at about this time the need of an intelligible rationale for the disposition of events. We shall consider these matters in a moment. But it ought to be noted first that in these two passages the primary concern is not with a philosophy of *life* but with "old" and "staid" Philosophy, which will make him a better *poet*. It is a more satisfactory *poetic* way of seeing or thinking that he desires, and Philosophy appears in both poems almost as a personified abstraction, or a companion, to provide him with an imaginative stability which he is aware of having lacked up to this point. In the immediate contexts of both poetic statements, there is an implied admission that he must temper such power as he now has, with whatever "Philosophy" may be, before he can achieve the authentic vision and utterance of the poet.

Considering the necessary relationship, however indirect, between what the poet experiences as a man and what he expresses in his writing, the personal problems of Keats's life at this period should probably not be overlooked. Some of them were trivial, others of considerable weight, but their cumulative effect was inevitably distressing.

One annoyance, which must be reckoned as a continuous background to all the other vexations of the time, was the correction and copying of *Endymion* for the press, a tedious process which continued through the first two-and-a-half months of 1818. After that, there was final proof correction, the matter of a suitable preface to be written (and rewritten), and the anxiety of awaiting, first, the late-April publication, and then the public response to it. In other words, although the exhausting six-month process of creative composition was over by the beginning of December 1817, there was an almost equally long period of busy-work, second thoughts, and authorial apprehension before the poet could free his mind of the most sustained and difficult undertaking of his career up to that time.[9] Added to the normal anxiety for the work's success, and the normal impatience attendant upon the copying process, were the difficulties of self-criticism, expressed in the rejected preface in words which every author will approve ("by repetition my favorite Passages sound vapid in my ears"),[10] and the greater self-knowledge, expressed in the whole of both prefaces, of final

[9] Keats twice expressed his impatience to be done with it, so that he might get on with new projects. Cf. *ibid.*, 239, 246.
[10] *Poetical Works*, p. xciii.

CRISIS

failure in a major attempt. However relieved the poet may have been at the completion of the arduous work of original composition, no one will suppose that the subsequent process, or the conclusions to which it led, gave him joy.

Simultaneously, and reaching back to the latter months of *Endymion's* composition, Keats had many other occasions for doubt and disappointment. Among his friends, Bailey was blocked in his first appointment to a curacy,[11] Reynolds was suffering a painful and protracted illness,[12] and Hunt was savagely maligned in the first of the *Blackwood's* articles "On the Cockney School of Poetry," from which quarter Keats himself correctly anticipated an attack.[13] Perhaps worse, the stability of the small social circle to which Keats belonged was being shaken by a general spirit of quarrelsomeness. As early as October 8, 1817, Keats commented on his friends' irritability, "every Body seems at Loggerheads."[14] This he followed with an account of petty bickering chiefly involving Hunt and Haydon. By January 13, 1818, Haydon and Hunt had "parted forever,"[15] and Haydon and Reynolds were exchanging "sharp" and "most cutting" letters.[16] Of the whole situation, Keats was able to say only, "I am quite perplexed in a world of doubts & fancies—there is nothing stable in the world—uproar's your only musick,"[17] adding, "I do not mean to include Bailey in this,"[18] though Bailey too had recently found occasion to be annoyed with Haydon.[19] Worst of all, Keats was himself involved in the general atmosphere of antagonism. Haydon cautioned Keats against letting Hunt see his progress

[11] *Letters,* I, 178-79.
[12] *Ibid.,* 236, 245, 247 and note [George Keats to JK].
[13] *Ibid.,* 179-80.   [14] *Ibid.,* 169.   [15] *Ibid.,* 205.
[16] *Ibid.,* 205.   [17] *Ibid.,* 204.   [18] *Ibid.,* 204.
[19] *Ibid.,* 183.

on *Endymion*,[20] while Hunt offended Keats by publicly intimating that he was to some extent the guiding genius behind the poem.[21] When subsequently shown the completed first book of *Endymion*, both Hunt and Shelley were more critical of it than Keats thought they had a right to be, and he attributed their disapproval to petty motives of revenge for his not having consulted them more often during its composition.[22] Even the venerated idol Wordsworth was, by his egotism, falling rapidly in the younger poet's esteem.[23] By the middle of March 1818, Keats had become so disenchanted with his friends' affectations and inadequacies as to declare, at least half in earnest, that they injured by their association the very arts with which they identified themselves.[24]

In the more intimate circle of his family, trouble was also gathering in several quarters. For one thing, Abbey had begun his systematic campaign to remove the younger sister Fanny from the influence of her poet-brother,[25] and for another, Tom Keats had begun to show alarming symptoms of the disease which was to carry him off before the end of the year in which *Endymion* was published. The poet's concern for his brother's condition (which his medical training no doubt enabled him to understand fully) was frequently expressed,[26] and at the end of the first week in March 1818 Keats went down to Devonshire to care for the semi-invalid. There, the nastiness of the climate and (as it seemed to him) the degeneration of the native race depressed him to the point where he fancied "the very Air of a deteriorating quality"[27] and felt as if "the Moon had dwindled in heaven."[28]

To a sensitive and responsive person whose whole pur-

[20] *Ibid.*, 169.   [21] *Ibid.*, 169.   [22] *Ibid.*, 213-14.
[23] *Ibid.*, 223-25, 237.   [24] *Ibid.*, 251-52.   [25] *Ibid.*, 214.
[26] *Ibid.*, 172, 186-87, 196, 212, 241, 244, 245, *passim*.
[27] *Ibid.*, 241.   [28] *Ibid.*, 242.

pose in life was centered in his art, and whose understanding and practice of that art were grounded in assumptions of a benign tendency in nature and a discernible and humanly attainable harmony in the universe of
which man and nature were correlative parts, these must
have been more than ordinarily disquieting experiences.
It is hardly surprising therefore to discover, in the "God
of the Meridian" lines and in the lines on Milton's hair,
those sudden and hitherto uncharacteristic outbursts expressive of a need for something more stable, less wholly
dependent upon idealized imaginative rationalization of
experience, than he had yet been able to attain in his
views of life and art.

What the new "Philosophy" was that would put all out
of doubt was never explicitly defined. In most of his
remarks on the subject, Keats seemed rather to be expressing a sense of need than choosing a specific course.[29]
The direction in which he was moving is discernible,
however, in a letter to Bailey of March 13, 1818, in which
he casually presented a tentative new formulation which
differed markedly from the old. Its chief difference is its
introduction of "reality" as a coefficient of value. Such
was the poet's growing incertitude about his accustomed
values that he found himself able to make the (for Keats)
rather startling remark, "I am sometimes so very scep-
tical as to think Poetry itself a mere Jack a lanthern to
amuse whoever may chance to be struck with its brilliance," and he went on: "As Tradesmen say every thing
is worth what it will fetch, so probably every mental pursuit takes its reality and worth from the ardour of the
pursuer—being in itself a nothing—Ethereal thing[s]
may at least be thus real, divided under three heads—

[29] His uncertainty about his philosophic destination is reflected
in his remark of April 27, 1818, that he will "ask Hazlitt in about
a years time the best metaphysical road I can take." *Letters*, i, 274.

Things real—things semireal—and no things—Things real—such as existences of Sun Moon & Stars and passages of Shakspeare—Things semireal such as Love, the Clouds &c which require a greeting of the Spirit to make them wholly exist—and Nothings which are made Great and dignified by an ardent pursuit."[30]

The passage has two scales of value, one for the ranking of elements which incite speculative activity, and the other, which is the final value, for the result of that activity. As far as impetus to speculation is concerned, value increases as immediate comprehensibility decreases. Objective substantiality is not the criterion, for a passage from Shakespeare, which is experienced solely as an idea in the mind of the reader or auditor, is clearly less tangible than a cloud. But a Shakespearean passage is more "real" than a cloud in that its completeness of statement brings speculation to rest,[31] while the amorphous variability of a cloud's more tangible substance is capable of providing

[30] *Ibid.*, 242-43. With reference to the Nothings, Keats concludes that these are the objects of pursuit which most clearly differentiate intellects, "insomuch as they are able to *'consec[r]ate whate'er they look upon*[.]' " Rollins [*ibid.*, i, 243n.] suggests comparison with Shelley's "Hymn to Intellectual Beauty" (13-14), "Spirit of Beauty, that dost consecrate / With thine own hues all thou dost shine upon." This is almost certainly the passage Keats had in mind in his misquotation, though Shelley sees the consecrating principle as outside the mind and inherent in the universal order, but intermittently accessible to human perception. Probably closer to Keats's idea is that which Wordsworth alluded to (deprecatorily) in the "Elegiac Stanzas" suggested by a picture of Peele Castle in a storm (15-16), where he spoke of "'The light that never was, on sea or land, / The consecration, and the Poet's dream." At the time (1805), Wordsworth was at approximately the same point of intellectual development as Keats was in the spring of 1818, doubtful of the sufficiency of his earlier formulations, and willing to submit his mind to the sterner discipline of the "real" world.

[31] Cf. Keats's comment of four months before, that Shakespeare "has left nothing to say about nothing or any thing." *Letters*, i, 188-89.

[190]

infinitely varying objective stimuli to the onlooker's imagination. The final value, however, the self-existent value to whose test ethereal musings must be brought, is "reality," for the statement begins with the pairing of "reality and worth." A thing that is "real" to begin with, therefore, already has its worth established. Other things, which are less "real" in their substantive identities, acquire worth in proportion as they acquire "reality" in the mind which takes them up and seeks to understand them. If the introductory remark about his skepticism of poetry's worth is relevant to what follows, Keats seems to be somewhat defensively attempting to find a value coefficient for such subjective experience as animates the poetic imagination by establishing its various kinds on a reality-scale. At its most "ethereal," the imaginative activity of poetry is granted to have only a personal reality-worth, i.e. it is valuable *if you think it is*, because it thereby achieves reality *for you*. But the more it demands of the greeting spirit, the less general "reality" it has, hence the less "worth." If such was his skepticism of ethereally oriented poetry, one must suppose, then, that a greater admixture of, or reference to, "reality" was what Keats hoped to acquire in the pursuit of Philosophy, and the impetus toward that pursuit can only have come from his sense that "reality" was somehow lacking in the formulation that had sustained him up to this point in his career.

The word "real," as a coefficient of value, was relatively new to Keats's vocabulary, but he retained it throughout the period of intellectual crisis which he was entering at the time of this formulation. It is clear from the examples he gives in this passage, however, that his conception of "reality" continued to embrace more than brute natural fact. In order to sharpen our understanding of the poet's drift, therefore, we might examine the other uses to which he put the word "real" at about this time. It first occurs, as a term of approbation, in a letter of September 14, 1817, where Keats thanks the Reynolds girls for having introduced him to "so real a fellow as Bailey."[32] Writing to Bailey himself, on January 23, 1818, Keats takes up a former topic of their conversation, the question of why woman should have to suffer. He sees no justice in it, yet he is obliged to acknowledge that "These things are," i.e. such suffering is an inescapable condition of existence, and he concludes helplessly with a comment on "how incompetent the most skyey Knight errantry [is] to heal this bruised fairness . . . ,"[33] thus opposing a fact to a pleasing fancy. Then, presumably through the association of juxtaposed ideas, he goes on, "Your tearing . . . a spirit-less and gloomy Letter up to rewrite to me is what I shall never forget—it was to me a real thing."[34] It was almost two months later that he wrote, again to Bailey, the passage cited earlier, in which he classifies speculative elements on a scale of reality. Two months after that, writing to Reynolds on May 3, he concluded the disquisition in which the "Mansion of Many Apartments" passage occurs with the comment, "I may have read these things before, but I never had even a thus dim perception of them. . . . After all there is certainly something real in the World—Moore's present to Hazlitt is real—"[35] And on July 13 he wrote to Reynolds, whose marriage was supposedly imminent, that the affectionate attachment of marriage and family ties is "real."[36] In all these instances, "real" connotes something like a capacity to move the heart for adequate human reasons, and it is presumably

---

[32] *Ibid.*, 160.   [33] *Ibid.*, 209.   [34] *Ibid.*, 209.

[35] *Ibid.*, 282. In a note at this place, Rollins accepts Holman's conjecture that the giver was not Thomas but Peter Moore, one of the managers of Drury Lane Theatre, and that the gift was a sum of money.

[36] *Ibid.*, 325.

therefore opposed to the sentimentality of such "skyey Knight errantry" as fulfills an imaginative longing without having any capacity for humane amelioration. Much of Keats's early poetry consisted of just such chivalric impulse, in either convention or intent. And while we must not overlook some badness in its writing, where it failed it was often because it embodied an ideal vision of human life rather than an experiential human truth. The movement toward "reality," then, is a movement away from conceptual and toward experiential cognition. With increasing frequency the poet would maintain the position that "axioms in philosophy are not axioms until they are proved upon our pulses,"[37] and that "Nothing ever becomes real till it is experienced—Even a Proverb is no proverb to you till your Life has illustrated it—"[38]

But at the time that Keats formulated his classification of "ethereal" things according to their "reality," he was merely tentatively exploring new ground. There is no evidence to suggest that he had yet abandoned his old formulation, and indeed, the sonnet "Four seasons fill the measure of the year," which he appended to his discussion of "reality" as an illustration of it, is primarily conceived in terms of the old view of a parallel development in man's intellect and nature's bounty, and only marginally in the light of his new concept of speculative reality. The sonnet, in fact, simply traces the decreasing dependency of the ripening intellect upon experience of the outer world, while it affirms, as always, the outer world of nature as the starting point for all speculative activity. The real crisis of Keats's intellectual commitment was yet to come. But its coming was not many days away.

On March 24, 1818, Keats wrote to James Rice: "What a happy thing it would be if we could settle our thoughts,

[37] *Ibid.*, 279.
[38] *Ibid.*, II, 81.

make our minds up on any matter in five Minutes and remain content—that is to build a sort of mental Cottage of feelings quiet and pleasant—to have a sort of Philosophical Back Garden, and cheerful holiday-keeping front one—but Alas! this never can be: for as the material Cottager knows there are such places as france [*sic*] and Italy and the Andes and the Burning Mountains—so the spiritual Cottager has knowledge of the terra semi incognita of things unearthly; and cannot for his Life, keep in the check rein" (*Letters*, I, 254-55). The letter is otherwise lighthearted, as appropriate to the tone established in the Rice circle, and the wonder is only that Keats could have brought himself to be thus serious in a quarter where wit and easy cynicism seem to have been the prevailing mode.[39] The passage is part of a continuous paragraph but is only slightly relevant to the subjects which precede and follow it. Were there any evidence of unusual disquiet in Keats's mental life (and I think we have seen that there was, and with sufficient cause), one might readily conclude that, despite his surface gaiety, the poet was undergoing so great an upheaval of his most deeply held convictions as to be unable wholly to suppress the mood. As it happens, we need not guess, for on the following day Keats wrote the verse epistle to John Hamilton Reynolds which marks his confrontation of facts that he had hitherto avoided because they did not accommodate themselves to the scheme of his Philosophical Back Garden.

The epistle "To J. H. Reynolds, Esq." has long been recognized for the crisis statement that it is, but two important aspects of it have not been recognized. The first

[39] Cf. *Letters*, i, 197; ii, 236. In the latter place Keats repeats to Rice, as amusing, a grossly morbid anecdote so unlike anything else in the whole range of his correspondence as to suggest that only the predilections of its recipient could have called it forth.

of these is the specific nature of the poet's complaint, and the second, closely related to the first, is the high degree of internal relevance among the poem's parts. Keats's apology to Reynolds for the "unconnected subject, and careless verse"[40] no doubt encourages the casual reader to see more disjunction among the parts than actually exists. The poem shows every evidence of having been composed in a mood of emotional agitation and sent to Reynolds without polishing and revision, and Keats's awareness that he was sending a rough draft, which he would not wish to have judged as a specimen of completed effort, was certainly the reason for his apology. This is, of course, not at all what is customarily read into his apology, i.e. that he had nothing particular in mind when he began to write, and that he consequently rambled from topic to topic until he finally hit upon something that he really wanted to say.

The poem opens with a dozen lines of incongruously juxtaposed image-elements which are represented as the passing fancies of a sleepless evening hour:

> Dear Reynolds, as last night I lay in bed,
> There came before my eyes that wonted thread
> Of Shapes, and Shadows and Remembrances,
> That every other minute vex and please:
> Things all disjointed come from North and south,
> Two witch's eyes above a Cherub's mouth,
> Voltaire with casque and shield and Habergeon,
> And Alexander with his night-cap on—
> Old Socrates a tying his cravat;
> And Hazlitt playing with Miss Edgeworth's cat;
> And Junius Brutus pretty well so, so,
> Making the best of's way towards Soho.
>
> (1-12)

[40] *Letters*, I, 263.

CRISIS

De Selincourt was put off by the "meaningless caprice"
of this beginning,[41] but it is customary to take Miss Lowell's tone of tolerant condescension and say that Keats set
out "solely to amuse and give pleasure to his sick friend,"[42]
and therefore simply began to prime the pump of composition with good-natured foolishness. There is indeed
an element of foolery in some of the images themselves,
yet it cannot be said that there is any spirit of nonsense
or merriment in the lines with which they are introduced.
They are "Shapes, and Shadows and Remembrances," suggesting rather the ghostly visitants of a haunted fancy
than projections of playful caprice. If they "please" the
random imagination, they equally "vex" it, for they come
(and the epithet plunges to the core of the poem) "all
disjointed." The imagination is not in harmony with its
impulses: it comprehends too much. It is incapable of
projecting a single ideal image, and finds itself toying
with possibilities by which the ideal is debased. The poet
does not say that he conjured up these visions for his own
amusement but that they "came before my eyes." The
first of them, a witch's eyes above a cherub's mouth, is
clearly morbid, and the others are all comically degraded
prototypes of ideal human qualities.

Should there be any remaining doubt about the poet's
pleasure or volition in these experiences, it is dispelled
in the following lines:

Few are there who escape these visitings—
P'erhaps one or two, whose lives have patent wings;
And through whose curtains peeps no hellish nose,
No wild boar tushes, and no Mermaid's toes:
But flowers bursting out with lusty pride;
And young Æolian harps personified,
Some, Titian colours touch'd into real life.—

41 E. de Selincourt (ed.), *Poems*, p. 538.
42 Amy Lowell, *John Keats*, I, 612.

[196]

CRISIS

The sacrifice goes on; the pontiff knife
Gleams in the sun, the milk-white heifer lows,
The pipes go shrilly, the libation flows:
A white sail shews above the green-head cliff
Moves round the point, and throws her anchor stiff.
The Mariners join hymn with those on land.

(13-25)

There are few who *escape* this sort of visitation, few whose emotional and imaginative self-containment is never threatened by perception of the absurd, the incongruous, and the malign. For these few, nature is simply the burgeoning of beauty ("flowers bursting out with lusty pride"), man is seen always in harmony with his world ("young Æolian harps personified"),[43] and all life is perceived with the vivid warmth of its representation in a painting by Titian.[44] For these happy few, life has all the serenity and self-sufficiency implicit in the ritual act which is described in the next three lines. For these happy few there is a readily perceived, acknowledged, and maintained rapport between man and the purposive forces which direct his life.

The image of religious sacrifice is a perfect vehicle for

[43] The symbolism of the Æolian harp, with the man who is perfectly attuned to the world of nature (normally the poet) as its analogous personification, is too familiar to require explanation. For a convenient brief summary of the convention, see M. H. Abrams, *The Mirror and the Lamp*, pp. 51-52.

[44] I must take exception to the universal view that the reference to Titian, in l. 19, represents Keats's confusion of paintings by Titian and Claude Lorrain. The poet neither says nor implies that Titian is the painter of the scene that immediately follows. On the contrary, he does say that for a few people life is not one thing but its opposite, the opposition being made concrete in the three images of ll. 17-19, the flowers, the harp, and the ideal colors of the painting transposed to "real life." (The last image is the more elegant equivalent of "looking at life through rose-colored glasses.") The whole quality of such a life is then objectified in the extended image of the sacrifice scene described in ll. 20-25.

[197]

the expression of this idea—and in the terms of its description there are some interesting ramifications. Keats is not here creating the image but adapting it to his purposes. He is describing a painting which happens to be appropriate to his meaning, and, while he is therefore limited by the picture's content, he is at liberty to select those elements of the picture which seem most relevant and to couch his description in what seems to him the most significant language. This being true, it should not be amiss to note that the brief passage includes the sun (and further, the sun mirrored in the instrument of human devotion), music, and wine—all central elements in the familiar Apollo-complex. That the juxtaposition of these elements is not fortuitous is certain, if Sidney Colvin is correct in his assertion that the picture described is Claude Lorrain's "Sacrifice to Apollo."[45] When one couples this Apollinian imagery with the recollection of Keats's view of the poet as mediator between the god and man, one whose poems are acts of devotion to the god, the function of the description, at least for Keats, becomes instantly clear. Those whose lives are filled solely with perceptions of universal harmony can go through life performing those ritual acts of devotion of which poems are the literary equivalent. By the practice of poetry they can effectually serve Apollo as his priests. But Keats is no longer one of these, for in this poem he has already opposed such people to others, like himself, who are tormented with a perception of disjuncture among the elements of life. For him there is no longer that harmony of vision objectified in the scene of sacrifice and in the hymn of praise shared, at the conclusion of the whole descriptive passage, by those on land and

[45] Sidney Colvin, *John Keats*, p. 264. Dorothy Hewlett concurs [*A Life of John Keats*, p. 156], as does E. C. Pettet [*On the Poetry of Keats*, p. 335].

sea. At this point in the poem Keats has not yet revealed
the final ground of his disenchantment; but in the employment of his accustomed imagery of harmony to represent a condition *un*like his own, he has revealed its
completeness.

Lines 26-40 offer a fairly literal, though subjectively
interpreted, description of another painting, Claude Lorrain's "The Enchanted Castle":

> You know the Enchanted Castle it doth stand
> Upon a Rock on the Border of a Lake
> Nested in Trees, which all do seem to shake
> From some old Magic like Urganda's sword.
> O Phoebus that I had thy sacred word
> To shew this Castle in fair dreaming wise
> Unto my friend, while sick and ill he lies.
>
> You know it well enough, where it doth seem
> A mossy place, a Merlin's Hall, a dream.
> You know the clear Lake, and the little Isles,
> The Mountains blue, and cold near neighbour rills—
> All which elsewhere are but half animate
> Here do they look alive to love and hate;
> To smiles and frowns; they seem a lifted mound
> Above some giant, pulsing underground.
>
> (26-40)

Though the power of Phoebus is called upon for the
"fair" representation of the picture (i.e. compositionally),
it is realized as anything but fair. The earlier morbidity
of mood returns in the gratuitous introduction of Ur-
ganda and Merlin, agents of sinister enchantment, and
in the description of mountains as the mere surface cov-
erings of a pulsing giant force gathering its strength just
out of sight of all that meets the eye. Nowhere in Keats's
poetry, up to this point, is there any equivalent for this
distrust of what nature presents to the eye. And never

before, in his treatment of the lore of enchantment, had Keats looked so directly at its malevolent side. The picture itself, as Claude painted it, is emotionally neutral, and without its title it would hardly be likely to give rise to any response not appropriate to landscape painting in general. Given its title, one may interpret the quality of its enchantment as one wishes, but the quiescence of every element in the picture, which is established and focused by the pensive human figure seated in the foreground, provides little reason for seeing it as anything but a charmed and charming dream vision. Keats's response is, beyond any question, perverse; and its causes, hinted at in the poem's beginning, will be fully manifest at its end.

In the last lines of this passage, Keats makes the peculiar remark that lakes, little isles, mountains, and rills seem, everywhere but in this painting, to be "but half animate," or half alive. Without the next two lines, it would be extraordinarily difficult to know what sort of life he meant to imply, but the parallel sentence elements that follow make his meaning quite clear. Here, in this picture, the elements of nature are alive "to love and hate / To smiles and frowns." In this vision of nature, the whole of human life is mirrored, the hate and the frowns as well as the love and the smiles; opposed tendencies are comprehended in a single configuration of nature. The landscape elements from which Keats hitherto would have abstracted assurance of benign harmony now provide a collective metaphor for the internal disharmony of the perceiving mind's own impulses. And it would be as well to emphasize that the mind which so conceives the innocuous landscape elements of the painting is its own unhappy place, torturing itself with imaginative inferences of evil from a source that does not overtly present them. Just as the poet, at the beginning of his poem,

could not sustain an uncorrupted fantasy, so now his contemplation of an object outside himself is marred by a
fantasy of its latent corruption.

Keats continues his poem with almost excessive imaginative insistence upon the disjointed and unintegrated:

> Part of the building was a chosen See
> Built by a banish'd Santon of Chaldee:
> The other part two thousand years from him
> Was built by Cuthbert de Saint Aldebrim;
> Then there's a little wing, far from the Sun,
> Built by a Lapland Witch turn'd Maudlin nun—
> And many other juts of aged stone
> Founded with many a mason-devil's groan.
>
> (41-48)

Not only is the building the product of different design-
ers but also, judging by the cultural implications of their
assigned identities, the motives of its builders were different. In the case of the "Lapland Witch turn'd Maudlin
nun" there is the same ambiguity of identity, or if one
prefers, the same tension of opposed tendencies, as has
been objectified in the building itself and in the scenery
which forms its backdrop. Whether convert or lamia, she
presents herself to the mind's eye in a single form, and
the truth of her nature cannot be known.

Having exploited the possibilities of one type of imaginative response, the poet begins in the succeeding lines
to consecrate what he looks upon by initiating an imaginative series of images and actions which begin where
the details of the picture leave off:

> The doors all look as if they oped themselves,
> The windows as if latch'd by fays & elves—
> And from them comes a silver flash of light
> As from the Westward of a Summer's night;

Or like a beauteous woman's large blue eyes
Gone mad through olden songs and Poesies—
   See what is coming from the distance dim!
A golden galley all in silken trim!
Three rows of oars are lightening moment-whiles
Into the verdurous bosoms of those Isles.
Towards the Shade under the Castle Wall
It comes in silence—now tis hidden all.
The clarion sounds; and from a postern grate
An echo of sweet music doth create
A fear in the poor herdsman who doth bring
His beasts to trouble the enchanted spring:
He tells of the sweet music and the spot
To all his friends, and they believe him not.
                                                (49-66)

The tone of these lines is chiefly pastoral and serene. The mason-devils give way to fays and elves, the magic casements reflect light that is significantly reminiscent of a summer evening's sunset in the west, a golden galley enters upon the scene and sets off the sweet music of a herald's clarion. As the poet's imagination operates on the materials of his immediate experience, we are carried back to the atmosphere of chivalry, fairyland, and verdurous nature.

There are, however, a few jarring notes. The beauteous woman gone mad from hearing the old songs, and the frightened shepherd whose friends refuse to credit his story of enchantment, do break the spell of poetic calm. Taken in their contexts, however, they must be judged inadvertent lapses, the sort of fault for which Keats apologized to Reynolds. A mad woman is an unhappy image, and a beautiful mad woman is even more painful, simply because more of what we desire is lost to us. In the mood in which Keats obviously wrote the poem, he was entirely capable of supplying such images, but it should be noted here that the woman and her condition are not the intended focus of attention. The woman, for poetic purposes, is merely an adjunct of her eyes, the flashing of which serves as one limb of a simile of which the other is the appearance of the castle windows. Having introduced the woman's "large blue eyes," the poet probably felt obliged to particularize his image and so added the subordinate detail of the madness induced by old poetry. By this latter detail, I believe, Keats intended to convey not insanity but rapture, for the image's function is parallel with that of the sunset image which precedes it. In the case of the herdsman's fear of the unaccustomed music, and his friends' disbelief of his tale, the effect calculated is, I think, that of the charm associated with naïve simplicity, rather than of genuine terror and misunderstanding. I am persuaded to these readings by the lines which open the next verse paragraph, "O that our dreamings all of sleep or wake / Would all their colours from the Sunset take," which introduce a shift of thought and mood. The emphatic word is the "all" of the first line, implying that *some* dreams, like the daydreams we have just seen, are pleasant, but that this is by no means true of *all* dreams. The discussion which follows is opposed in tenor to that which has immediately preceded it, and the transition lines establish the distinction in kind. We must therefore assume that, however sinister the momentary implication of the lines cited, their intention was in keeping with the implied intention of the passage as a whole.

The section of the poem which begins with the lines just cited makes explicit the complaint that has been variously objectified up to this point:

> O that our dreamings all of sleep or wake
> Would all their colours from the sunset take:

From something of material sublime,
Rather than shadow our own Soul's daytime
In the dark void of Night. For in the world
We jostle—

(67-72)

The two introductory lines, which would color all our
dreams with sunset hues, refer back on the most literal
level to the sunset coloring of the preceding passage. The
word "colours" is, however, obviously metaphorical, referring to general quality rather than to particular tints.
When we recall Keats's habitual association of sunset,
Apollo, and the creative process, the quality to which he
alludes in the sunset reference, here and in the preceding
passage, becomes clear. That is, it is clear in respect to
the problem of integrated personal vision that the poem
has single-mindedly explored up to this point. The poet
misses the harmony of vision that sunset has always embodied for him—the assurance that his theory of imagination is adequately confirmed by the visible evidence of
external nature, localized in the beauty and calm of sunset and epitomized in the concept of a fructifying god
who symbolically passes at the sunset hour from one dynamic sphere to the other, from the physical to the intellectual, thereby objectifying the analogical continuity of
the animating principle in both. All this is summed up in
the idea of a "material sublime," something in the material world commensurate with our capacity for interior
serenity and awe. The material sublimity of the sunset
is, of course, in terms of Keats's theoretical framework,
representative of the starting point in external nature for
that imaginative activity which culminates in the harvest
of poetry. It is opposed here by the jostling of the daytime, or ordinary world, by that clashing of human purposes which denies the wished-for principle of harmony.

However much one might desire continuous impulses of harmony for the imagination's nourishment, one's solitary meditations are perforce fed by all that the soul has experienced, and this must include conflict. Hence the grotesque visions with which the poem began and the images of conflict and uncertain identity by means of which the poet has presented its argument up to this point.

The poem was now, for all practical purposes, complete. It had come full circle in treating the problem posed at its beginning, and Keats seemed disposed in the next few lines to disclaim any pretense to validity in his ideas, as was his custom in those letters where he committed himself to passages of abstract speculation:[46]

> but my flag is not unfurl'd
> On the Admiral staff—and to philosophize
> I dare not yet!—Oh never will the prize,
> High reason, and the lore of good and ill
> Be my award. Things cannot to the will
> Be settled, but they tease us out of thought.
> (72-77)

He acknowledges his inability to deal authoritatively with philosophic problems *yet*, i.e. up to that point in his experience. Then, on second thought, he despairs of *ever* being able to master the "lore of good and ill,"[47] for he lacks sufficient faith in the mind's own power. "High reason" and "the lore of good and ill" together constitute

[46] Cf. *Letters*, I, 233, 243, 277; II, 80-81, 104.
[47] I here accept Garrod's and Rollins' reading, "lore," rather than Milnes' "love," which was followed by de Selincourt and others, because it seems to make better sense in context. In its literal denotation of "learning," it is precisely what Keats is talking about. If read as "love," it goes one step beyond the situation Keats describes, i.e. to the consequences succeeding upon the acquisition of that learning which he does not have.

the despaired-of prize; each is a supposed concomitant of the other, the latter dependent upon and following after the former. But things "tease us out of thought," i.e. tantalize us beyond the boundaries that thought can reach. (The concept of eternity is one such "thing," as the repetition of this expression in the "Ode on a Grecian Urn" tells us.) A judgment is thus passed on the ultimate incapacity of human reason, and one which affects, in turn, our understanding of the statement that "Things cannot to the will / Be settled. . . ." The question is not whether things can be settled as we should *like* them to be, but whether they can be settled *at all*, given the will to acquire intellectual means. If the means, i.e. human reason and understanding, are inadequate, there can be no efficacy in the exercise of the will.

Although the poem might have been left at this point to the reader's meditation, the poet's apology for his inadequacy to deal with its central problem had thus veered into a criticism of the inadequacy of reason as a mode of arriving at truth—which was just contrary to the whole idea that the poem had been intended to express. It was the imagination, as Keats had been accustomed to conceive it, that was failing him, and the poem had expressed, within certain limits, the nature and extent of that failure. No doubt aware of the incongruity of these last lines, and perhaps desiring to round out his new line of argument by considering in a parallel summary[48] the alternate mode of approaching truth, Keats then went on with what proved to be the poem's most concise statement of what is really its central problem:

[48] The introductory "Or" in line 78 places the passage on imagination parallel with that on reason, implying in its context a statement which might be paraphrased as, "Is it really the inadequacy of human reason that prevents us from arriving at truth, *or* is the difficulty perhaps inherent in the imaginative mode of seeking truth?"

Or is it that Imagination brought
Beyond its proper bound, yet still confined,—
Lost in a sort of Purgatory blind,
Cannot refer to any standard law
Of either earth or heaven?—It is a flaw
In happiness to see beyond our bourn—
It forces us in Summer skies to mourn:
It spoils the singing of the Nightingale.
                                        (78-85)

The difficulty is here attributed directly to the nature of
the imagination, which persuades us that there *is* a truth
transcending the evidences of our senses and the limitations of our reason but which is incapable of leading us
to it. The "proper bound" of imagination would appear
to be its capacity to provide pleasure, or "happiness."
When it attempts to go beyond this function and guide
us toward truth, it is delusive, leaving us in "a sort of
Purgatory blind," no longer creatures merely of the
earth (i.e. confined to the evidences of ordinary perception), but still far short of the ideal heaven of understanding. This conjecture, presented in question form,
culminates in the ultimate question: Is it possible that
the imagination "Cannot refer to any standard law / Of
either earth or heaven?" What it must have cost Keats to
confront the implications of this question can be measured by the extent to which his whole career, up to this
point, had been predicated on the assumption of a universal principle operative in both earth and heaven and
accessible to the properly oriented imagination. If the
poet were obliged to answer, and the very asking of the
question implies such an answer, that there is no such
law, then he would have no rationale for the continuance
of his poetic career and would either have to give it up
for sheer inanition or re-establish it on a radically new

foundation. It appears that Keats did consider giving up poetry, at least until he could ground his understanding on firmer principles.[49] But the direction in which he was actually to move appears by implication in the concluding lines of the verse-paragraph under discussion.

When the poet says that "It is a flaw / In happiness to see beyond our bourn," he is speaking about the over-extended imagination. And this, the imagination, is the antecedent of the subject-pronouns in the lines, "It forces us in Summer skies to mourn: / It spoils the singing of the Nightingale." The word that leaps out at us is, of course, "Nightingale." Here is a specific link with the theoretical formulation that is in question throughout the epistle, a tangible creature of the natural world, but one which had been laden with tremendous conceptual weight, in the earlier poetry, as both vehicle and symbol of the Apollinian idea. If the argument of the last eight lines is coherent and consistent, as we must assume it is intended to be, we can only conclude that the imagination, when brought beyond its proper bound, misleads us in much the same way that, in its ordinary mode, reason does, because *both* invite us to relate the objects of our experience to principles outside those of their own existential being. The legitimate pleasure of a summer day or a nightingale's song, one infers, consists in our immediate and unmeditated response. Since man is not a mindless creature, however, the imagination, stimulated by impulses of pleasure, may then provide trains of associated pleasure-images—but there it must stop. The moment that it attempts to etherealize, conceptualize, or relate to a larger whole the pleasures of immediate experience is the moment at which we lose the only verifiable truth about the nightingale, i.e. that its song

[49] Cf. *Letters*, i, 271, 274.

gives pleasure. Imagination can flaw our happiness by diverting our attention from the beauty of things as they simply are.

The lines which follow are almost always quoted out of context, as if the poet had merely been rambling up to this point, and had suddenly stumbled upon a serious theme. As a result, they have been universally misunderstood;[50] they actually serve as an exemplum of the argument on imagination just presented, which in turn grew out of the reflections on his flawed poetic vision which the poet had been developing from the very beginning of his epistle. In illustration of his last remarks, the poet goes on:

> Dear Reynolds, I have a mysterious tale
> And cannot speak it. The first page I read
> Upon a Lampit Rock of green sea weed
> Among the breakers—'Twas a quiet Eve;
> The rocks were silent—the wide sea did weave
> An untumultuous fringe of silver foam
> Along the flat brown sand. I was at home,
> And should have been most happy—
>
> (86-93)

In a setting of great natural beauty and serenity, the poet *should* have been happy,

> but I saw
> Too far into the sea; where every maw
> The greater on the less feeds evermore:—
> But I saw too distinct into the core

[50] The standard view of the passage is that it represents Keats's sudden coming to awareness of what Hoxie N. Fairchild, in the classic essay on the subject, calls the struggle-for-existence concept ["Keats and the Struggle-for-Existence Tradition," *PMLA*, LXIV (1949), 98-114]. While the concept certainly does enter the poem, it is by no means in the way or toward the consequences that this essay suggests.

Of an eternal fierce destruction,
And so from Happiness I far was gone.
Still am I sick of it: and though to-day
I've gathered young spring-leaves, and flowers gay
Of Periwinkle and wild strawberry,
Still do I that most fierce destruction see,
The Shark at savage prey—the hawk at pounce,
The gentle Robin, like a pard or ounce,
Ravening a worm—

(93-105)

Instead of accepting the scene before him as he found
it, he *conceptualized* it, and the morbidity of his conception continues to press upon him, so that, though he has
since "gathered young spring-leaves, and flowers gay /
Of Periwinkle and wild strawberry," these things cannot
give him pleasure. He is unable to find joy in even the
simplest elements of nature because his imagination has
placed them in a terrible conceptual interrelationship.
That this conception runs directly counter to that which
had dominated Keats's mind for so long is certainly con-
tributory to his melancholy, but the poem had already
rehearsed arguments enough about the conceptual mal-
function of his accustomed imaginative mode. In this
passage, which culminates in the investiture of innocent
experience with imaginative attributes not immediately
appropriate to it, the attack is not upon the inadequacy
of a particular conception but upon the conceptualizing
imagination itself. As the poet has just said, the power
of the imagination to alter the essential quality of experience destroys the experience's integrity. An incapacity
to look at the periwinkle without seeing the shark at
savage prey is clearly a derangement not of nature but
of mind.

The poet's final exclamation, before concluding on a

personal, sociable note, confirms this view of the passage's argument: "Away ye horrid moods, / Moods of one's mind!" (105-106) What he wishes away is the capacity of the mind to invest the world with its own coloring, or mood. By the qualification of "horrid moods" with "Moods of one's mind," emphasis is directed away from the possible source of discontent in the outer world to its probable source in the inner. It is not the world that is at fault but the mind that interprets the world. Thus, in the poem's conclusion we have the full resolution of the problem that had been only partially resolved at the point where the poem was, in all probability, first thought of as complete, i.e. at line 72.

Keats's tendency to worry a problem, once he got his teeth into it, a tendency that can be verified by referring at random to virtually any of the speculative passages in his letters, brought him at last to full confrontation of an issue which was so basic to the rationale of his poetic life that he could probably not have brought himself to face it by any more direct process. From beginning to end, the poem is concerned with the unhappy vagaries of imagination. But, where the initial trend of argument culminates in an attempt to place the blame on the external world's increasing tendency to intrude on the imagination's capacity for idealization, Keats's unflinching determination to have it out, once and for all, carried him past a tentative resolution, in which he merely accepted the malfunctioning of his own imagination, to a final resolution in which, with reluctance and pain, he recognized what a grossly distorting glass the unfettered imagination can become. One may doubt whether there exists anywhere else, in the whole of the world's literature, so dramatic a display of the mind of genius in the very act of coming to know itself.

FOUR

Transition

THE force of the shock that Keats had sustained in composing the Reynolds epistle is revealed in the letters of the following months. All the elements of emotional confusion are present—irritability and depression, indecision and lethargy, baffled self-evaluation and a sort of wild, wide-ranging casting up of programs for a fresh start. But the emotional abrasion had a polishing effect, and intermittently there are gleams of a new, reflective maturity emerging and replacing the old imaginative optimism.

Another letter to Reynolds, this time in prose, written about five weeks after the verse epistle, reveals most of what had been going through the poet's mind in the interval. Beginning with the complaint that he has "been in so uneasy a state of Mind as not to be fit to write,"[1] he moves quickly to the topic that has been most in his thoughts, the question of knowledge. "An extensive knowledge," he says, "is needful to thinking people—it takes away the heat and fever; and helps, by widening speculation, to ease the Burden of the Mystery: a thing I begin to understand a little. . . . The difference of high Sensations with and without knowledge appears to me this—in the latter case we are falling continually ten thousand fathoms deep and being blown up again without wings and with all [the] horror of a bare shoulderd Creature—in the former case, our shoulders are fledge[d],

[1] *Letters*, I, 275.

and we go thro' the same air and space without fear."[2]
Questioning whether knowledge can sustain one through
the emotional shocks of life,[3] and whether it may not in
the long run make one less happy,[4] he yet goes on, in the
Mansion of Many Apartments simile, to consider the
stages of normal growth in knowledge. He says that he
has passed through the "infant or thoughtless Chamber"[5]
and is just emerging from the "Chamber of Maiden-
Thought," in which the "thinking principle" is first awakened and we "become intoxicated with the light" therein,
and "see nothing but pleasant wonders."[6] It is a good
condition to be in, he says, but one cannot stay, for gradually one becomes aware "that the World is full of Misery and Heartbreak, Pain, Sickness and oppression—
whereby This Chamber of Maiden Thought becomes
gradually darken'd."[7] At that point, other possibilities
offer themselves, but one cannot see far enough to be
sure of which should be chosen. Such, he says, is his own
condition at the moment.[8]

It is, on the whole, a sound appraisal, and one clearly
indicative of the intellectual crisis through which Keats
was passing. A new awareness of substantial reality was
leading him out of his old intellectual chamber of intoxicating light, and he was looking forward to the grounding
of his speculative activity in solid knowledge. Simultaneously, he was writing verse of a kind wholly divorced
from either teleological or ideal consideration, verse committed entirely to the celebration of intense momentary
experience. The joys of friendship are thus celebrated in
the sonnet "To J.R.," of April 20 or 21,[9] in which the poet
wishes that "time itself would be annihilate" when he is

[2] *Ibid.*, 277. [4] *Ibid.*, 279. [6] *Ibid.*, 281.
[3] *Ibid.*, 277-78. [5] *Ibid.*, 280. [7] *Ibid.*
[8] *Ibid.*

[9] This dating was established by Amy Lowell, *John Keats*, i, 615-
18.

in the company of his friend; and in the fragment of an "Ode to May" (or Maia), of May 1, he considers the pleasure of composing poetry as entirely adequate to itself, without other reward, so long as he can be "Rich in the simple worship of a day."

On June 22 Keats set out with Charles Brown on the walking tour of the North which was to be one of the most interesting and satisfying experiences of his life. Despite the inevitable discomforts and inconveniences of their mode of travel, the poet responded with gusto to these new experiences of natural beauty and human conduct. Still, he did not leave his nagging preoccupation behind him, nor did he now in his verse fall back into the accustomed mode and attitude of his former expression. Admittedly, the poetry of the walking tour is all occasional, some of it mere entertaining doggerel, yet we have seen frequent examples of Keats's earlier extempore verse (e.g. "On the Grasshopper and Cricket," "Hence Burgundy," "God of the Meridian," "Lines on Seeing a Lock of Milton's Hair") falling repeatedly into a fixed conceptual framework. The verse of the walking tour, on the other hand, tends to be objective, given to literal description of what the poet sees, or to the recording of such unsystematic associations of ideas as spring immediately from the observed fact; or, when speculative, is openly hostile to the heightening tug of an idealizing imagination.

The sonnet "On Visiting the Tomb of Burns," for example, though almost impossible to unriddle in every detail, does in a few lines veer unmistakably toward the new orientation. Written "in a strange mood, half asleep,[10] the sonnet registers the poet's disappointment at his inability to *feel* anything at Burns's tomb:

[10] *Letters,* i, 309.

[214]

TRANSITION

The Town, the churchyard, & the setting sun,
The Clouds, the trees, the rounded hills all seem
Though beautiful, Cold—strange—as in a dream,
I dreamed long ago, now new begun
The shortlived, paly summer is but won
From winter's ague, for one hours gleam;
Through saphire warm, their stars do never beam,
All is cold Beauty; pain is never done.
For who has mind to relish Minos-wise,
The real of Beauty, free from that dead hue
Fickly imagination & sick pride
*   wan upon it! Burns! with honor due
I have oft honoured thee. Great shadow; hide
Thy face, I sin against thy native skies.
 * Illegible word.

The text of the poem is barbarous, particularly in matters of punctuation, but its essential statement is not too
difficult to find.[11] Though the poet visits the tomb at the
(hitherto inspirational) sunset hour, all nature seems
pale and cold to him. The tone is very like that of Coleridge's *Dejection* ode, but where Coleridge laments the
loss of his capacity to respond imaginatively to nature,
Keats appears to resent imagination's intrusion on what
should be an objective pleasure. The substantive beauty
of the scene is acknowledged, but to the mind of the
poet it *seems* cold, the summer *seems* a mere interval in
the normal sickness of winter, the sky *seems* incapable
of warmly glowing. The fault, then, does not lie with
the world of nature but with the fickle imagination's in-
vesiture of it with the mood that it brings to the scene.

[11] I use the text in *Letters*, I, 308, because, though imperfect,
and a transcript by John Jeffrey, it is the sole authority. Garrod's
emendations, while sometimes congenial to my reading (e.g. "Sick-
ly" for "Fickly" in line 11), actually make a coherent reading
more difficult than does the choppy text given here.

Implicit in the idea of imagination's fickleness is the correlative that, if one submits to its guidance, instead of to the external stimuli in the setting, one can be as easily cast down as raised up—there is no objective constant for the experiencing of beauty. And yet, the pain of such disappointment seems inescapable, for imagination plagues human understanding to the extent that the poet doubts whether *anyone* can look on "The real of Beauty" with the objective neutrality of the exemplary judge Minos. So deeply is imagination ingrained in human nature that all must expect its moody waywardness occasionally to defraud them of the world's authentic pleasures.[12]

The sonnet "To Ailsa Rock," written ten days later, is almost first-rate in conception and organization, despite a nagging querulousness of tone. Keats himself called it "the only Sonnet of any worth I have of late written,"[13] yet it is one which is seldom anthologized, even in collections which include numerous sonnets, some of inferior craftsmanship. I suspect that the reason for this customary omission is the editors' vague feeling that it isn't very "Keatsian," and indeed it is not, in the usual view of "Keatsian" as imaginative idealization of sensuous delight. This sonnet insists upon the deadness of the great rock, upon its inability to mean or to communicate anything beyond the fact of its great bulk:

Hearken, thou craggy ocean pyramid!
  Give answer from thy voice, the sea-fowls' screams!
  When were thy shoulders mantled in huge streams?

[12] John Middleton Murry [*Keats*, p. 206] interpreted the lines much as I do, i.e. that Keats's sin against Burns's countryside is "preconceived imagination." However, he concluded that Keats felt this to be a failure of empathic imagination, while I believe it more consistent with Keats's continuing mood to suppose that he did not wish to surrender to the arbitrariness of imagination at all.

[13] *Letters*, I, 330.

When from the sun was thy broad forehead hid?
How long is't since the mighty Power bid
    Thee heave to airy sleep from fathom dreams?
    Sleep in the lap of thunder or sunbeams,
Or when grey clouds are thy cold coverlid?
Thou answer'st not; for thou art dead asleep;
    Thy life is but two dead eternities—
The last in air, the former in the deep;
    First with the whales, last with the eagle-skies—
Drown'd wast thou till an earthquake made thee steep,
    Another cannot wake thy giant size.

There is an imaginative conception at work here, that of
the rock as a great lubberly sleeper, personified in the
apostrophe of direct address and in the ascription of a
forehead, shoulders, and other features of human anatomy, but there is no conceptual framework to which the
central idea can naturally be fitted. There are images
which not long before would have implied dynamic relationships, but here the sunbeams are things (among
many others) to which the great rock is indifferent, and
the voices of the sea-birds cannot speak to it or, on its
behalf, to man. The whole poetic statement is about as
objective as it could be, without losing its poetry, and
the imaginative conception in terms of which the particular identity of the rock is expressed is drawn not from
a prior conceptual orientation but from the poet's immediate response to the object; for he is, as nearly as
possible, seeing the object as in itself it really is.

The sonnet "Read me a lesson, Muse," composed on
the top of Ben Nevis on August 2, asserts directly man's
incapacity to read any lesson from nature but that of his
own ignorance:

Read me a lesson, Muse, and speak it loud
    Upon the top of Nevis, blind in mist!

[217]

I look into the chasms, and a shroud
   Vaporous doth hide them,—just so much I wist
Mankind do know of hell; I look o'erhead,
   And there is sullen mist,—even so much
Mankind can tell of heaven; mist is spread
   Before the earth, beneath me,—even such,
Even so vague is man's sight of himself!
   Here are the craggy stones beneath my feet,—
Thus much I know that, a poor witless elf,
   I tread on them,—that all my eye doth meet
Is mist and crag, not only on this height,
But in the world of thought and mental might!

The sonnet is rather stiff, with a Neoclassic tendency to use the natural imagery as mere confirmatory analogue of the intellectual argument, but the argument itself is explicit enough to pass without further comment. As a measure of the intellectual distance that Keats had recently traveled, however, one might compare this poet's experience on his mountain-top with that of the poet on another mountain-top, in "I stood tip-toe" (193-204), the poet "Who stood on Latmus' top, what time there blew / Soft breezes from the myrtle vale below" and won from his scanning of the skies those "golden sounds" in which the romance of Endymion and Cynthia found its earliest mortal expression.

Whatever their subjects or techniques of development, these three sonnets have one thing in common, and that is that there is nothing like them, in conceptual independence, in any of the serious poetry written before the epistle to Reynolds. In each of the three there is some manifestation of flight from imagination's tendency to invest the object with attributes or powers not its own. It is possible, of course, to see these poems as merely occasional expressions of passing moods, unmeditated, and therefore, with reference to Keats's rooted poetic principles, aberrant. That the tendency is genuine, however, and reflects a reasoned aversion to what had long been a poetic first-principle, is confirmed by a poem of the walking-tour period which we have skipped over in the sequence, the "Lines Written in the Highlands after a Visit to Burns's Country," which was appended to a letter to Bailey completed on July 22.

Before considering this poem in detail, we might recall for a moment the sudden flash of fear of imagination's power which had been expressed in "God of the Meridian," written about seven weeks before the Reynolds epistle. In that poem, having represented his soul as flown upward toward the sun-god, while his body remained pressed to the earth, the poet had reflected on his state:

> It is an awful mission,
> A terrible division;
> And leaves a gulph austere
> To be fill'd with worldly fear.
> Aye, when the soul is fled
> To high above our head,
> Affrighted do we gaze
> After its airy maze,
>
> . . . .
> And is not this the cause
> Of madness? . . .
>
> . . . .
> O let me, let me share
> With the hot lyre and thee,
> The staid Philosophy.
> (5-12, 16-17, 20-22)

One's consciousness of substantial identity, while in the very act of achieving imaginative fellowship with the highest essence, fragments the psyche and brings one to the verge of madness, for there is a terrible confusion of self-knowledge, i.e. of whether one's true nature is spiritual or substantial. The excitement of spiritual ascent on the wings of imagination momentarily persuades one that ultimate reality has been reached, yet there remains the sad fact of an unassimilable body's continuing presence in the world of time and space. There being no rational way to subdue that fact, the contrary fact must be proportioned to it. When the poet begs for more philosophy, then, he is asking for something to counterbalance the ascendancy of the imagination, something to heighten his assurance of reality in the phenomenal world so as not to lose his mind in the phantasmal world that imagination holds out to him. It is to this same problem, elaborated in greater detail and brought closer to resolution, that he returns in the "Lines Written in the Highlands."

The first half-dozen lines of this later poem describe the pleasure of visiting places renowned in history and legend. But even more stirring, the poet goes on (7-12), is a visit to the birthplace of someone who was great in former times. At such moments, the grandeur of imaginative conception is so powerful that "Forgotten is the worldly heart," and, in contemplation of the humane ideal, one is impervious to the song of birds, the sound of flowing water, the light of sunset, and all the influences of beauty in the natural world (13-24). It should not escape notice that the natural elements alluded to are those which until very recently had been symbolic of imagination's source in the substantial world, but which are now seen as the substantive beauties lost to a mind that leaves the real world behind in its imaginative involvement with ideality. Not only are these natural images no longer related members of an aesthetic system

oriented toward ideality, but they now stand collectively
as an *alternative* to the ultimate value which that system
had been created to achieve. The poet has not yet begun
to evaluate the experience, rather has recorded the plain
fact of it, that intensity in one kind tends to cancel out
the other kind altogether. Having stated the fact, however, he immediately places it in the context which, in
"God of the Meridian," had so terrified him:

> Aye, if a madman could have leave to pass a
>   healthful day
> To tell his forehead's swoon and faint when first
>   began decay,
> He might make tremble many a one whose
>   spirit had gone forth
> To find a Bard's low cradle-place about the si-
>   lent North!
> Scanty the hour and few the steps beyond the
>   bourn of care,
> Beyond the sweet and bitter world,—beyond it
>   unaware!
> Scanty the hour and few the steps, because a
>   longer stay
> Would bar return, and make a man forget his
>   mortal way.

> (25-32)

One must give in to these imaginative impulses infre-
quently, and then only briefly, for a too prolonged indulgence can literally deprive one of sanity through the
substitution of a phantasmal desideratum for that "sweet
and bitter world" which is proper to mortality.

And what then? Why should one fear the substitution
of a perhaps greater fulfillment for a lesser?

> O horrible! to lose the sight of well remember'd
>   face,

Of Brother's eyes, of Sister's brow—constant to
    every place;
Filling the air, as on we move, with portraiture
    intense;
More warm than those heroic tints that pain a
    painter's sense,
When shapes of old come striding by, and vis-
    ages of old,
Locks shining black, hair scanty grey, and pas-
    sions manifold.

                                              (33-38)

I believe that the key to these lines, though it is not
among them, is the word "real," in a slight variant of the
sense in which Keats was becoming accustomed to use it,
i.e. the "real" is that in the external world with which
one's affections are bound up. One may accept or reject
an abstract idea, but one cannot love it, cannot know it
with one's whole heart, in the same way that one loves
and knows those with whom affectionate experience has
been shared. Personification of the idea, even in an historical personage, does not alter its abstractness for *us*,
nor does its splendid embodiment in a work of art bring
us as close to a humanly viable truth as does the livelier
image of someone to whom we are bound in a reciprocal
intensity of feeling. The horror of flight to ideality, therefore, is that we substitute a concept which has no immediate anchor in the substantial world for one which
has, and we thereby lose the vivid authenticity of contact with the experiential springs of the human heart's
affections. Flight to ideal "reality" is thus a flight from
total experience, the substitution of an attenuated part for
a realized whole, the pursuit of chimera, and therefore
madness.

Keats's world is no longer what it was in the conceptual

view of "Sleep and Poetry" and *Endymion,* the staging
area for intuitions of a purer reality—a good and necessary, but incomplete, arena of experience. It is now for
Keats what it had become for Wordsworth, "the very
world, which is the world / Of all of us,—the place where,
in the end, / We find our happiness, or not at all!" (*The
Prelude,* XI, 142-44) And it is so because he had come
to find sufficient in it what Wordsworth had found (and
Wordsworth's statement perfectly expresses the dichot-
omy in Keats's mind), because he had found "Beauty—
a living Presence of the earth, / Surpassing the most fair
ideal Forms / Which craft of delicate Spirits hath composed / From earth's materials" (*The Recluse,* I, i, 795-
98). In the security of such a commitment the poet need
not fear too much the horrible possibility that has just
suggested itself to him:

> No, no, that horror cannot be, for at the cable's
>   length
> Man feels the gentle anchor pull and gladdens
>   in its strength:—
> One hour, half-idiot, he stands by mossy water-
>   fall,
> But in the very next he reads his soul's me-
>   morial:—
> He reads it on the mountain's height, where
>   chance he may sit down
> Upon rough marble diadem—that hill's eternal
>   crown.
>   ("Lines Written in the Highlands," 39-44)

The tug of affection for the world of mortal experience
will always have power to pull him back because it is
more deeply rooted in his mortal nature. Though he may
briefly be made "idiot" by his speculative fancy, his
natural identification with the world of solid substance

will never lose its power to recall him to himself. Still,
the danger must not be lightly dismissed:

> Yet be his anchor e'er so fast, room is there for
> a prayer
> That man may never lose his mind on mountains
> black and bare;
> That he may stray league after league some great
> birthplace to find
> And keep his vision clear from speck, his inward
> sight unblind.
>
> (45-48)

The keynote is repeated often enough to leave no doubt
about Keats's horror of the unfettered imagination. Belief in its truth is madness, plain and simple. The poet
leaves room for rare flights of exaltation, presumably to
fulfill an instinct of the soul to rise above its ordinary
experience, which, since it does assert itself, is natural
and must not be altogether denied. But the self-sufficient
beauty of the real world, of people and places one has
known and loved for themselves, is the only reality one
can cling to in mortal existence.

It is this objectivity of emotional commitment to primary experience that did duty for philosophy in Keats's
revised view of human truth, and it is this which in one
way or another governs the outlook of his major poetry.
It is not a "philosophy" in any ordinary usage of the
term which implies the systematic reconciliation of experiential factors with each other. It is, rather, the flight
from system in a willing acceptance of whatever response
the experience of the moment may bring forth. It pre-
tends to "know" nothing at all.

FIVE

Hyperion

BETWEEN the completion of *Endymion* in late November 1817 and the commencement of *Hyperion* almost a year later, Keats wrote none, or very nearly none, of the poetry by which his reputation lives. *Isabella* was completed in late April 1818, about the time of *Endymion*'s publication, but, with all its felicities acknowledged, it is yet not a poem of which Keats or the majority of his readers have thought very highly. Except for a few sonnets, everything else written in this considerable period was extemporaneous or occasional, and much of it is marked by the characteristics of such composition—incompleteness, internal disjunction, or surface roughness. There are things to be learned from some of these poems, but their value lies chiefly in their hints of what to expect in future poems and not in their absolute qualities as works of art. To some extent this hiatus in serious composition no doubt reflects the poet's disenchantment during this period with his hitherto governing ideas, and his consequent uncertainty about how, or on what basis, to proceed. But other factors certainly contributed to the meagerness of production, practical factors which interfered with the carrying out of plans already made. The long period of *Endymion*'s copying and correction, and the two-month interruption of the poet's normal activity by the walking tour, precluded his carrying through any sort of major work. And we know that another major work was taking shape in Keats's mind even before he had finished *Endymion*.

On April 10, 1818, in his revision of the Preface to *Endymion*, Keats wrote, "I hope I have not in too late a day touched the beautiful mythology of Greece, and dulled its brightness: for I wish to try once more, before I bid it farewel."[1] He was to touch it many times again, indeed he never did "bid it farewel," but the implication of this sentence, the very last he wrote in connection with the composition and publication of *Endymion*, is that a specific work was being projected. What this contemplated work was to be, and the nature of its treatment, we learn from a letter written several months earlier, on January 23, 1818, while Keats was copying *Endymion* for the press, in which he replies to Haydon's offer to paint a scene from *Endymion*: ". . . it would be as well to wait for a choice out of *Hyperion*—when that Poem is done there will be a wide range for you—in Endymion I think you may have many bits of the deep and sentimental cast—the nature of *Hyperion* will lead me to treat it in a more naked and grecian Manner—and the march of passion and endeavour will be undeviating —and one great contrast between them will be—that the Hero of the written tale being mortal is led on, like Buonaparte, by circumstance; whereas the Apollo in Hyperion being a fore-seeing God will shape his actions like one" (*Letters*, I, 207). Nothing about this statement is vague or groping. On the contrary, while the poet was still fully occupied, as he was to be for several more months, with the labor of preparing *Endymion* for publication, he had already made detailed plans for what was obviously to be his next major effort. That his title-figure and the protagonist he names belong to successive orders of classical deities indicates that his subject was to involve the war of the Titans and the Olympian gods. That Apollo is designated as the hero of a poem bearing the

[1] *Poetical Works*, p. 64.

name of his predecessor suggests that the contending
issues and forces of the titanic struggle will be represented by the virtues and powers of these two, and that,
in the "historical" certainty of Olympian supremacy,
Apollo's virtues and powers will determine the value-
scheme of the poem. It has been settled that the hero,
having a more comprehensive soul than the mortal hero
of *Endymion*, will be the forger rather than the follower
of his own destiny, and that the manner of treatment,
befitting the loftier strain of war, will be more spare and
direct than would have been appropriate to the romance
Endymion.

From this casually firm description of the projected
Hyperion two other significant facts emerge: (1) While
Endymion was still in process,[2] Keats was seriously con-
structing the framework and rationale of a poem whose
hero was to be the brother divinity of *Endymion*'s
heroine; and (2) in his discussion of it, Keats automatically tended to compare the projected poem with
Endymion. In short, he appears to have thought of the
poems as complementary. That the complementary *Hyperion* was not a happy afterthought, arrived at in the
process of casting about for a new topic as the long
labor of *Endymion* drew to an end, we know for a certainty from a line in *Endymion* itself, a line written some-
time in the middle of November 1817. Toward the end
of the poem, in a proleptic address which anticipates
Endymion's marriage to the moon-goddess, the poet con-
fides to his hero, "Thy lute-voic'd brother will I sing ere
long" (IV, 774). Moreover, de Selincourt, in his note on

---

[2] Although a fair copy for the printer was the chief end of
Keats's industry for some weeks following, he was also amending
the work poetically, e.g. the "fellowship with essence" lines (I,
777-81) were sent to the publisher a week after this letter to Haydon, as a substitution for the weaker passage that had originally
been submitted. *Letters*, I, 218-19.

this line, calls attention to the description of Oceanus in Book III (994-98) as evidence that Keats had "already thought on the subject of his next classical poem."[3] If we accept this conjecture as probable, we shall have traced *Hyperion*'s genesis back at least to late September 1817. De Selincourt also notes, without further comment, that the reference to Saturn in exile in Book II (994) is a "first suggestion of the picture with which Hyperion opens."[4] It is a slight allusion, one of almost innumerable interspersed references to more or less irrelevant classical deities in the Endymion story as Keats chose to treat it. There is no reference to the war between successive dynasties of gods, but Saturn would not have been in exile had there been no such war, and Keats certainly knew that there had been one, so let us say that the idea of *Hyperion* was at least latent as far back as late August 1817.[5]

But de Selincourt does not notice, and I cannot recall anyone who has noticed, the allusion in the first book of *Endymion*, where, suggesting the variety of "old songs" awakened by the "Eolian magic" of the wind, the poet says, "Bronze clarions awake, and faintly bruit, / Where long ago a Giant Battle was" (I, 791-92). The capitalization of "Giant Battle," adjective as well as noun, is inexplicable unless it was meant to intimate a specific battle involving Giants, and not simply any battle of great magnitude. It is evident from *Hyperion* itself that Keats confused in his own mind the battles of the Titans and the Giants, so there can be no objection on the score of its allusion to a different conflict than that treated in *Hyperion*. The capitalization was not preserved in the first published version, but the words *are* capitalized in the fair copy sent to the printer. The indication is thus that

---

[3] E. de Selincourt (ed.), *Poems*, p. 451.   [4] *Ibid.*, p. 436.
[5] For the date, see *Letters*, I, 149 and 148n.

Keats's original intention was to allude to that particular battle which had already claimed his attention. The reduction to lower case, and the consequent loss of allusion, may be attributed to a typesetter's inattention or to a last-minute proof change occasioned by the poet's observation that this specific allusion intruded on an otherwise generic catalogue of kinds of song. In either case, the presence of the battle in the printed version of the poem is less significant than the manuscript evidence of its presence in the poet's mind. As the chronology of composition of the first book of *Endymion* is unknown, assignment of an exact date to this allusion is not possible. With its inclusion, however, it is at least possible to say that references to the poem which Keats subsequently announced as his next major project appear in *Endymion* at every stage of its development.

It is not of very great consequence that we accept this means of establishing so early a date for the genesis of *Hyperion* in Keats's mind. But it does tend to confirm the impression, discussed in the second chapter, that in choosing the Endymion legend for his first long poem, Keats was consciously projecting and deferring a complementary poem of which Apollo would be the hero. He need not have had *Hyperion*, as such, in mind at the time, but these early and continuing allusions to the basic situation of *Hyperion* suggest that he was thinking about it, and perhaps to some extent planning it, concurrent with his work on *Endymion*. My reason for emphasizing the relationship of the two poems in their creator's mind is that it helps us to understand *Hyperion* generally, it explains a quite remarkable interruption, in this poem, of Keats's movement away from his old aesthetic formulation; and it gives us a clue as to why, really, Keats failed to complete *Hyperion*.

It can hardly escape notice that the old symbols, which

[229]

for half a year had been out of Keats's favor, reappear in
Hyperion with perhaps greater concentration and intensity than ever before. However, there is little emphasis
of this kind in the first two books, which are chiefly given
to approximations, developed in Keats's own way, of the
Miltonic epic situations. Their over-all movement is from
the awakening of the fallen deity, through his brief defiance of his fate, to the council of fallen deities and the
appearance of Hyperion, who seems to have been prepared for the role of champion, to oppose, like Satan, the
superior powers at whose hands the Titans have suffered
the loss of heaven. But Milton's purposes are not Keats's,
and, with increasing emphasis as the first two books develop, Keats stresses a thematic point of his own, i.e. that
the loss of godhead defines the condition of manhood.
What a wretchedly limited creature undeified deity becomes is simply what mortal man has always been:

> For I have seen my sons most unlike Gods.
> Divine ye were created, and divine
> In sad demeanour, solemn, undisturb'd,
> Unruffled, like high Gods, ye liv'd and ruled:
> Now I behold in you fear, hope, and wrath;
> Actions of rage and passion; even as
> I see them, on the mortal world beneath,
> In men who die.—This is the grief, O Son!
> Sad sign of ruin, sudden dismay, and fall!
>   (I, 328-36)

> There saw she direst strife; the supreme God
> At war with all the frailty of grief,
> Of rage, of fear, anxiety, revenge,
> Remorse, spleen, hope, but most of all despair.
> Against these plagues he strove in vain; for Fate
> Had pour'd a mortal oil upon his head,
> A disanointing poison.
>   (II, 92-98)

The point is not merely that the gods have fallen but that the change of condition is a change of kind, which, in turn, implies an unbridgeable gulf between the mortal and the divine. The easy optimism of Keats's earlier view, that man, by making a relatively simple adjustment of his understanding, can participate directly in the divine, is implicitly denied, for even the gods, once lost to godhead, are impotent and frail. And equally indicative of Keats's withdrawal toward objectivity in surveying the human condition is the admonition on how best to confront and triumph over the unmitigable fact:[6]

> Now comes the pain of truth, to whom 'tis pain;
> O folly! for to bear all naked truths,
> And to envisage circumstance, all calm,
> That is the top of sovereignty.

(II, 202-5)

Although there are touches of the old symbolic complex before the third book,[7] they tend to function more often as affective images than as symbols, rather as miniatures or vignettes of the life proper to deity than as natural exempla of divine intercourse with mortality through an elemental principle of harmony. There are exceptions, however, in those speeches which presage the coming of Apollo, such as Oceanus' designation of light as the essential element of original creation:

> From Chaos and parental Darkness came
> Light, the first fruits of that intestine broil,
> That sullen ferment, which for wondrous ends
> Was ripening in itself. The ripe hour came,
> And with it Light, and Light, engendering

[6] The speech belongs to Oceanus, who is generally acknowledged to be Keats's spokesman among the Titans.

[7] For example: i, 190-93, 203-8, 224, 340-41.

Upon its own producer, forthwith touch'd
The whole enormous matter into Life.
(II, 191-97)

Another exception is found in Clymene's account of the rapturous terror accompanying her premonitory experience of Apollo's power:

I stood upon a shore, a pleasant shore,
Where a sweet clime was breathed from a land
Of fragrance, quietness, and trees, and flowers.
Full of calm joy it was, as I of grief;
Too full of joy and soft delicious warmth;
So that I felt a movement in my heart
To chide, and to reproach that solitude
With songs of misery, music of our woes;
And sat me down, and took a mouthed shell
And murmur'd into it, and made melody—
O melody no more! for while I sang,
And with poor skill let pass into the breeze
The dull shell's echo, from a bowery strand
Just opposite, an island of the sea,
There came enchantment with the shifting wind,
That did both drown and keep alive my ears.
I threw my shell away upon the sand,
And a wave fill'd it, as my sense was fill'd
With that new blissful golden melody.
A living death was in each gush of sounds,
Each family of rapturous hurried notes,
That fell, one after one, yet all at once,
Like pearl beads dropping sudden from their string:
And then another, then another strain,
Each like a dove leaving its olive perch,
With music wing'd instead of silent plumes,
To hover round my head, and make me sick
Of joy and grief at once. Grief overcame,

And I was stopping up my frantic ears,
When, past all hindrance of my trembling hands,
A voice came sweeter, sweeter than all tune,
And still it cried, "Apollo! young Apollo!
"The morning-bright Apollo! young Apollo!"
I fled, it follow'd me, and cried "Apollo!"
                                        (II, 262-95)

These portend the entrance of Apollo, in the third
book, where all the old instrumentalities symbolic of harmony flock to the poet's aid in evocation of the Apollinian influence on the world of man. There, soothing the
atmosphere for the god's introduction, the poet calls upon
the Muse to leave the rage and grief of fallen divinity
and "touch piously the Delphic harp" (III, 10). If she
does so, "not a wind of heaven but will breathe / In aid
soft warble from the Dorian flute" (III, 11-12), for "'tis
the Father of all verse" who comes (III, 13). To fit the
scene for his coming, the poet urges that "the clouds of
even and of morn" be freed (III, 16), that "the red wine
within the goblet boil" (III, 18), and that all the trees of
Delos rejoice, the olive, the poplar, the palm, "and beech,
/ In which the Zephyr breathes the loudest song" (III,
25-26), for "Apollo is once more the golden theme" (III,
28). The coming of the god to the place of full deification
had begun when he "left his mother fair / And his twin-
sister sleeping in their bower, / And in the morning twi-
light wandered forth" (III, 31-33). The poetry of earth is
never dead, and it sang to the god on the morning of
his glory:

The nightingale had ceas'd, and a few stars
Were lingering in the heavens, while the thrush
Began calm-throated. Throughout all the isle
There was no covert, no retired cave
Unhaunted by the murmurous noise of waves,

[233]

> Though scarcely heard in many a green recess.
> He listen'd, and he wept, and his bright tears
> Went trickling down the golden bow he held.
> (III, 36-43)

Mnemosyne, goddess of memory and mother of the Muses, then appears, and Apollo, while he does not recall ever having seen her before, knows that he has heard the presence of her divinity in nature:

> Sure I have heard those vestments sweeping o'er
> The fallen leaves, when I have sat alone
> In cool mid-forest. Surely I have traced
> The rustle of those ample skirts about
> These grassy solitudes, and seen the flowers
> Lift up their heads, as still the whisper pass'd.
> (III, 53-58)

Perhaps he has dreamed of her. Yes, she tells him,

> Thou hast dream'd of me; and awaking up
> Didst find a lyre all golden by thy side,
> Whose strings touch'd by thy fingers, all the vast
> Unwearied ear of the whole universe
> Listen'd in pain and pleasure at the birth
> Of such new tuneful wonder.
> (III, 62-67)

If his nature is such that even his casual touch of the lyre awakens the universal harmony, how, she asks him, can he weep? He tells her that

> For me, dark, dark,
> And painful vile oblivion seals my eyes:
> I strive to search wherefore I am so sad,
> Until a melancholy numbs my limbs:
> And then upon the grass I sit, and moan,
> Like one who once had wings.—O why should I

Feel curs'd and thwarted, when the liegeless air
Yields to my step aspirant? why should I
Spurn the green turf as hateful to my feet?
Goddess benign, point forth some unknown thing:
Are there not other regions than this isle?
What are the stars? There is the sun, the sun!
And the most patient brilliance of the moon!
And stars by thousands! Point me out the way
To any one particular beauteous star,
And I will flit into it with my lyre,
And make its silvery splendour pant with bliss.
                                        (III, 86-102)

Apollo, with all his latent powers, is not yet a god. Therefore he must suffer the frustrations of his desire for fellowship with the essences which the beauty of the external world convinces him exist. Like Keats, as he was
before the Reynolds epistle, he feels the necessity of joining himself to some principle higher than that of mere
earthly experience, and his instinct tells him that it is
with the lyre that he can best place himself in harmony
with the beauty he beholds. But, like the Keats who was
to speak in the opening lines of the "Ode to a Nightingale," his power is incommensurate with his yearning desire, and he is left numb and dazed by the struggle of his
spirit to free itself from the bondage of mere sense. Because he is a god *in posse*, his limitations can be overcome, however, and, gazing upon the face of the silent
goddess before him, he feels a sudden infusion of that
"Knowledge enormous" which accompanies and characterizes ascent to a higher condition of being:

Knowledge enormous makes a God of me.
Names, deeds, gray legends, dire events, rebellions,
Majesties, sovran voices, agonies,
Creations and destroyings, all at once

Pour into the wide hollows of my brain,
And deify me, as if some blithe wine
Or bright elixir peerless I had drunk,
And so become immortal.

(III, 113-20)

After a few more lines, descriptive of the agony of dying into immortality, the poem breaks off, leaving us in lasting ignorance of how Apollo was to exercise the powers of his new identity.

Among the passages from Book III cited above, virtually every symbolic element comprehended in Keats's original aesthetic formulation appears: pure light; the sun at rising and setting; the moon; the twin-sister of Apollo; the ripening process; wind, sea, bird-song, and the undifferentiated sounds of nature as evidence of informing divinity; wine, both literal and figurative; gold; heroic deeds; music; indeed, all the linked components of universal harmony. The question that naturally arises is whether, given this plethora, Keats's retreat from his earlier systematic formulation was in fact absolute. I think it was, and that the later poems which we examine will demonstrate that it was, but to say so is not the same as to say that Keats was happy with his inability to reconcile theory and experience. The recurrence of all the old elements here, in all the old relationships, can probably be accounted for in the first instance by the fact that this is the poem that Keats had been planning to write for almost a year-and-a-half. In its original conception, paired in rationale with *Endymion*, it was to have been the full and definitive rendering, at the highest level of expression, of those truths about life and art which *Endymion* was to have embodied in a poetry of lesser kind. *Endymion* was to be beautiful, *Hyperion* sublime; but each was conceived as an aspect of the truth embodied in the other.

Considering the radical shock which his intellect had sustained, that Keats came finally to write the poem at all is evidence, I think, that he had arrived at least hopefully at an intellectual plateau. Somewhere, he thought that he divined a possibility of salvaging the old synthesis, if not entirely, with such adjustments as might reconcile the old and new views of human experience. His recent preoccupation with knowledge, his acceptance of brute fact, and his attempts to formulate a viable concept of reality are evident in *Hyperion*, even as he goes about the ritual incantation of the familiar symbol-elements. Oceanus' Stoic assertion that the only way to rise above life's evils is, in effect, willingly to acknowledge their inescapability; Apollo's summing-up of his less-than-divine condition as one of "aching ignorance" (III, 107); and his subsequent deification through the putting on, or taking in, of enormous knowledge; all these reflect Keats's new orientation toward experience. Had he been unable to persuade himself that this sort of knowledge was conformable with the quality of revelation promised by the old synthesis, he might never have begun a poem based on assumptions which, in their original form, he could no longer accept as tenable.

The fact is, of course, that at the poem's first great climax it was abandoned. Since Keats probably knew that it contained some of his finest individual passages of poetry, and therefore must have considered it promising, commentators have been at some pains to find an explanation. The matter was once thought to have been adequately explained by Keats's objection to the poem's excessively Miltonic style,[8] but as it now seems virtually certain that the poet's comment applies, rather, to *The Fall of Hyperion*,[9] critical conjecture has had to proceed

[8] *Letters*, II, 167.
[9] See below, Chapter 7, note 5.

with scarcely a clue from the poet himself.[10] Indeed, there is little to refer to beyond his remark, in a letter, that "I have not gone on with Hyperion—for to tell the truth I have not been in great cue for writing lately."[11] And yet, in the sentence which precedes this one, he promises to send to his brother and sister-in-law "The Eve of St. Agnes" and, if he finishes it, "The Eve of St. Mark," both of which he obviously *had* been in cue for writing. The inference, then, is that he had not been in cue for writing the sort of poem that *Hyperion* was intended to be.

[10] Among those who see the problem in terms not incompatible with mine, C. D. Thorpe [(ed.), *Poems*, pp. 309-10], suggests the possibility of Keats's discontent with the direction his poem was taking in its third book, i.e. veering away from epic action toward the expression of incongruous aesthetic ideas, which dated back as far as "Sleep and Poetry," through the person of a Keats-like Apollo who seemed to be developing into a prototype of the poet rather than of the hero; Joseph Warren Beach [*A Romantic View of Poetry* (Minneapolis, 1944), p. 131], sees the abandonment as evidence of Keats's continuing difficulty in reconciling philosophically opposed points of view; Northrop Frye [*Fearful Symmetry: A Study of William Blake* (Princeton, 1947), p. 325] considers one of the major unresolved problems in Keats's mind to have been "how to give the theme of the poetic mind the same significance in *Hyperion* that it had had in *Endymion*"; and Kenneth Muir ["The Meaning of 'Hyperion,'" *John Keats: A Reassessment*, ed. by Kenneth Muir (Liverpool, 1958), p. 108]—reading *Hyperion*, in the light of *The Fall of Hyperion*, as a statement of the necessity for the poet-dreamer to become the ameliorating poet-hero, and interpreting the deification of Apollo as a voluntary assumption of human suffering—believes simply that, in resolving the issues so far treated in the poem, Keats had "reached the limit of his experience" at the point where he stopped writing. Of this last it may be said that to interpret deification as a movement toward human suffering seems to be to apply an inverted New Testament allegory to a poem clearly oriented toward a contrary emphasis, but that Keats does seem to have been concerned, not only in the poem but in his own mind, to reestablish the poet as an ameliorative figure.

[11] *Letters*, II, 62.

What was intended, as we have already suggested, was a reaffirmation of the epistemological and aesthetic principles treated in *Endymion*, tempered by and newly grounded in the objective attitude toward experience and the more circumscribed view of the possibilities of human knowledge which had preoccupied the poet for some months before he undertook *Hyperion*. As the event was to prove, this was manifestly an impossible task. For the unique virtue of the old construction was that it assured human access to the experience of ideality, while the whole tendency of Keats's more recent thought was toward the intense appreciation of local experience as a self-justifying end, relatable to other experiences of the same kind but in no way accessory to experience of a higher kind.

The irreconcilability of the conflict lies on the very surface of *Hyperion*, for the first two books reiterate in a variety of ways the absolute distinction between the conditions of divinity and mortality (i.e. they represent the poet's more recent views), while the third book represents Apollo as passing from a condition like mortality to one of deity (i.e. performing the prototypal action which the poets, in Keats's old view, would imitate). One immediately wonders why, if the not-yet-god Apollo can achieve divinity, the fallen gods should not be able to reachieve it. The only negotiable answer is Oceanus' dictum that "first in beauty should be first in might" (II, 229), i.e. heaven is preempted to those who fulfill an antecedent condition of superior being. If this excludes the gods of inferior beauty (as the rationale of the poem's completed portion makes clear that it does), it must also exclude mankind, whose inferiority is implicitly defined by the very conception of such a state as godhead.

As the poem developed, then, Keats's newer views had become predominant, and the demonstration of Apollo's ability to make the transition from phenomenal to ideal understanding, instead of establishing a pattern for man to follow, had been justified by an argument which excluded man from the possibility of doing so. Keats's abandonment of the poem resulted, therefore, from his abandonment in the first instance of those conceptual views in terms of which it had originally been projected, and in the second instance from his inability to adapt to each other, as he had tentatively hoped he might, his old and new views of the functional limits of human understanding.

Keats's temper and attitude in the last weeks before quitting the poem altogether, during which time he scarcely worked on it at all, are revealed in the letters:

> I am . . . in a sort of qui bono temper, not exactly on the road to an epic poem. . . . I have come to the resolution never to write for the sake of writing, or making a poem, but from running over with any little knowledge and experience which many years of reflection may perhaps give me. . . . What Imagination I have I shall enjoy, and greatly, for I have experienced the satisfaction of having great conceptions without the toil of sonnetteering. . . . I am three and twenty with little knowledge and middling intellect.
>
> (*Letters*, II, 42-43)

> I have been at different times turning it in my head whether I should go to Edinburgh & study for a physician; I am afraid I should not take kindly to it, I am sure I could not take fees—& yet I should like to do so; it is not worse than writing poems, & hanging them up to be flyblown on the Reviewshambles—
>
> (*Letters*, II, 70)

Though a quarrel in the streets is a thing to be hated, the energies displayed in it are fine; the commonest

Man shows a grace in his quarrel—By a superior being
our reasoning[s] may take the same tone—though erro-
neous they may be fine—This is the very thing in which
consists poetry; and if so it is not so fine a thing as
philosophy—For the same reason that an eagle is not
so fine a thing as a truth—Give me this credit—Do you
not think I strive—to know myself? Give me this credit
—and you will not think that on my own accou[n]t I
repeat Milton's lines

"How charming is divine Philosophy
Not harsh and crabbed as dull fools suppose
But musical as is Apollo's lute"—

No—no for myself—feeling grateful as I do to have
got into a state of mind to relish them properly—Nothing ever becomes real till it is experienced—

(*Letters*, II, 80-81)

I am still at a stand in versifying—I cannot do it yet
with any pleasure—I mean however to look round at
my resources and means—and see what I can do without poetry—

(*Letters*, II, 84)

The whole appears to resolve into this—that Man is
originally 'a poor forked creature' subject to the same
mischances as the beasts of the forest, destined to hard-
ships and disquietude of some kind or other. If he im-
proves by degrees his bodily accomodations and comforts—at each stage, at each accent there are waiting
for him a fresh set of annoyances—he is mortal and
there is still a heaven with its Stars abov[e] his head.

(*Letters*, II, 101)

He cannot work on his epic poem. He will not write any
more poetry until he can ground it in an increased knowledge and experience. He is young and really knows very
little. In fact, he will not write any more poetry at all.

[241]

He will find another means of livelihood. Philosophy is better than poetry anyway. What counts is the "real," and that depends entirely upon experience of life. Man is helpless in the world, absolutely condemned to his mortality, with heaven forever beyond his reach.

All this is strange talk from a man who had, in fact, just finished writing "The Eve of St. Agnes."[12] One would suppose that a poet capable of that degree of perfection might look with some optimism on the continuation of his career. But Keats must have recognized that "St. Agnes" is, as a recent writer has characterized it, "a masterpiece of artificial atmosphere."[13] Its music, its play of contrasts, its evocation of mood are incomparable, but in the last analysis, its felicities are all merely verbal. One hears the rising and quite proper chorus of outrage at the word "merely." Yet, when one considers the excellences of "St. Agnes" in the perspective of that kind of poetry which Keats had been trying unsuccessfully to write in *Hyperion*, and when one recalls the extent to which Keats had habitually looked upon the vocation of the poet as that of the light-bringer, it is easier to see why his failure to work out the intellectual problems of *Hyperion* should have overshadowed completely the satisfaction possible to him in the composition of "St. Agnes." It was not in his nature to rest content with poetry that merely entertained. Just as he had meditated giving up poetry exactly a year before, after the Reynolds epistle had forced him to abandon his guiding conception of its worth, the failure to reestablish that conception in modified form in *Hyperion* led him again to the fear of poetry's being an unjustifiable pursuit. We may feel, and Keats came increasingly to feel, that verbal skill, like virtue, is

[12] Which he revised in September, however. *Ibid.*, 157.
[13] Howard Moss (ed.), *Keats*, The Laurel Poetry Series (New York, 1959), p. 14.

its own reward; but in this time of depression he could only say, in the sentence which follows the first quotation in the series above, "It is true that in the height of enthusiasm I have been cheated into some fine passages, but that is nothing."[14]

[14] *Letters,* ɪɪ, 43.

SIX

My Demon Poesy

THE poems of Keats's *annus mirabilis* have all had richly varied afterlives of critical commentary, and none has had a fuller range of posthumous existences than the maddeningly simple "La Belle Dame Sans Merci." Other poems, poems which assert things directly, have given rise to a greater quantity of criticism, but such criticism has tended to dwell primarily upon the authenticity and utility of the assertions. Thus, there is an enormous literature questioning the meaning of the proposition that beauty is truth; and then, whatever is decided, questioning further whether this is in fact what the poet wished to assert; and finally, however *this* is resolved, questioning whether the statement is truly an organic part of the poem in which it appears. One may ask how, *precisely*, are the poet and the dreamer distinct? Or, *in what sense* does philosophy unweave the rainbow? Or, *did* Keats intend us to interpret the poems in the light of these statements? It depends upon what Keats means by poet, dreamer, philosophy; upon the *personae* of the poems in which the statements are made; and upon the relevance of the statements to the imaginative contexts with which they interact. Such questions and considerations are essential to criticism, and the more fundamental the assertions with which they concern themselves, the greater is likely to be the bulk of considered opinion upon them. The assumption that lies behind this ceaseless critical activity is that the poems "mean" something and that what they "mean," or at least the direction in which meaning lies, can be ascertained by proper understanding of the mooted assertions.

In the case of "La Belle Dame," however, nothing whatever is asserted. A woebegone knight reveals that he has found complete fulfillment in love, only to be left in agonizing despair by his subsequent abandonment. We realize, as he does not, that what had seemed to be perfect felicity was actually his cruelly delusive enchantment by a demon. No single line or phrase in the poem can fairly be taken as summing up its point; one responds to the whole poem or not at all. Almost everyone does in fact respond to the evocative power of its imagery, diction, and incantatory rhythm, and feels simultaneously the simple narrative's insidious call for interpretation. But the situation, abstracted from its presentational details, is so basic to general human experience that interpretation of the poem inevitably falls into an equally basic formulation, such as that it is "expressive of the ashes to which are turned, so often, the worldly hope men set their hearts upon."[1] Now, this is a perfectly respectable reduction of the poem to the level of prose statement, and no matter how one chooses to word it, very little could substantively be added to it. The trouble is that the reduction is so drastic, that it is, however true, almost grotesquely incommensurate in emotional size with one's direct experience of the poem. The childlike, sing-song rhythms of the ballad meter do not wholly contain, indeed they contrast, the rich and eerie implications of the poem's multitudinous images. The truncation of each stanza's closing line impels the reader into a repeatedly opening metrical void in which something is going unsaid (a trick that Keats had learned three years before, from Haydon's suggestion that he abbreviate the thirteenth line of "Great spirits now on earth are sojourning"). One

[1] C. D. Thorpe (ed.), *Poems*, p. 340n.

feels an intensity, a pressure from within, which threatens constantly to erupt from the poem's disciplined understatement.

Given so much to ponder and so little to discuss, criticism has been driven to find its meanings outside the poem, guided by minimal cues within it. Since the poem is narratively concerned with a love encounter, and Keats was by this time deeply involved in his passion for Fanny Brawne, one set of critics has assumed that the poem is intended to be a commentary on love and its effects, and it has sought the specific nature of this commentary in varying interpretations of Keats's own emotional commitment at the time.[2] Other scholars have looked for clues to meaning in the "sources" from which the poet might have drawn his particulars of language and action, that meaning presumably residing unalloyed in the pil-

[2] For example: Amy Lowell [*John Keats*, II, 225] considers the poem's perfection to be evidence of an exuberant creative freedom resulting from a brief period of perfect felicity in Keats's relations with Fanny. Sidney Colvin [*John Keats*, p. 350], on the other hand, thinks the poem a "masterpiece of romantic and tragic symbolism on the wasting power of Love." This he attributes to a cause, which is later elaborated by C. L. Finney [*Evolution of Keats's Poetry*, II, 590-93], that the theme expresses Keats's fear of the debilitating effect on his work of his love for Fanny Brawne. Within this attitudinal context, E. C. Pettet [*On the Poetry of Keats*, pp. 213-19] implies a direct confrontation of the issue and the acceptance of love's baneful consequences, insofar as the knight-at-arms' death orientation at the poem's end is consonant with what Pettet takes to be a habitual association in Keats's own mind of his commitment to Fanny with death. Miriam Allott [" 'Isabella,' 'The Eve of St. Agnes' and 'Lamia,' " in *John Keats: A Reassessment*, ed. by Kenneth Muir, pp. 47-48], less inclined than some others to read narrative as *cri de coeur*, finds on the surface of the poem a pattern of sleep, enchantment, waking and disillusion which is elsewhere operative in Keats's narrative treatment of love experience, and which she considers to be correlative with an "obsessional sequence of emotions" aroused by the recurrent difficulty of reconciling the ideal and the actual.

laged originals.[3] Unfortunately, while many of the attributed sources of words and phrases commend themselves, their eclectic abundance militates against coherent interpretation, so that we are left simply to conclude that Keats was well read in poetry and, however unconsciously, remembered what was most memorable in its effects.

Among the source hunters there is one, however, whose suggestions are more promising. On the hypothesis that the poetry was habitually distilled from Keats's immediate experience of literature and life, Robert Gittings has made some compelling contributions to our knowledge and our speculations about Keats. He does not, unhappily, persuade us always, as the considerable success of his hypothesis occasionally leads him to venture where he cannot reliably guide. Although the present case is one of these, it will be worth a moment, I think, to see how he proceeds with "La Belle Dame."

When Keats sat down to write the poem, Gittings notes, among his recent experiences was an evening of cards, several nights before, Richard Woodhouse being among the players. And, we are told, *"It is not too much to imagine* him often being the odd man out as the other four played, and browsing to some effect among Keats's rough drafts of poems. . . . In that time Woodhouse *evidently* extracted from Keats the manuscripts of *The Eve*

[3] As a considerable anthology of the world's literature has been called to this fruitful service, it might be sufficient here merely to indicate that the principal attributions will be found in: E. de Selincourt (ed.), *Poems*, pp. 526-27; Amy Lowell, *John Keats*, II, 220-25; C. L. Finney, *Evolution of Keats's Poetry*, II, 595-99; E. R. Wasserman, *The Finer Tone*, pp. 68-75; and E. C. Pettet, *On the Poetry of Keats*, pp. 217-19, this last departing from the customary "source" method to suggest merely that the fifth canto of Cary's Dante gave Keats the conceptual framework for the expression in the poem of his uneasiness over his relationship with Fanny Brawne.

of *St. Agnes* and of the unfinished *Hyperion.* . . ."[4] And further, Keats *"must at least have glanced through"* his manuscripts when he gave them to Woodhouse.[5] These concentric circles of supposition lead us to the core assertion, that Keats rediscovered in "The Eve of St. Agnes," on this occasion, the title of the song which Porphyro sang to Madeline in stanza 33 ("La belle dame sans mercy," of course), and the word "manna," which occurs in stanza 30 of "St. Agnes" and was compounded into "manna dew" in "La Belle Dame."[6] These details became fused in his mind with a few others garnered from his recollection of "The Eve of St. Mark," his current reading in Burton's *Anatomy of Melancholy*, a review that he had just written of John Hamilton Reynolds' anticipatory parody of Wordsworth's "Peter Bell," perhaps some lay sermonizing by John Taylor at the card table, meditations on his current relations with Fanny Brawne, and, most centrally, his recent rereading of Wells's "Amena" letters to Tom Keats.[7] From this welter of immediate experiences, Gittings says, the poem was then precipitated.

The critical technique here employed is, of course, essentially that of John Livingston Lowes in *The Road to Xanadu*, though with a somewhat heavier emphasis on social experience than was Lowes's wont. The point of special interest, however, is the suggestion that, in several particulars, Keats was *his own* source. The attempt to locate the origins of a poet's work in himself, rather than in innumerable other people, commends itself to an intraorganic view of the poetry-making process in a way that much source hunting does not. But Gittings is left with several embarrassments, not the least of which are the

[4] Robert Gittings, *John Keats: The Living Year*, p. 114. Italics mine, here and in the next citation, except for those used in titles.
[5] *Ibid.*, p. 116.
[6] *Ibid.*
[7] *Ibid.*, pp. 113-23.

awkwardness of multiple suppositions for which there is no evidence, and the dubious Lowes assumption that suitably ticketed mental particulars constitute a reliable guide to the workings of the creative imagination. And perhaps one may be permitted just a touch of irritation at the curiously condescending notion that it was necessary for Keats, in order to be in possession of his own knowledge, to rediscover it in some previously written form. Might we not suppose that if Keats knew the title of Chartier's poem and the word "manna" in January 1819, he still knew them three months later?

Indeed, we might press the particular a bit farther. Finding the word "manna" in "La Belle Dame" and in "The Eve of St. Agnes," Gittings is obliged to imagine Woodhouse, as odd-man-out in a five-man card game, browsing among Keats's manuscripts and requesting the loan of some of them, and Keats, before parting with them, hurriedly rereading the manuscripts and making special note of a song title and the word "manna" in one of them. But the word occurs as "manna" in "St. Agnes," where it is one item in a cargo of delicacies transported across half the world for a nocturnal love-feast; and it is compounded into "manna dew" in "La Belle Dame," where it functions as one of a demon's agencies of mortal enchantment. The dramatic situations are contrary, the thematic and tonal purposes are contrary, the forms of the images which include manna are unlike, and the words themselves are different, "manna" and "manna dew." Now, it does happen that the compound form which appears in "La Belle Dame" occurs elsewhere in Keats's poetry, specifically, in *Endymion*, I, 766, "He seem'd to taste a drop of manna-dew." There is no evidence that Keats had recently been rereading this part of *Endymion*, but there is ample evidence that he was the author of it. Among people who write or regularly speak in public, it is a common experience to find themselves falling into patterns of vocabulary and discourse which they have used in earlier treatments of a given subject, and Keats was demonstrably no exception. Indeed, almost all writers on Keats have commented on the extent of verbal recurrence in his works, formal and informal, and the present study has been much concerned with one of the most pervasive of these patterns. One might hope too for agreement that Keats's work does in many ways constitute an organic whole, that he frequently returns to former themes and reworks them, in effect holding dialogues with himself in which he matches his current level of understanding against an earlier view of the same subject. The proper question to ask, then, is not whether we can prove that Keats had recently been rereading *Endymion*, but whether the precise verbal echo of *Endymion* in "La Belle Dame" occurs in an analogous context. If not, "manna dew" becomes simply a compound in Keats's vocabulary; if so, perhaps we can penetrate farther than has yet been done into what might be called the intellectual dynamics of the later poem.

If we return, then, to the *Endymion* context, we find the situation thus: the despondent Endymion has been entreated by his sister Peona to confess the cause of his melancholy. Endymion has replied with an account of his first dream and of the sense of estrangement from the natural world with which it left him. After a pause, in which Peona meditates the best way to undertake a protest which she fears will be vain in any case, she gently upbraids Endymion as follows:

'Is this the cause?
This all? Yet it is strange, and sad, alas!
That one who through this middle earth should pass
Most like a sojourning demi-god, and leave

MY DEMON POESY

His name upon the harp-string, should achieve
No higher bard than simple maidenhood,
Singing alone, and fearfully,—how the blood
Left his young cheek; and how he used to stray
He knew not where; and how he would say, *nay*,
If any said 'twas love: and yet 'twas love;
What could it be but love? How a ring-dove
Let fall a sprig of yew tree in his path;
And how he died: and then, that love doth scathe
The gentle heart, as northern blasts do roses;
And then the ballad of his sad life closes
With sighs, and an alas!—Endymion!
Be rather in the trumpet's mouth,—anon
Among the winds at large—that all may hearken!
Although, before the crystal heavens darken,
I watch and dote upon the silver lakes
Pictur'd in western cloudiness, that takes
The semblance of gold rocks and bright gold sands,
Islands, and creeks, and amber-fretted strands
With horses prancing o'er them, palaces
And towers of amethyst,—would I so tease
My pleasant days, because I could not mount
Into those regions? The Morphean fount
Of that fine element that visions, dreams,
And fitful whims of sleep are made of, streams
Into its airy channels with so subtle,
So thin a breathing, not the spider's shuttle,
Circled a million times within the space
Of a swallow's nest-door, could delay a trace,
A tinting of its quality: how light
Must dreams themselves be; seeing they're more slight
Than the mere nothing that engenders them!
Then wherefore sully the entrusted gem
Of high and noble life with thoughts so sick?

Why pierce high-fronted honour to the quick
For nothing but a dream?"

(Endymion, I, 721-60)

The sum of Peona's argument is that Endymion has
demeaned himself by forsaking the active life of valor for
the pursuit of love, and more than that, for a love that is
phantasmal, engendered in a sick fancy which has lost
the ability to distinguish between dreams and reality.
That Endymion's pursuit of the visionary goddess represents Keats's then-normal view of the imagination in pursuit of ultimate beauty and truth is implicit in the *form*
of Peona's acknowledgment that Endymion's impulse is
grounded in universal experience. Using the habitual
Keatsian referents, she says that she too has been charmed
by the sunset hour, has gazed upon the "western cloudiness" and felt her imagination stirred by cloud-shapes of
"gold rocks" and "gold sands" and been led by these to
splendid visions. The difference between her and Endymion is that she reckons this play of the fancy to be
no more than just that, and does not wish to "mount /
Into those regions," thereby placing her affections and
hopes for felicity in such fantasies. Endymion's pursuit
of love, a love that "doth scathe / The gentle heart, as
northern blasts do roses," and its displacement of the
real world by a world of imagination, are thus characterized as pernicious.

Stirred by this challenge, Endymion rouses himself, and

amid his pains
He seem'd to taste a drop of manna-dew,
Full palatable; and a colour grew
Upon his cheek, while thus he lifeful spake.

(Endymion, I, 765-68)

What he speaks is the speech on "fellowship with essence," in which he defends the authenticity of love and

[252]

imagination as modes of achieving a "self-destroying" spiritual reality which beggars that inferior kind centered in a consciousness of selfhood in the substantive world. Since he has the last word, Endymion is clearly to be taken as the winner of the argument.

In "La Belle Dame," on the other hand, we might say that Peona wins the argument. If we abstract the general characteristics of situation, we find the *Endymion* episode and "La Belle Dame" to be identical. A man of valor (Endymion / knight-at-arms)[8] has been reduced to a state of dejection and torpor by an experience of perfect love (Endymion's dream / knight's adventure) with a lady who proved to have no fixed existence in the world of substantial nature (moon-goddess / belle dame). In addition to these radical similarities, the two poems share a number of lesser similarities. In both, the lady is wholly compliant, indeed, as much the aggressor as the man (*End.*, I, 633-36, 653-57; "Belle Dame," 19-33). In both, the lovers move with their ladies from the place of meeting to a place of love-making which is associated in its accompanying imagery with a mountain cavern (*End.*, I, 640-50; "Belle Dame," 21-22, 29). In both, after the fulfillment in kisses the man falls asleep (*End.*, I, 672-78; "Belle Dame," 33). In both, the disappointed lover is identified by paleness of complexion (*End.*, I, 727-28; "Belle Dame," 2, 9-12), and birds and roses are employed as images correlative with the lovers' despondence (*End.*, I, 698-703, 733-34; "Belle Dame," 4, 11-12). In both, "manna-dew" is associated with commitment to the experience (*End.*, I, 765-68; "Belle Dame," 26), in the former identified with the vigor which returns to Endymion when he defends his commitment, and in the

---

[8] Because of its greater particularity in descriptive detail, I use the original text, of April 1819, rather than the revised version published in *The Indicator* thirteen months later.

latter used as an agency to induce commitment. There
are other similarities, but there is no need to press them.
The argument does not depend upon an assumption of
interchangeable symbolic equivalents but upon awareness of a common nexus of poetic elements which occur
when, and indeed because, the poet's mind is engaged
with the same essential problem. Given this fact, there
remains one enormous difference between the poems: in
Endymion the narrative experience is good; in "La Belle
Dame" it is evil.

The primary basis for this judgment is, of course, the
conduct of the narratives themselves. Endymion is given
the opportunity to justify his experience, but no one justifies the experience of the knight. Indeed, he is warned
by the spirits of her past victims that he is in the evil
power of an enchantress.[9] Furthermore, Endymion's ex-

[9] Most readers will be aware, here, of my fundamental disagreement with Wasserman's interpretation of the dream-figures as symbols of life, presented in the imagery of death on the principle that,
in spiritual terms, life in the body *is* death [*The Finer Tone*, p.
75]. Because they are called Kings, Princes, and warriors, Wasserman wishes to identify them with worldly "Men of Power," an expression used by Keats a year-and-a-half earlier to designate "those
who have a proper self" [*Letters*, I, 184]. To the extent, and it is
considerable, that Wasserman deems this sense of self-identity the
poem's negative pole, it is worth noting that the poem shows every
sign of having been composed directly into the letter which is its
sole autograph source, and that this letter is the same one in
which, on the same day, Keats advanced his "vale of Soul-making"
hypothesis, in which he commends, as better than the Christian,
the view of the world as a place where self-identity is *gained*. In
any case, on the basis of his interpretation of the death-figures as
life-figures, Wasserman concludes that "The knight's inherent
weakness in being unable to exclude from his visions the self-
contained and world-bound mortality dissipates the ideal into
which he has entered momentarily . . ." [*The Finer Tone*, pp. 76-
77]. It seems to me that this misreads what happens in the poem.
The portentous figures do not intrude on the rapturous interlude
with the fairy's child but appear as warning figures in a sleeping
dream, much as (to take an example with which Keats was inti-

perience is not over. Although the power of his vision has temporarily estranged him from the world of nature, the narrative will go on to a reconciliation of the real and ideal worlds for Endymion, and to a pragmatic justification of Endymion's affirmative idealism. In the case of the woebegone knight, the poem ends with his enchantment still in force as he sits, emptied of all capacity for significant action and oblivious to the natural processes of the world around him, waiting for another experience of what we have every reason to suppose will never come to him again. He is, in fact, just what Peona said Endymion would become if he did not mend his imaginative ways, a heroic figure lost to valor, wasted by love, and so much in the grip of a malign fantasy and out of touch with the real world as to be hardly even sane.

Under the circumstances, I think it is very hard not to infer as the theme of "La Belle Dame" the anti-theme of its prototype in *Endymion*. In the light of what we have seen of Keats's shifting values in the interim between the two poems—of the rejection, in the epistle to Reynolds, of imagination as a guide to truth, and of the very real fear, in "God of the Meridian" and "Lines Written in the Highlands after a Visit to Burns's Country," that the spirit which leaves the world too far behind, in its flight toward ideal experience, hovers on the verge of madness—it is

---

mately familiar) Hector appears in Aeneas' dream to warn him truthfully of the imminent destruction of Troy. But even discounting the literary validity of truthful dreams, it does seem that, if the knight is asleep when he receives his dream-visitors, his will may be supposed to be in abeyance and therefore not subject to our moral judgment. Further, in terms of tone, the Kings, Princes, and warriors, and the associated emblems of death, are perfectly appropriate to the poem's romantically haunting medieval atmosphere. Indeed, one would be hard put to think of what other characters they could be given which would not spoil either the unity of tone or the point, i.e. that even the mightiest of men have been overcome by this demon.

not too much to say that precisely what *Endymion* affirms and "La Belle Dame" denies is the holiness of the heart's affections when they are made correlative with the truth of imagination.

A few weeks after writing "La Belle Dame," Keats returned to its theme in the "Ode to a Nightingale."[10] My own view of the latter poem's total statement corresponds generally with those of C. L. Finney, who sees it as Keats's admission of "the inadequacy of the romantic escape from the world of reality to the world of ideal beauty,"[11] and E. R. Wasserman, who believes that "the core of the poem is the search for the mystery, the unsuccessful quest for light within its darkness . . . [which] leads only to an increasing darkness, or a growing recognition of how impenetrable the mystery is to mortals."[12] Despite obvious differences in orientation, these views are easily reconcilable, and each in its own way fairly represents the poem as a whole. However, since both writers shed entirely different kinds of light on the means by which the ode makes this essential statement, it may not be amiss to attempt illumination of yet another kind. My understanding of the poem's development is rooted in the per-

[10] Robert Gittings [*John Keats: The Living Year*, p. 132] plausibly conjectures the date to have been April 30, though it makes little difference here whether we accept this or the usual assumption that it was written about two weeks later.

[11] *The Evolution of Keats's Poetry*, II, 632.

[12] *The Finer Tone*, p. 222. While I am willing to accept the general terms in which Professor Wasserman represents the problem, I must again dissent from the details of his reading. To avoid tedious argument, I will merely suggest that his whole interpretation becomes untenable if his reading of the 35th line should be mistaken; and that reading depends upon the assumption of a peculiarity in typographic emphasis which, if actually present, must be unique in English printing. This argument, in turn, is supported by the apparent mistaking of a transcript of the poem, in another hand, as an early working draft by Keats himself.

suasion that Keats is here, as in the Chapman's Homer
sonnet, making his statement in terms which are wholly
intelligible on the public level but which have an additional significance for him, and that these terms, given
the history of their previous use by Keats, fully define
the inner problem with which the poem concerns itself.

My centers of immediate interest are the two key images, those of nightingale and wine. The first stanza is
given to the literal nightingale, the second to literal wine,
and the rest of the poem to the interaction of figurative
equivalents for both. It will be recalled that both elements were assimilated to Apollo in Keats's early poetry.
As the unseen singer, a virtually disembodied voice in
nature, expressing in harmonious tones the latent principle of beauty in the natural world, the nightingale functioned in the same mediatory way that Apollo functioned
in Keats's over-all mythopoeic theory of poetry. Such perceptible beauty as the nightingale's song in the natural
world tuned the poetic sensibility to the universal principle of harmony, in which spirit the imagination could
contemplate a homogeneous world of ideal forms and
conceptions, could perceive the essential relationships of
the mundane and the divine. Wine, on the other hand,
as the distilled essence of that ripeness to which Apollo
brought the fruits of the earth, served as the physical
counterpart of poetry, the distilled essence of that ripeness to which Apollo, speaking through the voices of the
natural world, brought the perceptive and contemplative
mind. And both wine and the poetic imagination, in their
own spheres, were capable of producing a kind of intoxication. In Keats's earlier synthesis of the poetry-making process, then, the nightingale and wine were symbolic representations of cooperating agencies, originating
respectively outside and inside the mind, which together
were capable of leading man toward supernal truth.

However, by the time Keats wrote the Nightingale ode he had had a full year's change of mind and heart about his original poetic principles. In testimony of this, even if all the evidence of the letters were lost, nothing more would be necessary than the "sort of rondeau," beginning with the line "Bards of Passion and of Mirth," written four or five months before the Nightingale ode.[13] In this poetic disquisition on "the double immortality of Poets"[14] Keats returns to the setting of the Apollo ode, the poets' Elysium. Poets enjoy one immortality there, in eternal communion with the incorruptible ideal forms of beauty which in their earthly forms are perishable, and another immortality in the poetic works which live after them on earth. At first glance the rationale of this seems not far removed from that of the earlier formulation. The difference is the all-important one of mutual exclusiveness, for in this poem there is absolutely no commerce between the spheres of heaven and earth. Heaven is the place where the ideal is realized, and earth is the place of inferior copies. The works the poets left behind them on earth do not point the way through sense perceptions of beauty to understanding of divine principles, but speak

> To mortals, of their little week;
> Of their sorrows and delights;
> Of their passions and their spites;
> Of their glory and their shame;
> What does strengthen and what maim.
> ("Bards of Passion," 30-34)

What the poets enjoy in the Elysian afterlife is a world, *un*like the one left behind,

[13] As it was copied on January 2, 1819, into a letter to George and Georgiana, as a poem recently written, it presumably belongs to December 1818.
[14] *Letters*, II, 25.

[258]

> Where the nightingale doth sing
> Not a senseless tranced thing,
> But divine melodious truth;
> Philosophic numbers smooth;
> Tales and golden histories
> Of heaven and its mysteries.
>
> ("Bards of Passion," 17-22)

It is to this Elysian world that the nightingale sings "divine melodious truth," and not to the world of mortal life, where, however much one might wish it otherwise, the nightingale is patently no more than "a senseless tranced thing."

Having committed himself to such a disjunction, so wholly contradictory to any previous implication of the nightingale image in his poetry, but so thoroughly in keeping with the anti-conceptualizing bias that had been constant since the Reynolds epistle, it is almost inconceivable that the nightingale should ever again function for Keats in the old way. I believe that it does not in the Nightingale ode, that it is used there as a sort of laboratory control for the running of an experiment which will test the poet's earlier theory of the poetic imagination. If we keep this functional analogy in mind, it may simplify the process of analysis.

The poem opens with what would once have been the situation most conducive to poetic truth, the poet alone, perceiving and responding to the voice of an agent of beauty in external nature. The agent is the nightingale, which is in that relationship to the hearer which is customary in the poetry through *Endymion*, "in some melodious plot / Of beechen green, and shadows numberless," that is, out of sight, her presence known only by its beautiful effects. The poet is reacting with that stifling excess of "aching pleasure" that he speaks of in the "Ode on

Melancholy," which was written at about the same time. In view of what comes soon afterwards in the poem, it is easy to mistake the mood here by supposing the poet to be rationalizing a simple desire for escape from mortal pain. But to do so is to anticipate the poem and to alter the conditions of its experiment. Keats is playing fair here: not disguising as sensibility a weak-kneed desire for escape, but placing himself in his own prototypal position of exposure to that natural beauty which will lead him to seek a yet higher consummation. The poem's validity depends upon faithful adherence to the experiential sequence. We may believe the poet, then, when he says that " 'Tis not through envy of thy happy lot, / But being too happy in thine happiness" that he feels depression.[15] He is, according to his old formulation, what the poet must be, the acutely sensitive listener whose total response to the voice of beauty in the natural world brings about his identification of himself with the essential source of his intense pleasure. Thus far we have the archetypal situation of the pre-*Endymion* relationship between poet and nature. It remains only for the poet to be moved to participation in that higher principle of harmony of which the earthly music is an emanation.

In the second stanza, as the second step in the over-all process, the desire to do so is originated: the poet yearns to complete the Lethe-wards transition, cut his ties of memory with the real world and enter empathically into the world of ideal harmony suggested by the song. It should be clear that the nightingale, while remaining the natural source of beauty, has already begun to be repre-

---

[15] Cf. Wordsworth, "Resolution and Independence," 22-25:

> . . . from the might
> Of joy in minds that can no further go,
> As high as we have mounted in delight
> In our dejection do we sink as low. . . .

sentative of something more than itself. The "forest dim"
into which the poet would fade away with the nightingale cannot be a literal forest of bark and branches and
dirt, where a senseless, tranced bird of feather and bone
sings an unconscious song, for these physical realties are
part of the world the poet wishes to leave behind. Clearly,
his desire is for another world, a world which his imagination has conceived on the organic beauty of the song
he hears, but one where, he is willing to believe, an im-
perishable singer communicates divine melodious truth
of a kind intuited in the beauty of the earthly bird's song.
For the fulfillment of this desire to shake off the world's
clogs, the normal human anodyne is wine, and this the
poet proposes to himself—though not without a hint of
ambiguity. Unless we wish to brutalize the poem by reading "the true, the blushful Hippocrene" literally to mean
that the intoxication of wine is the real source of poetic
imagination, we must see that the poet has already begun
to idealize this image too.

The third stanza is primarily a catalogue of elements
to be escaped from, and together they represent the idea
of mutability. The desire for escape and the earthly imagery in which the idea of mutability is embodied are explicit, but it is well to remind ourselves here of the poem's
"laboratory" strategy. The poetic statement does not *begin* here, it *arrives* here. The idea of escape from an inferior earthly condition, indeed the very awareness of its
inferiority, *follows upon* the conceiving of a higher one.
Faithful to the terms of his experiment, the poet has
come to the same point of earthly loathing, and for essentially the same reason, as Endymion after his vision
of ideal beauty.

In the fourth stanza, when escape is achieved, it comes
not through wine but imagination, "Not charioted by
Bacchus and his pards, / But on the viewless wings of

[261]

Poesy." As in "Hence Burgundy, Claret, and Port," the poet has renounced earthly wine for a more intoxicating stimulant, a beverage perhaps brighter and clearer.

Now, if we compare what has been done, up to this point, with some characteristic lines from "Sleep and Poetry," we can see our experimental conditions more clearly. In the earlier poem the imaginative process is ardently and confidently described in the form of a petition:

O Poesy! for thee I grasp my pen
That am not yet a glorious denizen
Of thy wide heaven; yet, to my ardent prayer,
Yield from thy sanctuary some clear air,
Smoothed for intoxication by the breath
Of flowering bays, that I may die a death
Of luxury, and my young spirit follow
The morning sun-beams to the great Apollo
Like a fresh sacrifice; or, if I can bear
The o'erwhelming sweets, 'twill bring to me the fair
Visions of all places: a bowery nook
Will be elysium—an eternal book
Whence I may copy many a lovely saying

. . . .

And many a verse from so strange influence
That we must ever wonder how, and whence
It came. Also imaginings will hover
Round my fire-side, and haply there discover
Vistas of solemn beauty, where I'd wander
In happy silence, like the clear Meander
Through its lone vales; and where I found a spot
Of awfuller shade, or an enchanted grot,

. . . .

Write on my tablets all that was permitted,
All that was for our human senses fitted.
Then the events of this wide world I'd seize

Like a strong giant, and my spirit teaze
Till at its shoulders it should proudly see
Wings to find out an immortality.
                ("Sleep and Poetry," 53-65, 69-76, 79-84)

What the poet desires, here and in the Nightingale ode, is the intoxication of Poesy, which is initially made possible by some element in the natural world that gives pleasure to the senses. The anticipated consequence in both is the destruction of isolated selfhood through spiritual absorption into the ideal world. So far, given the inevitable differences in situation and expression, the processes are virtually identical, as projected in the two poetic statements.

It is at this point, however, that theory and experiment diverge. According to the "Sleep and Poetry" prognosis, what should follow from this is a life of "visions" and "imaginings" capable of yielding up from the most ordinary earthly settings ("bowery nook," "fire-side") as much of sublime universal truth as is "for our human senses fitted." The poet should grow from strength to strength until his spirit has achieved such angelic understanding as to "find out an immortality." What actually happens in the Nightingale ode is quite otherwise.

Having fulfilled the specified conditions, the poet does indeed find himself in a lovely imaginative world, an idealized version of the world from which he has pictured the nightingale's song as issuing. And yet, for all the richness of imagery in the fourth and fifth stanzas, the joy, if it is joy, is strangely muted. One is struck, for instance, by the fact that what is seen in the imaginative vision includes nothing that the real world does not supply, the difference being simply that the imagination is capable of calling up these phantasmal entities at will. And the vision is obscured by darkness. Even though the

[263]

poet had asked to fade into the "dim" forest of "shadows numberless," a subtle shock is conveyed at the point where, having flown in imagination to the region of the queen of light, the poet suddenly (and, considering the conceptual value of "light," ominously) exclaims, "But here there is no light," and speaks of the "glooms" surrounding him. Hence, he "cannot see" but must "guess" at the presence of what his vision supplies. In the ideal world of imagination he must still uncertainly supply the objective truth of his own vision. The diction is slow and heavy, weighted with the retarding effect of more, and more intricately combined, polysyllabic words than occur in either of the enveloping stanzas, and is dragged down emotionally by words and phrases that, at some level of consciousness, make funerary suggestions: "flowers are at my feet," "incense," "embalmed darkness," "fading," "cover'd up," "murmurous haunt." Perhaps no reader of the poem has been unmoved by the fifth stanza's simple gorgeousness, but however powerfully it renders the "things" it describes, one observes that, in the context of the total experience, they are forced through a series of conceptual and expressive baffles in such a way as thoroughly to subdue the sense of fulfillment which the experience was supposed to supply.

The ominous death-hints of the fifth stanza are brought into focus in the sixth, at which point we find the imaginative process reaching its peak not in exultant triumph but in complete despair. The internal logic of the developing process, and the emotional bias of the terms in which it has found culminating expression, tempt the poet to the very brink of annihilation, not of self*hood* but of absolute *self*. Darkling adrift in a numbly realized half-world of idealized sense experience, the poet thinks for a moment that it would be so easeful, so pleasant, simply to drift out of life, having as one's last contact with the physical world the ecstatic song of the nightingale. And it is just here that the dream begins to break up. "Still wouldst thou sing, and I *have ears in vain*— / To thy high requiem *become a sod*" (italics mine). The brutal fact is that escape from the world of mutability entails as a necessary correlative the loss of that same world's beauty. Nothing is extenuated or substituted or promised to succeed this fact. No poet's Elysium is offered, no hereafter in which to have one's happiness "repeated in a finer tone,"[16] nothing but absolute loss and dissolution. The poet would, himself, become no more than mere earth. The desire for a dying into higher life becomes a denial of the real principle of the bird's song, which is beauty in *this* world. Like the Apollo of *Hyperion*, the poet has perceived a beauty in the natural world which has suggested to his imagination a superior world of immutable beauty, to which he has achingly aspired. Unlike the god, however, who can die into the life of ideality, the poet is obliged to confront the ultimate fact of his mortality, that a human being can die only into death. Imagination, which was supposed to have supplied an escape from the reality of earthly mutability and an ascent to a higher level of truth, has merely brought the poet to a perilous confrontation of the final truth of earthly reality.

Stanza seven reiterates this realization in various ways. The first two lines, "Thou wast not born for death, immortal Bird! / No hungry generations tread thee down," reassert in an implied comparison one aspect of the truth to which the poet has just been brought. The bird (or properly, its song, for which "Bird" is simply metonymous) was not born for death, unlike man, who *was* born for death. The song goes on, but the listeners have it each for but a brief hour before being trodden down in death. The remainder of the stanza illustrates this general truth

[16] *Letters*, I, 185.

concretely. The song is available to the poet "this passing night," i.e. in his transitory moment, just as in "ancient days" it was available to "emperor and clown" and to the sad-hearted Ruth, a stranger in an alien land. All accidental human distinctions are leveled in the three examples. Whatever might have been true about the emperor's, clown's, and lonely stranger's other relations with the world, the one relation with it that they shared equally was the fact of having lived in it, and therefore of having had the opportunity to experience, each in his passing moment, the beauty which, in *his* passing moment, the poet is *now* enjoying. When the poet becomes what they have long since become, the song will be as utterly lost to him as it has long since been lost to them. The essential distinction is not between those who dwell on higher and lower spiritual planes; the essential distinction is between the living and the dead.

Thus far the seventh stanza clearly ratifies the inescapable truth of human mutability and the recognition of the unmystical, unidealizable sense-beauty of the song which the poet had been forced to accept at the end of the previous stanza. The final lines, however, "The same that oft-times hath / Charm'd magic casements, opening on the foam / Of perilous seas, in faery lands forlorn" seem at first glance to exist on another plane. Merely to characterize them admiringly as "magic" or "pure poetry," and not attempt to ascertain their relevance, is to leave the laboratory before the experiment is over, and to miss the connecting link between the development of the poem up to this point and the plain statement of its theme in the concluding stanza. Since the poet has had his poem very much under control until now, there is no reason to suppose that it suddenly rises up and has its will of him. If we can see that the earlier portion of the stanza has been doing what a stanza ought to do, that it has been moving on from the point arrived at in the previous stanza, and in the direction pointed to by that stanza, we owe the poet the assumption that these lines are also relevant to the total statement he has been making.

In that spirit we can note that, while the visually concrete elements of these lines are the "casements," "foam," and "seas," they are merely components of a whole region that is now deserted, forsaken, forlorn. And this region is "faery land." Since the nightingale, whose song was heard in ancient times by the emperor, the clown, and Ruth, and is now being heard by the poet, is, after all, emphatically a bird of the real world, there appears to be an inconsistency here—*unless* the abandoned faery land is that presided over by "the Queen-Moon . . . on her throne, / Cluster'd around by all her starry Fays" (36-37), the world of Cynthia, now forlorn, which existed once, in the good old times of, say, Spenser, when the authenticity of the poetic imagination did not have to be called in doubt. In those past times the poet could successfully employ his imagination to transmute the beauty of the real world into ideal forms and create charming new worlds for the purified objectification of the highest human truths. But *this* poet, in *his* time, cannot. He must forsake, as he has just forsaken, the never-never land of imagination, where one is tempted to leave the world which contains all the beauty that mortal man can ever surely know. These lines therefore complete the poet's rejection of that world which, at the beginning of the poem, he had desired to enter, and from which, after realizing its implications, he had already withdrawn after the disappointment of his successful entry. The lines are also wholly in keeping with the total development of the stanza which they conclude, referring like the earlier lines to a context of time-past, but excluded, by the truth on which the earlier lines are grounded, from continuing validity in the truth of time-present.

The opening lines of the eighth stanza, "Forlorn! the very word is like a bell / To toll me back from thee to my sole self," complete the dissociation of singer and listener, leaving the poet alone to reflect with wonder on the whole experience. His sole comment on the experience, his only judgment of it, is, "the fancy cannot cheat so well / As she is fam'd to do, deceiving elf," which clearly places the evaluative emphasis neither on the qualities of the song itself, nor on any principle represented by the song, but on the role of the imagination as a mode of enlarging and apprehending the intuitions generated by the world of physical sensation. *This* has been the real subject of the poem. What the poet actually heard under the plum-tree in Brown's Hampstead garden occupies no more than a few lines at the beginning and end of the poem. Within that framework, the poem puts to the empirical test the theory of poetry which had originally been embodied in the Apollinian imagery complex, and employs, as primary functional ingredients, several images closely identified with that complex. While there is no reason to suppose that Keats intended the Nightingale ode as an answer to the specific lines from "Sleep and Poetry" cited at the beginning of this discussion, they represent an earlier and optimistic view of the process which the Nightingale ode rejects as unworkable. The "enchanted grot" to which the imagination was to lead him, in the "Sleep and Poetry" lines, had been visited a few weeks before the ode, in "La Belle Dame," in the company of a "faery's child" whose proffered felicity proved to be deceitful. She was, in fact, close kin to the "deceiving elf" who almost led the poet to his destruction in the Nightingale ode, before he realized again, what he had first acknowledged in the epistle to Reynolds, that the beauty of this earth is its own excuse for being, and that the imagination that tries to make it something more can only deprive us of even that small portion of ascertainable good that human life can truly offer.

A few weeks later in the summer of 1819 Keats began *Lamia*,[17] the third in his varied triad of poems expressing what had clearly become his demonic view of the poetic imagination. There was a time when critics of the poem, taking their cue primarily from those lines concerned with Philosophy's unweaving of the rainbow (II, 229-38), saw it, however equivocally, as in some sense an affirmation of the imagination against philosophy (i.e. reason or science). Indeed, so conveniently and often have these lines been plucked from context in order to assert some generalization about Keats or Romanticism, that the formula persists in the average "lay" reader's mind even today. However, closer students of Keats's work have moved toward a more balanced view, taking into account the poem's full development and seeing in the whole an acknowledgment on Keats's part of the validity of philosophic truth, and even of its supremacy where it comes in conflict with the merely apparent truths of imagination.[18]

[17] On July 11 he told Reynolds that he had completed the first section [*Letters*, II, 128]. Since his chief project at the time was the composition of *Otho the Great*, the 397 lines of *Lamia* were probably slow in coming. E. de Selincourt [(ed.), *Poems*, p. 453], Sidney Colvin [*John Keats*, p. 405], and C. L. Finney [*Evolution of Keats's Poetry*, II, 667] assert, and Robert Gittings [*John Keats: The Living Year*, pp. 147-49] documents, the probability that Keats had begun composition before he left for the Isle of Wight on June 27.

[18] E. de Selincourt [(ed.), *Poems*, p. 459] advises caution in inferring Keats's whole attitude from a few lines, and suggests that the poet, as a general proposition, would have recognized philosophic and imaginative truths as of separate and unconflicting kinds. Joseph Warren Beach [*A Romantic View of Poetry*, p. 128] approaches closer to the balance within the poem when he says that Keats "was not an enemy to reason, but . . . a friend to love," and that, however "disparaging are his references to the philosopher," he presents Apollonius as "an honest sage" who "has no

There are few critics, of any persuasion, however, who seem altogether easy in their conclusions, probably because what the narrative's characters *are* and what they *do* seem not always in perfect harmony; and, in fact, the poet's comments on various aspects of their being and doing seem not always, at all levels, to be consistent. I suspect that the length of time during which the poem was in process (late June to early September), and its being intermittently taken up and laid aside, account in some measure for the variety of sympathies expressed. At the same time, however, I believe that a consistent over-all scheme can be demonstrated, and I cannot subscribe to Finney's view that, owing to changes in the poet's life in the interval between composition of the two parts, the second part expresses attitudes which are in actual conflict with those of the first.[19] But in addition to the effect of the intermittent process of composition, there is another quality, which might fairly be called Shakespearean, that works against unity of thematic impression. That is, Keats

---

choice but to expose the cheat." C. D. Thorpe [(ed.), *Poems*, pp. xliii-xliv] is the most extreme, and in his conclusion the most solidly convincing, of the mediators: "The facts . . . seem to be that Keats was here dealing with two falsities. Lamia and Lycius represent an existence of phantasy—pure dream. Apollonius, on the other hand, stands for cold and factual reasoned knowledge." Keats, he goes on, had elsewhere expressed his disapproval of both extremes. When, in the poem, one triumphs over the other, all we can conclude is that here is "Keats the realist speaking, a man trained in hospitals and disciplined by the rigours of a life filled with unhappy facts." This view of Thorpe's, qualified by a necessary additional distinction between Lamia as deceiver and Lycius as deceived, together with Beach's suggestion that Apollonius is simply doing what it is his nature and function to do, gives us a sound basis for evaluation of the poem's development in the parts. For a defense of *Lamia* against oversimplification in terms of any of its internal commentary, see Bernice Slote, *Keats and the Dramatic Principle* (Univ. of Nebraska Press, 1958), pp. 166ff.

[19] *Evolution of Keats's Poetry*, II, 667, 679-703.

so far entered into sympathetic identification with his characters, in themselves and in their responses to each other, that their reality is heightened at the expense of their allegorical simplicity.[20] To have treated this as a defect is a charge I should not wish to have laid upon me.

It must be observed, then, before looking at her negative qualities, that Lamia is frequently a pathetic and sympathetic character. In her serpent-form, she pines for beauty of a higher kind than her own, and for the fulfillment of love. In her woman-form, despite a few questionable passages, her love for Lycius frequently seems genuine, if rather self-centered, and her deception of him is also apparently for love's sake, not for the sake of doing him harm. She does bring her lover a temporary happiness, and when her lord insists upon a public marriage which she recognizes as the beginning of the end of her felicity, she is nonetheless, as someone has remarked, the dutiful model of female submission admired by Keats's English contemporaries. She is also artlessly and sentimentally feminine in her distress at Lycius' mental wandering from the pleasures of passion to a concern with the "noisy world" of events in which a man has his larger scope (II, 40-45). And her exposure by Apollonius is certainly rendered in such a way as to call up all our sympathy for tender femininity heartlessly destroyed.

All these things are true; the poem is so managed as to elicit our favorable response to these qualities. But they merely provide dramatic insights into basic emotion-bearing situations, irrespective of particular character, and are not the plenum of data for the final evaluation of Lamia, the particular character. Shylock, Iago, Edmund, Claudius, all have moments of pathos, or sim-

[20] This is, of course, vital to the dramatic mode of composition. For a most interesting reading of the poem in terms of its dramatic oppositions, see Bernice Slote, *Keats and the Dramatic Principle*, pp. 138-53.

plicity, or grandeur, but they are "as if" moments in the total dramatic experience. We respond to the qualities because they are humanly affecting wherever we encounter them, but in the long run they only heighten our awareness of "what might have been," had the character been other than he patently is. Lamia is, after all, *a* lamia, and the sympathy we instinctively feel for her at certain moments is rather an evidence of our amiable social instincts than of her merit, which must be judged in the context of our whole knowledge of her.

That knowledge includes, first of all, the entire complex of traditional literary and folk association attached to the idea of a lamia, in which the creature is almost universally considered malign.[21] It includes, further, Keats's own characterizing comments, that "She seem'd, at once, some penanced lady elf, / Some demon's mistress, or the demon's self" (I, 55-56), and that she is a "cruel lady" (I, 290). That she is some sort of sorceress we know from the beginning, for she has made Hermes' beloved nymph invisible (I, 100).[22] Magic may, of course, be

[21] For a good recent summary of the tradition, see Bernice Slote, *op.cit.*, pp. 142-44.

[22] Although Professor Wasserman very shrewdly estimates both the thematic function and the structural weakness of the Hermes/nymph section [*The Finer Tone*, pp. 158-59], his attempt to equate the nymph with ideal beauty, unseen by the sensually oriented seekers but perceptible to the "passionate intensity" of the god [*ibid.*, pp. 159-61], seems unlikely in the context. For one thing, Hermes is just as sensually motivated as the fauns and satyrs from whom Lamia has hidden the nymph. For another, Hermes does not ultimately find the nymph because of any superior quality of his own, either manifested directly or perceived by Lamia's insight to be worthy of reward. The power to make the nymph visible is Lamia's, not his, and she does him that favor because he is in a position to do one for her, *quid pro quo*. Had he refused her, his "passionate intensity" could have gone blackberrying for the rest of the summer with no more fulfillment than the satyrs'. While Professor Wasserman might legitimately protest that I am here reading the poem with brutal literalness, I must insist that I do

white or black, but it is not reality, and its virtues must be judged by its effects in the real world. The final and irrefutable effect of Lamia's magic is that Lycius is destroyed by his belief in it. Moreover, he is destroyed by a cheat, for what breaks his heart is the loss of something that he never really had, because it never really existed in the way that he was willing to believe it did. It was not capable of substantial existence in the real world and therefore existed only in his fancy, the result of a spell cast upon him by the sorceress to convince him of a truth which was no truth, but mere illusion.

From the very beginning of their relationship Lycius is entranced, literally. At his first sight of Lamia he takes her for a goddess, and she encourages his belief. She threatens to leave him because the coarse pleasures of earth are inadequate to her ethereal nature, and "He, sick to lose / The amorous promise of her lone complain, / Swoon'd, murmuring of love, and pale with pain" (I, 287-89). And how does she react?

> *The cruel lady, without any show*
> *Of sorrow for her tender favourite's woe,*
> But rather, if her eyes could brighter be,
> With brighter eyes and slow amenity,
> Put her new lips to his, and gave afresh
> *The life she had so tangled in her mesh.*
> (I, 290-95, italics mine)

---

so in order to counteract his initial excess of interpretive attenuation. I take it as a critical axiom that any interpretation, however appealing, which is out of harmony with the literal data from which it proceeds is untenable. Judging by his repeated but unexplained use of the word "miracle" to fill in the rational gaps in his interpretation of this episode, I suspect that Professor Wasserman also subscribes to this irritating axiom. Despite these objections, however, I think there is a middle ground that we can both comfortably occupy.

The deliberate and unimpassioned entrapment of her prey is clearly not calculated to arouse associations of natural and heart-warming love. But more immediately relevant is the effect upon Lycius, for "he from one trance was wakening / Into another" (I, 296-97). He is awakening from the trance of his swoon, but not into the world of reality; it is a tranced world of sheer illusion into which he is wafted by the spell of the song she sings as he returns to consciousness. From that point on, Lycius accepts every deceit she practices on him, "And every word she spake entic'd him on" (I, 326). She persuades him, at least for the moment, that she is "a woman, and without / Any more subtle fluid in her veins / Than throbbing blood" (I, 306-8), though we already have been told that hers is not truly woman's but "elfin" blood (I, 147). He believes "that the self-same pains / Inhabited her frail-strung heart as his" (I, 308-9), though we have just seen her bending with glittering eyes over his unconscious form, "without any show / Of sorrow" for his woe. Lamia has not, in her metamorphosis, become a real woman but is "playing woman's part" (I, 337) because she coolly "judg'd, and judg'd aright" (I, 334) that her success with Lycius depended upon his faith in such a misapprehension. The enchantment continues on the way back to Corinth:

> The way was short, for Lamia's eagerness
> Made, *by a spell*, the triple league decrease
> To a few paces; *not at all surmised
> By blinded Lycius*, so in her comprized.
> (I, 344-47, italics mine)

Lycius meets Apollonius, who is frankly acknowledged to be "my trusty guide / And good instructor" (I, 375-76), but, under the spell of Lamia, Lycius suddenly sees him as "The ghost of folly haunting my sweet dreams"

(I, 377). The palace to which they retire is not a real palace that has merely been obscured from the eyes of the curious, but a "fairy roof" supported by continuous strains of music "as fearful the whole charm might fade" (II, 123, 124). Literally enchanted through the whole period of their relationship, Lycius is so lost to reality as to see everything in exactly the reverse of its true nature, accusing Apollonius at the wedding feast of such "Unlawful magic, and enticing lies" (II, 286) as Lamia has in fact been perpetrating, and of fixing "demon eyes" (II, 289) upon his beloved, a savage irony which is immediately made manifest in the event. The charm of fantasy must be, and is, broken by the clear eyes of truth. Judging from the richness of the poem's descriptions, we may feel that Keats was reluctant to find it so, but that is nevertheless the conclusion to which he relentlessly leads us.

Most readers of the poem would probably grant, without the foregoing chain of specific references, that Lamia holds Lycius by a spell greater than that of natural beauty; and most have probably been aware, too, that, whatever tender moments of human-like feeling she is given, there is a sinister quality in her whole association with Lycius. I think there can be little doubt, however, that Keats had for his creation more than a folklorist's or tale-spinner's concern, that she was not made sinister out of mere fidelity to the tradition that has considered her so, or because the narrative is made more gripping and suspenseful by that means. I think, rather, that she was originally chosen, and that the poem was constructed around her, precisely because in tradition her alluring beauty is false and her effect on human life pernicious. And I think further that, having such a received character, she was chosen because she was intended specifically to represent Keats's revised view of the poetic imagination.[23] The critical problem is compounded by the fact that she is not only the poetic imagination but has a dual identity, as imagination with respect to Lycius, and as a typical victim of imagination in her own person and conduct. Here Keats was perhaps being overly ambitious, yet the logic of his conception, given his former view of the poet's ameliorative social function, is not hard to see. The poet, who lives in his imagination and creates from it structures which stimulate the imaginations of other men, may wish to believe that he has achieved a higher than mortal truth, and that he is leading others to that truth. In fact, however, he is a self-deceiver and a deceiver of others, because the truth he imagines is not viable in the world that is given to our mortality.

As herself a victim of imagination, consider the pattern of Lamia's actions in the light of Keats's former synthesis and its symbols. First of all, she has the capacity, which she often exercises, of imaginative vision:

> But first 'tis fit to tell how she could muse
> And dream, when in the serpent prison-house,
> Of all she list, strange or magnificent:
> How, ever, where she will'd, her spirit went;
> Whether to faint Elysium, or where
> Down through tress-lifting waves the Nereids fair
> Wind into Thetis' bower by many a pearly stair;
> Or where God Bacchus drains his cups divine,
> Stretch'd out, at ease, beneath a glutinous pine;
> Or where in Pluto's gardens palatine
> Mulciber's columns gleam in far piazzian line.
> And sometimes into cities she would send
> Her dream, with feast and rioting to blend;

[23] For essentially the same basic view, though grounded in a different rationale and much more specifically correlated with events in Keats's professional life, see C. L. Finney, *The Evolution of Keats's Poetry*, ii, 698-700.

And once, while among mortals dreaming thus,
She saw the young Corinthian Lycius
Charioting foremost in the envious race,
Like a young Jove with calm uneager face,
And fell into a swooning love of him.

(I, 202-19)

Like Adam, who "awoke [from his dream of Eve] and found it truth,"[24] she has, in some unspecified way, come to know that Lycius does exist in the real world. Inspired by his beauty, she desires to leave the lower world of serpenthood and rise to the relatively more spiritualized world of human life, where she can participate directly in the beauty which both imagination and the extrapolated evidence of her senses have prefigured for her as a superior kind of existence. Her wish accomplished, by metamorphosis, she enters into the full life of illusion, in which, like the poet in the fifth stanza of the Nightingale ode, she does briefly enjoy the higher world. That her excursion into human existence is, for her, the equivalent of participation in ideality is made explicit in an autograph variant of II, 44-45, where Lamia, fearing that Lycius may be drawn back to the real world, anticipates the end of her idyll: "Too fond was I believing, fancy fed / In high deliriums, and blossoms never shed!"[25]

As with the poet of Keats's earlier visioning, music (poetry) gives substantial body to her ideal world. The faery palace whose sole support is music (II, 122-23), in which Lamia and Lycius have their transitory ideal existence, is the metaphorical representation of a poem, created by Lamia, whose every rift she carefully loads with ore:

Lamia, regal drest,
Silently paced about, and as she went,

---

[24] *Letters*, I, 185.   [25] *Poetical Works*, p. 204n.

> In pale contented sort of discontent,
> Mission'd her viewless servants to enrich
> The fretted splendour of each nook and niche.
> Between the tree-stems, marbled plain at first,
> Came jasper pannels; then, anon, there burst
> Forth creeping imagery of slighter trees,
> And with the larger wove in small intricacies.
>
> (II, 133-41)[26]

The aerial assistants who enable her to do so, though "'tis doubtful how and whence / Came, and who were her subtle servitors" (II, 117-18), are the exact equivalents of the "gentle whispering / Of all the secrets of some wond'rous thing / That breathes about us in the vacant air" (29-31) in "Sleep and Poetry," which, in that poem, were to eventuate in "many a verse from so strange influence / That we must ever wonder how, and whence / It came" ("Sleep and Poetry," 69-71). But no longer does the confidence of that former time permit the poet to suppose that such agency or action has any real efficacy; it can only "dress / The misery in fit magnificence" (*Lamia*, II, 115-16). The poet can adorn life, but he cannot escape it, for, as Keats was to say in another poem, on which he was perhaps working concurrently with this part of *Lamia*, the poet is one "to whom the miseries of

[26] C. L. Finney, *Evolution of Keats's Poetry*, II, 700, has suggested that the lines which follow,

> Approving all, she faded at self-will,
> And shut the chamber up, close, hush'd and still.
> Complete and ready for the revels rude,
> When dreadful guests would come to spoil her solitude
>
> (II, 142-45)

allude to "the public who did not appreciate Keats's poems," a suggestion I welcome as entirely appropriate to the palace-poem equation, though Keats's remarks about the public, during this period [*Letters*, II, 144, 146], suggest not so much his annoyance with adverse criticism from the public as they do a sense of indignity in the very act of submitting his poems for public perusal. But the strains are mixed.

the world / Are misery" (*The Fall of Hyperion*, I, 148-49).

What precisely happens to Lamia, when the Apollonius-reality enters, we don't know—she simply disappears. She may go back to the serpent-state in which she properly belongs, though one line, "Then Lamia breath'd death breath" (II, 299), hints at her complete destruction. It is enough, however, to recognize the pattern, to see that the world of human life, which for Keats had once been the world to be left behind in pursuit of the higher world opened up by imagination, was itself, for Lamia, the higher world to which imagination gave access. In keeping with Keats's matured view of the imagination, however, only brief participation in the higher world was possible for her, just as for Lycius it was possible only briefly to inhabit with her what he took to be the higher world of gods and goddesses.[27] The penalty both had to pay for their refusal of reality was its forfeiture altogether, and, with that, the forfeiture of every possibility contained in it, including that of imaginative vision.

Lamia's role as imagination with respect to Lycius is comprised in her role as reality-substitute, though there are specific touches which clarify the identity. Her agony in the transformation from serpent to woman is reminiscent of Apollo's painful dying into the life of divinity (*Hyperion*, III, 124-36), and she emerges not only beautiful but

> of sciential brain
> To unperplex bliss from its neighbour pain;
> Define their pettish limits, and estrange

[27] That Lycius came to believe he was enjoying with Lamia an experience of the divine is manifest in II, 85-88:

'Sure some sweet name thou hast, though, by my truth,
'I have not ask'd it, ever thinking thee
'Not mortal, but of heavenly progeny,
'As still I do. . . .'

Their points of contact, and swift counterchange;
Intrigue with the specious chaos, and dispart
Its most ambiguous atoms with sure art.

(I, 191-96)

That is, she is possessed of such superior knowledge
(though undoubtedly at a lower level) as signified the
deification of Apollo (*Hyperion*, III, 113). She is thus in
the potential Apollinian relationship with Lycius of inspirer to inspired. This potentiality is realized in the
poem's early action, her effect upon Lycius being of the
kind, and manifested through such means, as Apollo's
upon the poetic mind in Keats's earlier aesthetic. Where
the song of Apollo was heard in the music of natural
forms and inspired the poet with a desire for union with
the ideal, Lamia sings to Lycius (I, 249), as a natural
woman (I, 336-37), "A song of love, too sweet for earthly
lyres" (I, 299) and inspires in him the desire for union
with the divine world which he supposes her to represent (II, 86-88). Significantly, in terms of the old formulation's symbols, their first meeting, with its attendant
enchantment of Lycius, takes place at early evening (I,
233-37), and we see them at the peak of their felicity,
just before the world of reality begins the encroachment
which will culminate in their destruction,

in the even tide,
Upon a couch, near to a curtaining
Whose airy texture, from a golden string,
Floated into the room, and let appear
Unveil'd the summer heaven. . . .

(II, 17-21)

Lycius' spirit, at that moment, is in a "golden bourn" (II,
32), free from the "noisy world" (II, 33) which stands
in contrast to it and which, at exactly that point, Lycius
begins to feel encroaching on his happiness.

Ominously, Lycius' end is anticipated at his first meeting with Lamia, when he protests that "if thou shouldst fade / Thy memory will waste me to a shade" (I, 269-70), i.e. he will be reduced to that condition toward which Peona found Endymion tending, after his heavenly vision, and in which the knight-at-arms was left after his encounter with *his* "belle dame sans merci," or "cruel lady."[28] The elf-demon-faery Lamia, neither pure essence nor true mortal but an intermediate entity participating in both worlds, cannot have any valid and enduring relationship with the human Lycius, for their relationship is subject to the same objection as is the imagination in the epistle to Reynolds: when brought beyond its proper bound and used as a mediator between human limitations and ideality, it cannot be referred "to any standard law / Of either earth or heaven" ("To J. H. Reynolds, Esq.," 81-82).

It is at this point, I think, that the relevance of the introductory Hermes episode to the whole becomes clear. From the time of the Reynolds epistle, Keats had repeatedly acknowledged that the standard laws of earth and heaven were separate and unmediable. Where the poetic dreamer of "Sleep and Poetry" could believe in imagination's power to carry him "to the great Apollo" (60) "to find out an immortality" (84), and where Endymion, after suitable indoctrination in imagination's proper mode of exercise, could achieve union with his visionary ideal, no poetic agonist created after the Reynolds epistle succeeds in assimilating both worlds to his own spirit.[29] In-

[28] Miriam Allott [" 'Isabella,' 'The Eve of St. Agnes' and 'Lamia,' " *John Keats: A Reassessment*, pp. 56-57] and E. C. Pettet [*On the Poetry of Keats*, pp. 229-31] also remark the functional similarity of Lamia and the Belle Dame, and Pettet [*ibid.*, and note] contributes several illuminating details to an Endymion-Lycius parallel.

[29] One reader has justly pointed out that Keats clearly intended Apollo to do so, in *Hyperion*. I have let the generalization stand

deed, I can think of only two completed poems written after mid-1818 in which any kind of fulfillment at all is attained, "The Eve of St. Agnes" and the ode "To Autumn," both of which celebrate conspicuously tangible and earthly gratifications. The rest, in one way or another, either assert directly that the earthly nightingale is a "senseless tranced thing" or demonstrate the inevitable frustration of trying to make it something more. In the context of this continuing orientation, the Hermes episode of *Lamia* has pointed relevance to the poem's main action, for Hermes is a god. In the world of the immortals, as distinct from the world of man, the nightingale sings divine melodious truth. It is for men to question their perceptions of supernal beauty, "Was it a vision, or a waking dream?" ("Ode to a Nightingale," 79) Of the gods it may be asserted that "It was no dream; or say a dream it was, / Real are the dreams of Gods, and smoothly pass / Their pleasures in a long immortal dream" (*Lamia*, I, 126-28). There is more than one irony in the lines depicting Lycius' fury at Lamia's reluctance to celebrate a public wedding:

> Fine was the mitigated fury, like
> Apollo's presence when in act to strike
> The serpent—Ha, the serpent! certes, she
> Was none.
>
> (II, 78-81)

Certes, he was no Apollo, either, and the allusion underscores the incongruity between his world of passion and that of the god whose action introduced the narrative.

---

because, while Keats began with the "historical" knowledge that Apollo did come to full power with the other Olympian gods, he yet broke off his own poem at precisely the point where the functioning and rationale of the change, in such humanly applicable terms as he had once confidently asserted, would have required an explanation that he was no longer capable of giving.

The function of the Hermes episode, then, is to serve as a thematic contrast to the parallel action which follows it on a lower plane. While Hermes and Lycius are both lovers of creatures whose existence is in spheres other than their own, they have nothing else in common. The ideality of passion can be achieved by the god simply because the ground of his existence is essence itself. There is nothing for Hermes to reach up for, so he reaches down, without loss of his own essential divinity, for the real achieves the ideal in his own proper being. For Lycius, however, a mortal, the belief that he too can span the levels of existence is necessarily illusory. In imagination he can, or in the palace of art built by the imagination he can, *for a time*. But the attempt to substitute permanently the values of imagination and art for those of the mortal world is an attempt to usurp the prerogatives of godhood through the denial of manhood. Its consequence must be what Lycius finds it, not merely the temporary sublimation of identity in visionary beauty, but absolute self-annihilation.

Perhaps the best commentary on the revised hierarchy of values embodied in *Lamia* is a statement Keats made in a letter written to Bailey at about the time (August 14) that he was taking up the second, or Apollonius, part of the poem: "I am convinced more and more every day that (excepting the human friend Philosopher) a fine writer is the most genuine Being in the World."[30] The expression is interesting not only for its strikingly appropriate parenthesis but for its wording. To be the "most genuine Being" in the world is to have identity in a superlative degree, is to be "real." When we recall Keats's repeated use of the word "real" as a standard of value during the year or so preceding, and when we consider the uniform attitude toward the life of imagination implicit in the

[30] *Letters*, II, 139.

constant "elfin" metaphors of "La Belle Dame," "Ode to a Nightingale," and *Lamia*, the poet's increasingly firm conception of what he expected from "philosophy" becomes clear. It constitutes an acceptance of the world *as it is,* not as metaphysically conceived but as experientially known. This by no means implies rejection of poetry or of the antecedent imaginative activity necessary to its creation, but it does place limits on what it is possible for poetry to be or do in the world for which it is intended. Lamia's palace is a perfect poem, and Lycius' lending of his spirit to it is without fault, in itself.[31] It is when he attempts to remove himself from the "real" world altogether, to live eternally, as a mortal, the life of a god, that he seals his own doom. For imagination has a "proper bound" beyond which lies madness or some other form of essential annihilation of the self.

Keats had come a long way, in opinion if not in time, from that point at which he could speak of the poet as one who has no identity,[32] who is distinguished from Men of Power by that fact,[33] who lives a life of continuous prefigurative futurity,[34] and who uses this world primarily

[31] The description of the palace as a "purple-lined palace of sweet sin" (ii, 31) is certainly pejorative, but in a sense which hardly seems to apply to this discussion. The diction of the line implies, at least to me, a comment on sexual rather than intellectual morality, and was arrived at, judging by the apparent difficulty of composition at that point [cf. *Poetical Works,* p. 203n.], perhaps more out of expediency than conviction or relevance.

[32] *Letters,* i, 386-87.   [33] *Ibid.,* 184.

[34] *Ibid.,* 184-85. This is the passage containing all the famous phrases about the holiness of the heart's affections, the truth of imagination, Adam's dream, a life of sensations rather than of thoughts, happiness on earth repeated in a finer tone hereafter, etc. Some critics have lifted from it what they could use, while others have attempted to build a coherent rationale from the jumble of its parts, but almost no one has been able to leave it alone. For a sampling of its commentaries cf. Werner W. Beyer, *Keats and the Daemon King* (New York, 1947), pp. 124-25, 306-308; H. N. Fairchild, *The Romantic Quest* (New York, 1931), pp. 412-14; C. L.

as a springboard for metaphysical leaps into a better
one.[35] The "vale of Soul-making" letter[36] and Keats's remarks, later in 1819, about his relationship with the
poetry-reading public[37] reveal an increasingly strong concern with personal identity. And the three poems we
have just examined reveal the extent to which the poet
was capable of turning upon what had been his deepest
convictions in order to assert the necessity of maintaining identity in the world of phenomenal experience,
against the pernicious tendency of the mind to hide from
itself and from reality in perpetual fantasy. The philosopher, the reminder of our mortal identity, is a better hu-

---

Finney, *Evolution of Keats's Poetry*, I, 299-302; Richard Harter
Fogle, *The Imagery of Keats and Shelley* (Chapel Hill, 1949), pp.
194-95; Newell F. Ford, *Prefigurative Imagination of John Keats*,
pp. 20-38; H. W. Garrod, *Keats*, pp. 37-40; C. D. Thorpe (ed.),
Poems, 177-78n.; Earl R. Wasserman, *The Finer Tone*, pp. 102-
104, *passim*. There is reason enough to leap at the rich concatenation of key Keatsian terms here, and most critics handle it with
circumspection; but those few who fail to take into account its
extemporaneous and provisional nature, and who use it as a measur-
ing device in the analysis of Keats's poetic practice throughout his
whole career, generally learn what it means to eat one's bread in
sorrow.

[35] As in the "Sleep and Poetry" lines cited above (53-65, 69-76,
79-84) or the *Endymion* lines (I, 777-81):

> In that which becks
> Our ready minds to fellowship divine,
> A fellowship with essence; till we shine,
> Full alchemiz'd, and free of space. Behold
> The clear religion of heaven!

[36] *Letters*, II, 102-104, in which Keats sees human life as a
process of friction between the innocent soul and its experiential
vicissitudes, toward the end of creating individual identity.

[37] For example, "Who would wish to be among the common-
place crowd of the little-famous—who are each individually lost
in a throng made up of themselfes?" [*Letters*, II, 144]. And "My
own being which I know to be becomes of more consequence to
me than the crowds of Shadows in the Shape of Man and women
that inhabit a kingdom" [*Letters*, II, 146].

man friend than even the poet. To the extent that the poet can bring us sustaining visions of a beauty often lacking in our lives, he is, like the Grecian urn, a friend.[38] But when we lose ourselves in these, we need a better friend, one who, at whatever cost to our spurious felicity, will free us from such delusion as robs us of our mortal identity. If we remark that, in the case of Lycius, disenchantment ended in annihilation, we must also observe that it was not Apollonius' fault. He destroyed the delusion; Lycius destroyed himself, by his commitment to it. The knight-at-arms of "La Belle Dame" was last seen undergoing a more protracted form of the same process, and the poet of the Nightingale ode was saved from a similar fate only by his sudden flash of insight into the real meaning of leaving the world behind. Philosophy, reality, the willingness to see the world not as metaphor or symbol but as the necessary arena even of our dreaming, is the first requisite for understanding what must always be the ultimate concern of poetry—the *human* condition.

[38] For more detailed discussion of this ode, see the Appendix.

SEVEN

Final Assault

TO the extent that Lamia's pleasure palace is equatable with a poem, and she with the imagination that brings it into being, she may be considered, from one point of view, the generic poet. But she does not do, in her creation, what Keats himself does in the creation of which she is a part; that is, she does not tell the truth. The consequences are clear, and a serious moral problem is thus posed for every practitioner of the poetic art. If Lamia, by seeming to promise more than she can fulfill, defines poetic irresponsibility, what are the resources and limitations of the responsible poet? In *The Fall of Hyperion,* the revised version of what had originally been conceived as his most heroic statement about the nature and function of the poet, Keats turned his attention to the direct clarification of the problem.

It cannot be said that the attempt was wholly a success, for there are indications that Keats had not yet made up his mind about what he believed—and, in any case, this draft too remained unfinished. But there are a number of positive elements to consider. For example, the poem opens with the assertions that dreams, visions of a better world than ours, are natural to human kind (I, 1-4), that they *should* be preserved (I, 4-7), and that poetry is the only available means for the preservation of such imaginative adventures (I, 8-11). Indeed, it is concluded that the ability to have such visions is the mark of a comprehensive human soul (I, 11-15). Imagination, as such, is thus ratified as a normal and proper human faculty.

The poet then represents himself as imaginatively present in a sense-paradise:

> Methought I stood where trees of every clime,
> Palm, myrtle, oak, and sycamore, and beech,
> With Plantane, and spice blossoms, made a screen;
> In neighbourhood of fountains, by the noise
> Soft-showering in mine ears; and, by the touch
> Of scent, not far from roses. Turning round,
> I saw an arbour with a drooping roof
> Of trellis vines, and bells, and larger blooms,
> Like floral censers swinging light in air;
> Before its wreathed doorway, on a mound
> Of moss, was spread a feast of summer fruits,
> Which nearer seen, seem'd refuse of a meal
> By Angel tasted, or our Mother Eve;
> For empty shells were scattered on the grass,
> And grape stalks but half bare, and remnants more,
> Sweet smelling, whose pure kinds I could not know.
> Still was more plenty than the fabled horn
> Thrice emptied could pour forth, at banqueting
> For Proserpine return'd to her own fields,
> Where the white heifers low. And appetite
> More yearning than on earth I ever felt
> Growing within, I ate deliciously.

(I, 19-40)

The beauty of the trees and flowers is seen, of the splashing fountains is heard, of the roses and foods is smelled, and of the angelic banquet is tasted. That the poet should imaginatively yield to these temptations of sense and partake of the delicacies before him indicates that he is alive to the pleasures of the senses. And this too is apparently requisite to the visionary poet, for, did he not yield to

[288]

their attractions, he would not finally drink the potion (I, 41-46) that delivers his consciousness to the ultimate vision. Thus far, then, we are within the *Endymion* and pre-*Endymion* preserve, acknowledging the desirability of a sensorium attuned to beauty in the external world and of a capacity for imaginative vision. There is also, in the poet's "pledging all the Mortals of the world, / And all the dead whose names are in our lips" (I, 44-45) before he drinks, the bias of both *Endymion* and the later poetry toward the values of human life.

At this point, however, there is a sharp break with the earlier formulation, a break signalized by an action which is to be emphasized by reiteration in a parallel action within the next hundred lines. Having drunk the potion found among the banquet meats, the poet begins to fight its effects:

> No poison gender'd in close monkish cell
> To thin the scarlet conclave of old men,
> Could so have rapt unwilling life away.
> Amongst the fragrant husks and berries crush'd,
> Upon the grass I struggled hard against
> The domineering potion; but in vain:
> The cloudy swoon came on, and down I sunk
> Like a Silenus on an antique vase.
>
> (I, 49-56)

This is the first of the two actions. Awakening in heavenly surroundings, and seeing in the distance a temple toward which his curiosity impels him, the poet arrives at its base, where a shrouded figure tells him that he must mount the steps before him or die where he stands. Then,

> suddenly a palsied chill
> Struck from the paved level up my limbs,

And was ascending quick to put cold grasp
Upon those streams that pulse beside the throat:
I shriek'd; and the sharp anguish of my shriek
Stung my own ears—I strove hard to escape
The numbness; strove to gain the lowest step.
Slow, heavy, deadly was my pace: the cold
Grew stifling, suffocating, at the heart;
And when I clasp'd my hands I felt them not.
One minute before death, my iced foot touch'd
The lowest stair; and as it touch'd, life seem'd
To pour in at the toes: I mounted up,
As once fair Angels on a ladder flew
From the green turf to heaven.

(I, 122-36)

This is the second. In these closely juxtaposed passages
the poet is twice threatened with the loss of conscious
identity. In both cases, he fights against it with his whole
being. It is true that he does not know, in either case,
that such loss may be necessary to revelation, so it cannot be said that he prefers lower to higher imaginative
experience. But his instinct, whenever his being, or selfhood, or identity is threatened, is to fight for its preservation. A "dying into life" motif is present here, but it is
not like Apollo's, in *Hyperion*, for the same reason that
it is not like the immolation of the self in poetry which
stands as the desideratum of "Sleep and Poetry," i.e. it is
wholly involuntary. The ideal of the poetry through *Endymion* was transcendence of the world and of the conscious identity of self in the world, through an imaginative mingling of one's own essence with the essential
beauty of the universe. The ideal now is rather a willingness to *risk* such self-loss in the exploration of imaginative vistas (the poet does imaginatively expose himself
to the consequences of drinking an unknown potion and
inspecting an unfamiliar landscape) while yet maintain-

ing an identity to the fixed nature of which these experiences will have relational relevance. There is nothing "natural" about the process by which the poet is vouchsafed his visions in *The Fall*. He is distinguished from the rest of mankind not by his special attunement to the first principles of a harmoniously constructed universe but by his spiritual curiosity and intrepidity. Neither does he at starting "know" anything beyond the ordinary—but he is *willing* to know.[1]

[1] Regardless of his reason for doing it, it is worth calling attention to the reiterated refusal of death in this poem, if only to give pause to those who find a death-wish latent in Keats's mature aesthetic, e.g. in varying degrees, H. N. Fairchild, "Keats and the Struggle-for-Existence Tradition," *PMLA*, LXIV (1949), 100-103; E. R. Wasserman, *The Finer Tone*, pp. 193-96; Robert Gittings, *John Keats: The Living Year*, p. 102; David Perkins, *The Quest for Permanence*, pp. 251-53. Wherever the death-wish argument is advanced, one is likely to find it supported by part or all of the last four lines of the sonnet "Why did I laugh," which is about the only place in Keats's poetry where an unambiguous commitment to death can be found:

> Yet would I on this very midnight cease,
>   And the world's gaudy ensigns see in shreds;
> Verse, fame, and Beauty are intense indeed,
> But Death intenser—Death is Life's high meed.

I have never been able to make sense of this sonnet, in any terms at all, with this reading, but find it infinitely more manageable in Rollins' transcription of its only autograph [*Letters*, II, 81], in which the concluding four lines are given (with my italics below) as:

> Yet *could* I on this very midnight cease,
>   And the world's gaudy ensigns see in shreds.
> Verse, fame and Beauty are intense indeed
> But Death intenser—*Deaths* is Life's high mead.

The correction of "would" to "could" changes an apparent desire to the contemplation of a possibility, while "Deaths," since a plural is impossible in the construction, becomes possessive. The sonnet's complete statement (q.v.) then becomes readily intelligible, i.e. "I don't know why I do some things, but any attempt to discover the laws to which I am obedient must end in frustration, since, however great my achievements or perceptions, death will ultimately claim them." Needless to say, this is hardly the expression

Keats's tentative arrival at such an estimate of the poetic character was almost inevitable. From "God of the Meridian" and the "Lines Written in the Highlands" through "La Belle Dame," the "Ode to a Nightingale" and *Lamia*, the country of the imagination had held a fearful place in the poet's consciousness. Having no longer his former capacity to rationalize it as continuous with and illuminative of experience of the natural world, he had been forced to abandon his former plan to represent it so in *Hyperion*. Yet, recognizing in himself a strong propensity for visionary dreaming, and feeling it harmless, perhaps even valuable, so long as it should not lead to a spurning of the earth, Keats here came to momentary rest in a view of the poet as adventurer on the frontiers of spirit, which does represent at least a tenable working hypothesis for the deliberate exercise of imagination.

It is impossible to say, of course, that this is precisely what Keats had in mind. I consider it probable but will rest content if others acknowledge it as merely possible, given the direction of the poet's movement and the nature of his aesthetic problem. In any case, *should* this have been the first step toward the provisional working out of a new view of the poet's role and his means of filling it, there remained yet another problem. Granted the poet's curiosity and intrepidity in blazing spiritual trails, for what end should he cultivate these qualities?

---

of a death-wish. But it *is* consistent with the attitude to which Keats gave passionate expression aboard the *Maria Crowther*, when he had abundant reason to wish an end of his struggles: "I wish for death every day and night to deliver me from these pains, and then I wish death away, for death would destroy even those pains which are better than nothing. Land and Sea, weakness and decline are great separators, but death is the great divorcer for ever" [*Letters*, II, 345]. This acquiescence in life as it is, because of an intolerable alternative, is somewhere present in all of Keats's mature poetry.

The colloquy with Moneta, which follows the poet's ascent of the temple steps, tries to provide a rationale, though Keats was obviously having trouble in formulating his distinctions. The basic attempt is to assimilate to the poet the qualities of the hero. Having been represented in action as one who greatly dares the unknown, the poet is defined in the ensuing discussion as one who, when he is wholly what he should be, does so not for the mere pleasure of the adventure but on behalf of mankind. Keats had, of course, always thought of the poet as the benefactor of mankind. But where his earlier view of the poet's role had seen him chiefly as either putting his audience in touch with the eternal principle of harmony, or, as in the epistle "To My Brother George" (67-109), so moving the emotions of his readers as immeasurably to heighten their appreciation of life, his tentative new view comprehended something like direct ameliorative action in the public arena.

There is some slight foreshadowing of this orientation in the poet's pledging of all mankind, and especially its heroes, just before drinking the potion which will remove him from their realm. Although it is not stated, it is obliquely implied, in the otherwise gratuitous insertion of the toast, that the action of drinking is done not entirely on his own behalf. The verbal exchange with Moneta clarifies the point:

'None can usurp this height,' returned that shade,
'But those to whom the miseries of the world
Are misery, and will not let them rest.
All else who find a haven in the world,
Where they may thoughtless sleep away their days,
If by a chance into this fane they come,
Rot on the pavement where thou rotted'st half.—'

(I, 147-53)

There are two kinds of people, those who acknowledge and are affected by the bitterness of human life, and those who are comfortable in the world and insensitive to its evils. Interestingly, both can achieve access to this heaven of imaginative vision, but only the socially conscious visionaries, once there, have further access to the residuum of truth (the temple) located at its center.

The kind of truth to be found there is implicit in the name and character of Moneta. Since the poet addresses her as "Shade of Memory" (I, 282), and her heavenly function appears to be the preservation of Saturn's memory in the universe (I, 221-27, 243-48), she is related to poetry through her likeness to Mnemosyne (Memory), mother of the Muses, who presided over Apollo's deification in *Hyperion*.[2] In her original identity, however, she is a Roman goddess of counsel, or warning, and is therefore emblematic of public wisdom. And in her character in the poem, she is the epitome of universal sorrow (I, 256-82), a sorrow which yet radiates a "benignant light" (I, 265), beams "like the mild moon" (I, 269), and fills "with . . . light / Her planetary eyes" (I, 280-81). In joining the imagery of light to the idea of sorrow, the poet thus commends her to us as a bringer of truth through conscience, or through sympathy with the suffering which is as old as the world. In her whole charac-

[2] Sidney Colvin [*John Keats*, pp. 447-48 and note], suggests that Keats's recent reading in *Auctores Mythographi Latini* may have provided a clue for the unorthodox association of Mnemosyne and Moneta. Most commentators have assumed that Keats meant them to have the same poetic functions and that he interchanged names because they were simply early and late designations of the same classical deity. I have found no warrant for supposing them identical in antiquity, and in the poems they have virtually antithetical functions: Mnemosyne sympathetically schools the rising god in the lessons of usurpation; Moneta preserves the remnants and the memory of the overthrown god's reign, and schools the visionary poet in the lessons (insofar as poetry is a social act) of social responsibility.

ter, then, she enlightens the conscience of those who look into her eyes (and these can be only the socially conscious visionaries) by drawing them into sympathetic remembrance of the whole history of sorrow and suffering in the world, so that the lessons of the past may not be lost to those living men to whom the poet will transmit his revelation. Abstracting from the allegory the practical means toward realization of this principle, one infers two necessities incumbent upon the poet: he must attempt to *know* what has happened, and he must *feel* what he knows as if it were a part of his own experience, i.e. in Keats's sense of the word, it must be "real" to him.

The significant remainder of the poem's revision (I, 154-210) consists primarily in the attempt further to refine the distinctions, first, between men of action and of vision, and then, between socially purposeful and mere self-indulgent visionaries. There has been some question whether Keats intended one section of this (I, 187-210) to remain in the poem,[3] but, however that may be, he did write the lines, and they are in keeping with the distinctions between true poet and mere dreamer which he had already made.

Having passed over this hortatory and definitional introduction, the purpose of which, aside from its value to the poet himself, is apparently to lay a valid claim on the reader's attention to the mythological history to follow, the poem picks up the narration of the first *Hyperion*, carries it to the introduction of Hyperion himself, and again breaks off. The reason, I think, was the same as that for the original version's having been left incomplete. Keats was again approaching the point where Apollo would have to be introduced, and, while he had tentatively refined his aesthetic ideas, in the introduction

[3] Cf. E. de Selincourt (ed.), *Poems*, pp. 517-19, 583-84, and John Middleton Murry, *Keats*, pp. 238-49.

to this poem, to the point where he could justify the writing of such poetry (or of poetry, at all), there was still no place in his scheme for the conception of Apollo which had originally governed his choice of this poetic subject. Hyperion had to fall, and he had to be replaced by a benevolent god of universal beauty and harmony. To the extent that Keats might succeed in rendering such an Apollo, he would be false to the values he had held (or true to values he had not held) ever since the Reynolds epistle of a year-and-a-half before. And, through a shift of dramatic emphasis from the sadness of the fall to the fulfillment of a higher value in a better god, he would be false to the humane aesthetic rationale which he had just formulated for the purpose of justifying his poem. For a moment, he had seemed to clarify the issues of poetic truth and responsibility with which *Lamia* had confronted the poetic imagination. In themselves, the new positions were satisfactory, but there seemed no point at which they could be reconciled with the inherent values of the poem he was actually writing, so he abandoned the attempt.[4] He could have proceeded in the tragic vein, and let Apollo develop as something like the upstart bully that the Titans saw in all the Olympian gods, but this he was incapable of doing. Somewhere inside himself he still felt that, whatever the limitations of his own understanding, the supremacy of Apollo was right. And he had reasons.

On September 21, 1819, Keats announced in a letter to Reynolds that he had given up *The Fall of Hyperion*.[5] In

---

[4] Kenneth Muir ["The Meaning of 'Hyperion,'" *John Keats: A Reassessment*, p. 120] suggests a possibly related difficulty: that Keats had already used up in his induction those ideas that should have been climactic.

[5] *Letters*, II, 167. He calls it "Hyperion," but in his letter of the same day to Woodhouse he encloses "a few lines from Hy-

the same letter, he commented on the beauty of the autumn season, adding that he had composed upon the subject on the previous Sunday, that is, two days before. What he had composed was, of course, the ode "To Autumn," which he did not include in the letter to Reynolds but sent to Woodhouse in a letter of the same date.[6] In this poem (and one wonders whether he realized it), he truly achieved a resolution in practice of the problems he had been unable to reconcile in theory.

The whole poem is a celebration of fruition and fulfillment in the process of time. It is the intense moment at the climax of the old seasonal cycle, upon which Keats had built so much of his intellectual system, that occupies our whole attention in the poem. And behind the rich bounty of its harvest stands Apollo, "the maturing sun," whom Keats, with apparent restraint, kept out of sight, presenting him almost entirely in terms of his beneficent effects.[7] The first stanza is heavy with the burgeoning fulfillment of nature's own potentialities for growth, the effect being emphasized poetically through abundance of "growth" verbs, i.e. *load, bless, bend, fill, swell, plump, set budding, o'er-brimm'd.* The mood is one of dynamic composure, created by the use of such organically active verbs for the representation of an extremely slow process which is rendered at an almost static moment of near-completion.

---

perion" which are in fact from *The Fall* [*Letters*, ii, 171]. There can scarcely be any doubt, then, that the poem he had been working on was *The Fall*, that it was customarily identified by him and his friends by the ambiguously abbreviated title, and that it was that poem which he had abandoned.

[6] *Letters*, ii, 170-71.

[7] Keats eliminated several direct and indirect allusions to the presiding power, i.e. "While bright the Sun slants through the husky barn" (15); and "a gold" altered to "barred," "gilds" altered to "bloom" (25). See notes to *Poetical Works*, pp. 273-74.

The second stanza introduces man and his fulfillment to the scene, through the personification of Autumn in terms of man's harvest activities, winnowing, reaping, gleaning, and pressing cider. The serenity and quietude of the first stanza are maintained by the presentation of each activity at a moment or in a posture of ease, thereby shifting emphasis from the hard work of harvest to the blessing of its abundance. Autumn is "sitting careless" on the granary floor during the winnowing process, sleeping between furrows during a break in the reaping activity, carrying upright the full basket of gleanings instead of bending in aching agony over the stubble, and sitting for hours "with patient look" beside the richly oozing cider-press.

In the final stanza, the peace and serenity accompanying the idea of fulfillment for both nature and man in the harvest season are objectified in an harmonious orchestration of natural sounds at the sunset hour. One by one the natural "instruments" are introduced, each one taking up and swelling the muted chorus; first the gnats are heard, then the lambs, the crickets, and the robins, and finally, the "gathering swallows twitter in the skies," the last image of the poem raising our eyes upward from the earth and its creatures, toward that heavenly region from which is ultimately derived this natural plenitude and human peace.

This is, I think, the only perfect poem that Keats ever wrote—and if this should seem to take from him some measure of credit for his extraordinary enrichment of the English poetic tradition, I would quickly add that I am thinking of absolute perfection in whole poems, in which every part is wholly relevant to and consistent in effect with every other part. To give Keats this credit is not to diminish the rest of his achievement but in fact to place him in a company of laureled peers whose membership will vary with the literary experience of individual readers but whose numbers will always be few. Keats could not have written the poem had he not gone the steps we have been tracing. The ode contains the benignant commerce of heaven and earth, the ripening agency of the sun-god, the cycle of the seasons, harvest, the sunset hour of peace and beauty, and at that hour, the harmonious *concors discordia* of external nature. To the extent that these are centered in the personification of the autumn season, they exist in a conceptual interrelationship. So far, Keats's earlier exercises in aesthetic hermeneutics stood him in good stead. But the beauty and truth of the elements wrought into this concatenation are self-existent and self-justified. They do not lead anywhere but into the grateful heart of man. And for this, Keats's protracted and often bitter-hearted discipline in objectivity of perception and statement is the cause. The return to aesthetic intellection in *The Fall of Hyperion* reflected a habit of mind and artistic conscience which extended over the poet's whole career; but, as the event proved, final solutions were not to be found by such means. Thought had already done its work for him. And when he could no longer explain to himself why, or how, or to what end he wrote poetry, the silent well of his knowing sent up from its depths the poem in which all the searching fervor of his life is serenely and gloriously inurned.

Appendix

SINCE I have been tracing a major preoccupation of Keats's thought through those poems in which it seems to be the central thematic issue, I have not wished to digress into commentary on less relevant poems, however interesting they may otherwise be. Nonetheless, I do recognize the interest that a number of them have, for abundantly sufficient reason, and I would not wish, in any case, to be suspected of having ignored significant poetry because of a presumed embarrassment to my argument. I therefore include this additional discussion.

Aside from the two *Hyperions* and "To Autumn," which make their own claims to consideration, my reason for having chosen to discuss the mature poems that I did must be obvious: they are united by a common demonic metaphor which, with its folklore implication of will-o'-the-wisp lurking just beyond the immediate general understanding of pernicious influence, ideally represents the dangerous and delusive light which Keats then felt the imagination to shed. Keats was an experimenter, of course, and did not always play the same tune on the same string, so that some of his poetry, at every stage of his development, has other reasons for being than those with which we have been chiefly concerned here. Other poems, and "major" ones, are quite consistent with the spirit and attitude we have been discussing. Both kinds are represented in the handful that no doubt merit discussion here: "The Eve of St. Mark," the odes on "Melancholy," on "Indolence," and to "Psyche," the "rondeau" "Fancy," and the "Ode on a Grecian Urn."

While "The Eve of St. Mark" has been long and justly

admired for the perfection of its texture, it is clearly remote from the sort of considerations that have been oc-
cupying us. Because it is not only unfinished but scarcely
more than a prologue to whatever action was intended
to follow it (if any had in fact been definitely conceived),
it is not possible even to speculate about its inherent implications. Keats himself referred to it casually as "a little
thing,"[1] and implied that insofar as it had any purpose it
was simply atmospheric, being designed to capture "the
spirit of Town quietude" and "give you the sensation of
walking about an old country Town in a coolish evening."[2] Moreover, the poet seemed wholly uninterested
in going on with the poem, however prosperously it might
have been begun.[3] One may suppose, then, that whatever impulse brought this fragment into being was grati-
fied in the execution, and that that impulse was indeed
what Keats said it was: an attempt to create with poetic
tone the quality of experience normally associated with a
certain set of external elements. I am much of Robert
Gittings' mind, that "It is a 'made' poem, and it comes to
an end when Keats has exhausted the impressions out of
which such a poem could be made. . . ."[4] It is, if not an
"occasional" poem, a poem resulting from a mood, either
immediate or induced. When the mood passed, or its materials were used up, composition stopped; hence, the
question of purpose or significance hardly enters in. But
I am humanly weak enough to observe that, whatever
may have been the poem's purpose, there are stylistic
manifestations in it of Keats's continuing objectivity. No
matter what subjective effect the poem's imagery is in-

[1] *Letters*, II, 62.   [2] *Ibid.*, 201.
[3] See his comments at the two places cited above.
[4] *John Keats: The Living Year*, p. 92. Though all would not
agree with Gittings' certainty about the social experience out of
which he believes the poem to have been made, his discussion of
its physical materials is extremely illuminating [*ibid.*, pp. 86-91].

tended to have on its readers, in the poem itself the imagery is rendered not only concretely but often with elaborate attention to detail. If one observes that the same may be said of the imagery in "I stood tip-toe," it must also be observed that the imagery there subserves an ideal aesthetic function, while it is not readily conceivable how the imagery of such a poem as "The Eve of St. Mark" could be made to do so. Indeed, the poet's few comments on his poem are solidly rooted in concern for the texture of here-and-now.

The "Ode on Melancholy" projects a more ambiguous image of the poet's mind. It concerns itself centrally with the subjective, with a state of mind and emotion, and it not only does not reject but seems actually to celebrate, in something like masochistic triumph, the unhappy truth of inner experience that is its subject.[5] That subject itself, the unity and functional interdependence of opposed states of feeling, was one of Keats's reflective preoccupations throughout his career, first appearing in one of his earliest known poems (the 1814 "Fill for me a brimming bowl") in an inversion of its customary later orientation: "I should have felt 'the joy of grief.'" One of course recognizes that this paradox of feeling is simply microcosmic of that essential paradox of physical and spiritual simultaneity in human existence which Keats's early epis-

[5] For those with psychoanalytical propensities, I hasten to add that I use the term "masochistic" to describe only the tone of the poem, not the character of the poet. One must not forget that Keats is here deliberately assuming the values appropriate to the convention within which he begins the poem, those implicit in the cult of sensibility's relishing of Gothic horrors. He does not recommend melancholy as a desirable state, merely says, in effect, "If that is what you seek, I can suggest a better method than yours." Indeed, some elements of the first stanza, and most of the canceled stanza that originally opened the poem, suggest that he began in a vein of amused condescension toward the attitude but soon found himself on the way to making a serious statement, so canceled the clownish beginning.

temological aesthetic was intended to resolve. The question is whether the imaginative act of the poem itself constituted in the poet's mind anything like the resolution which he had earlier considered feasible.

I don't think so. For one thing, the poem does not promise any sort of resolution; rather, it asserts, as was Keats's current wont, the inescapability of the experiential process it describes. Any suggestion that the pain we feel in the knowledge and presence of beauty's inevitable attrition can be converted to a quality of experience that is beyond attrition and pain would be a betrayal of the very point that the poem exists to make. The mental and emotional condition described neither transcends nor interprets the physical facts—it grows out of them and achieves meaningful expression through them. And the imagery is proportioned to this need, concrete, carrying its own implications, integrated to and by the value-scheme established by its own concatenation within the poem, but not to any scheme outside the poem's own self-validating system. The rain that "hides the green hill in an April shroud" depends almost entirely upon the word "shroud" for the fulfillment of its effect, though the concreteness does not lie in that word (which is rather a conceptual diffusion-lens for the main image) so much as in the process of visualization that the word forces us into. The real shroud's practical function and its association with death compel a visualization of the rain's both hiding and darkening the green hill, which, once done, certifies on our emotions the novel implication that the earliest and most promising stages in the natural process are already premonitory of its inevitable melancholy conclusion. This image of the rain's nourishing the life of nature for an ultimate extinction binds the concretion itself to the poem's dominant metaphorical pattern of feeding to the end not of vigor but of debility, the parasite

Melancholy flourishing upon us in proportion as we flourish upon the world of external beauty. Clearly, the world of nature has ceased utterly to be conceived as a mediatory instrumentality in man's spiritual ascent. I very much doubt that this was the conceptual point foremost in Keats's mind as he wrote, but *what* he wrote reveals the current bias of his mind and is conceptually consistent with what he was writing in other works at about the same time.

It is unlikely that the "Ode on Indolence" has ever been anyone's favorite poem, and it is certain that it was not Keats's. Why he excluded it from the 1820 volume we do not know, but it is repetitious and declamatory and structurally infirm,[6] and these would be reasons enough. Still, it was written by Keats, and, judging by its strophic form and the number of images and expressions it shares with the other odes of May 1819, it is an expression of the same mind that conceived the greater odes. That mind, it is quite clear, has at least momentarily disengaged itself from commitment to poetry, as either a means of self-expression or an avenue of truth. Robert Gittings, relating the mood of the ode to that of the sonnet "Why did I laugh," supposes love to be the major problem with which the poet was concerned, a choice between Fanny Brawne and Isabella Jones, and poetry (with its cause and effect of ambition and fame) to have been brought into consideration because of the poet's association of poetic composition with Mrs. Jones.[7] One must be willing to grant a great deal to Mr. Gittings' speculations about Mrs. Jones before acceding in such an interpretation, and

[6] To savor its structural infirmity one has only to read its stanzas in the order printed by H. W. Garrod, and then in the additional orders of the two transcripts, as indicated in *Poetical Works*, p. 447n., and attempt to discriminate among them on the basis of one's own relative responses.

[7] *John Keats: The Living Year*, pp. 102, 146-47.

one must be willing to translate rather than absorb the poem's own emphasis. What the poem says is that the poet wishes to forgo emotional intensity of all kinds for the duration of his indolent spell, these intensities being represented by the two common to all men, and therefore to him (Love, Ambition), and by the one that is his particular goad (Poesy). There is no reason whatever to suppose that the three figures who represent these intensities are intended to body forth real actors in the drama of Keats's life, or that the poem is intended to express anything more than such a quality of experience as Keats himself elsewhere attributed to it. In an earlier letter he had spoken of the delight of indolence in terms which were ultimately to supply the framework of the poem, and there he had commented that the happiness of such emotional and intellectual neutrality "is a rare instance of advantage in the body overpowering the Mind."[8] The emphasis is, of course, the reverse of Keats's earlier idealizing attitude toward physical experience. As transitory as the isolated experience out of which the poem grew may have been,[9] the emphasis of the statement about it is consistent with Keats's general movement away from intellectualized conceptualization in his reaction to the external world. Indeed, the emphasis of his remark is where the emphasis of his ode is, and three months after writing the former remark he wrote another, that the "Ode on Indolence" may be taken as representative of "my 1819 temper."[10]

Of the "Ode to Psyche" I could not say more to the point than has already been said by Mr. David Perkins,

[8] *Letters*, II, 79.

[9] Since the poem is separated by about two months from the letter in which the experience is discussed, and the poem's basic image introduced, it is clear that the possible brevity of the experience is less significant than the evident duration of its influence.

[10] *Letters*, II, 116.

to whose full discussion I refer the reader.[11] That part of his acute and subtle analysis which is most applicable to our present concern is his identification of Psyche, on one level, with the visionary imagination. The problem that he sees Keats struggling with in the poem is the validation and justification of a quality of imaginative experience that quite frankly exists only in an isolated corner of the mind, having no relevance to the world of external action and perhaps no truth to offer even the visionary dreamer himself.[12] One of the more telling suggestions of this last point is the poem's reference to the "fond believing lyre" of former times, from which, if "fond" is felt to have any of its traditional meaning of "foolish," some wry self-mockery of the poet's trust in his imaginative visions must be inferred.

One may doubt whether the Psyche of the poem does herself represent the visionary imagination, but it is happily unnecessary to chop logic on this point. Whatever, if anything, she represents, there can be no doubt about the poem's main import, that the poet piously dedicates himself to a continuing imaginative veneration of her memory, which he calmly and firmly distinguishes entirely from conditions in the external world. There is no pretense at any time that this imaginative activity will be useful either in ameliorating human suffering or in conducting the poet himself toward a higher than mortal understanding. At the same time, the poem is wrought with an intensity that bespeaks firm and open-eyed commitment to the imaginative activity which is both cele-

[11] *The Quest for Permanence*, pp. 222-28.
[12] *Ibid.*, pp. 226-28. Anthony Hecht ["Shades of Keats and Marvell," *Hudson Review*, xv (1962), 65] agrees that "the reality of the imagination" is the ode's central problem, though he takes another view of the poem's representation of discontinuity between imagination and the world of fact, that is, that without such connection there can be no real facing of the problem at all.

brated and manifested in it. It is clear, then, that the poem, while not claiming for the imagination any of the values that Keats had once attributed to it, does make a more ardent commitment to the exercise of imagination than he had for some time permitted himself to make (with one exception, noted below), or would ever permit himself to make again. The question that naturally arises is whether this unique point of view is indicative of a major change or is merely a position taken for the sake of exploiting a particular poetic subject.

I have always felt, without specific reference to the present consideration, that the "Ode to Psyche" is more than anything else an experimental poem. Since at least the beginning of the year, Keats had been concerned to develop a form in which one idea could be "amplified with greater ease and more delight and freedom than in the sonnet—"[13] and for several weeks, during March and April, he had been experimenting with the sonnet form itself. Concurrently with these experiments, or as a culmination of them, he wrote the "Ode to Psyche," which is well on the way to becoming, but has not yet achieved, the form in which his five major odes are written. This latter form, on the road to which "Psyche" seems clearly to be the halfway house, is composed of strophic units resembling foreshortened sonnets, seemingly made up of structural elements borrowed from both the Shakespearean and the Petrarchan traditional sonnet forms.[14] If, as the sonnet experiments and their subsequent adaptation to the uniquely Keatsian ode strophe suggest, the poet's

[13] *Letters*, II, 26.

[14] Keats's adaptation of sonnet form to ode is discussed by H. W. Garrod, *Keats*, pp. 80-94; M. R. Ridley, *Keats' Craftsmanship: A Study in Poetic Development* (Oxford, 1933), pp. 195-207; W. J. Bate, *The Stylistic Development of Keats* (New York, 1945), pp. 126-32; and Thomas E. Connolly, "Sandals More Interwoven and Complete: A Re-Examination of the Keatsean Odes," *ELH*, XVI (1949), 299-307.

major concern in his composition at the time was with physical structure, then almost any topics would serve the experimental purpose. He might even indulge the self-forbidden luxury of plunging into an imaginative experience that he did not trust but which it was his nature to enjoy—so long as he did not permit his treatment of the chosen subject to hint any utility for the experience beyond the immediate pleasure of the indulgence itself. Whether this is or is not what he thought, he was in fact consistent in the "Ode to Psyche" with the principles first realized in the Reynolds epistle, for he does not in the ode bring the imagination beyond its proper bourn of immediate self-gratification in its momentary exercise; he does not refer it to any standard law of earth or heaven. The poem is as unintellectualized and amoral as the greater part of "Fancy," the poem that apparently began the period of formal experiment which culminated in the odes, and which comes closer than any other to the attitude that is manifested in the "Ode to Psyche."

"Fancy" was one of two poems in an octosyllabic couplet form that Keats described as "a sort of rondeau" and which he offered, at the beginning of the year, as examples of his experiments to find a more flexible brief form than the sonnet.[15] The other such "rondeau," presumably written at about the same time, was "Bards of Passion," in which that strict distinction was made between the earthly and heavenly nightingales' songs which characterized and governed all of Keats's mature work.

It is not possible to date the poems' composition exactly, but some reasonable inferences can be drawn from scraps of evidence, and I think the attempt is worth making. The form tells us almost nothing, for Keats had been using it intermittently throughout his writing life—the 1814 "Fill for me a brimming bowl" is in it, as are five subsequent whole poems and several others in large part,

[15] *Letters*, ii, 21-26.

before the end of 1818.[16] The one thing that all these earlier poems in the form have in common, however, which is not shared with the two later ones, is a certain lack of seriousness, or intensity, or emotional commitment. Perhaps because of its Hudibrastic associations, Keats seemed instinctively to adopt this form when his mood was playful or fancifully speculative, or when his subject was, to his mind, unworthy of dignified treatment, as, for example, was frequently for him the representation of his own erotic desire. Since the form was not new in his practice, then, one must infer that the reason for his considering "Bards of Passion" and "Fancy" as experimental poems was that he was using their form with a new intent, i.e. he was trying to compose serious verse in it.

Since we cannot set an approximate date to Keats's interest in the possibilities of the form, we are thrown back upon other kinds of evidence, most of which is negative. The poems make their appearance in a letter to George and Georgiana Keats, in a portion of it dated by Keats as Saturday, January 2, 1819. They were not composed spontaneously in the letter-writing process, as some of his verses were, for, a few lines before the first one appears, he promises to copy into the letter for them "one or two little poems you might like," and then, after a few rambling remarks on other matters, announces, "Here are the Poems."[17] Presumably they did not exist before the previous November 1st, for they are not included in the last letter to George and Georgiana, written

[16] The poems written entirely in this form are: "Fill for me a brimming bowl," *To***** ("Hadst thou liv'd in days of old"), "Give me women, wine and snuff," "Robin Hood," "Lines on the Mermaid Tavern," and "On Visiting Staffa" ("Not Aladdin magian"). Those predominantly in the form are: "Welcome joy, and welcome sorrow," "Fairy's Song" ("Shed no tear"), and " 'Tis the witching hour of night."

[17] *Letters*, II, 21.

October 14-31, in which he humorously complained of such a dearth of news that he might have to fill up his pages by copying out Mother Hubbard or Little Red Riding Hood.[18] Had he had any poems about, he would no doubt have used them for filler. Between these extremes are the months of November and December 1818. There is no evidence of Keats's having written anything during November, nor should anything be expected, for, as Keats himself said when he was considering writing a prose tale, in mid-October, "in the way I am at present situated I have too many interruptions to a train of feeling to be able to w[r]ite Poetry—"[19] The way in which he was situated included such components of emotional unease as the recent publication of the bitterest attacks upon him in *Blackwood's* and the *Quarterly*, his nursing of his brother Tom through an illness that was to be terminated in death within six weeks of the date of writing, and his involvement with Fanny Brawne, which was to culminate in some sort of mutual understanding in about two months' time. Under such circumstances we may suppose that when he says, in the middle of December, eleven days after Tom's funeral, "I am passing a Quiet day—which I have not done a long while—and if I do continue so—I feel I must again begin with my poetry,"[20] he is speaking of the resumption of an activity left off for some time through a period of extreme disquiet. It was probably during this brief time, then, between December 18 and the beginning of January, that the two "rondeaux" were composed. It was also the time, as Brown later recalled it, during which the bulk of *Hyperion* was written.[21] We may presently find this significant.

As to the seriousness of the two "rondeaux," "Bards of

[18] *Ibid.*, I, 401.   [19] *Ibid.*   [20] *Ibid.*, II, 12.
[21] *Keats Circle*, II, 65.

Passion" has been previously discussed, in connection with the "Ode to a Nightingale," but the acceptance of that argument may seem to proscribe the acceptance of this one, as "Fancy" is a poem of radically different conceptual character. Where "Bards of Passion" defines the mutually exclusive limits of ideal and mundane experience, and thereby implies the folly of imaginative adventuring, "Fancy" does not merely urge the imaginative life but at one point hints its efficacy in the pursuit of truth. For the most part the poem is one of pure escape, arguing in a variety of ways that Fancy supplies the deficiencies of ordinary earthly experience. Before going on to the more aggressive passage, let us simply note that, as in the "Ode to Psyche," there is no utility, beyond the satisfaction of personal preference, asserted for this view, and that this view is by all odds the predominant one in the poem.

In lines 5-8, however, something more is implied. In the text that Keats copied out for his brother and sister-in-law in January 1819 [*Letters*, II, 21], the lines are as follows:

> Then let winged fancy wander
> To wards heaven still spread beyond her—
> Open wide the mind's cage door
> She'll dart forth and cloudward soar.

There is a certain ambiguity here. The implication could be metaphysical, that imagination in one of its functions seeks out the heavenly mysteries—though it is not directly implied that the search is necessarily successful. Or, the implication may be simply visual, since the "heaven" that is "cloudward" may be no more than the natural heavens overhead. In the version published in the 1820 volume, however, the ambiguity is eliminated, the second line having been altered to, "Through the thought still

spread beyond her," which makes clear the original intention to suggest that, whether or not imagination successfully enters into the heavenly haven of truth (and
"Through" may denote success), at least one of its functions is to make that exploratory attempt. In other words,
this poem *seems* to contradict the immediate implications of its experimental companion-piece and the long-
range drift of Keats's entire intellectual development.

One might observe, however, that the two views expressed in "Fancy" manifest the same sort of patching
together of incongruous ideas as Keats attempted in *Hyperion*. While the ideas contained in the two poems are
essentially different, both introduce at some point the
same hopeful conception, alien to both their unlike arguments, of mortal access to immortal understanding. Given
the probability that "Fancy" was composed during the
period of most intense work upon *Hyperion*, and given
our awareness of the irreconcilability of the issues that
Keats hoped to harmonize in *Hyperion*—issues which
perhaps he was beginning to see as hopeless—there
should be nothing to surprise us in the possibility that
Keats broke the hard labor of highly serious composition,
at some point, and indulged himself in an argument of
contrary import, urging not stern acceptance of life but
irresponsible imaginative relief from it, and that, in the
process, he tried to assimilate to it the very idea which
loomed as the central problem in his increasingly difficult composition of *Hyperion*. The temptation newly to
insist in these poems upon that idea, the idea of human
access to immortal understanding, cannot have been less-
ened by the death of his brother Tom, which provoked
him to the uncharacteristic remark, "I have scarce a
doubt of immortality of some nature [or] other—"[22]

As he published it in the 1820 volume, it is obvious

[22] *Letters*, ii, 4.

that Keats had his reasons for liking the poem. Yet its escapism was not in tune with his workaday understanding, and its hint of intellectual utility in the process of escape was no more functional or persuasive in this cameo than in the great canvas of *Hyperion*. And so, I suspect, having tried on a small scale to do what he could not do on a large one, and finding the experimental result, however charming, equally unpersuasive, he made another essay in the same form, "Bards of Passions," this time adhering to the uncompromising truth that was emerging as the thematic center, and the ultimate destroyer, of *Hyperion*. This, I say, is what I suspect, and it can be neither proved nor disproved. All that is certain is the core, that "Fancy," like the concurrent *Hyperion*, attempts to reconcile discordant elements, one of which is alien to the purposes of both and out of harmony with the poet's currently prevailing ideas; and that the otherwise irresponsible and impractical spirit of the experimental "Fancy" was indulged in just once more in Keats's poetic career, at the culmination of that period of experiment which "Fancy" had inaugurated, i.e. in the "Ode to Psyche."

Prudence and economy suggest that the "Ode on a Grecian Urn" be dealt with only briefly here, as the battle lines of criticism are clearly drawn, and I have little more to do than to signify on which side I take my stand, and why. The central issue is, of course, whether the two last lines are to be understood as a single thematic summary of the whole poem's import, or whether they are divisible into a statement by the urn and a counterstatement by the poet, or his speaker in the poem.

I must say that the logic of the poem's argumentative development and the textual evidence on which any conclusion must be based both compel me to read the lines as statement and counterstatement. As every proponent of the contrary reading has seemed to have been aware, to read them as a single unit of statement is to make non-sense of the poem as a whole. From beginning to end, the poem demonstrates that the kind of beauty that the urn has is incommensurate with the kind of truth that men must live by. To suppose that the ending of the poem suddenly reverses the implications of the evidence that has been so painstakingly amassed is to assert that one of Keats's best-controlled poems is finally a muddle.

As for the logic of the poem's development, it deals throughout with the ambiguities of seeing and knowing and ultimately of being. The urn is at once a self-contained, serenely still and integrated entity and the messenger of a vigorous, noisy, impassioned existence somewhere else in space and time. From the very beginning, what it is and what it tells us are different kinds of truth because representative of different modes of being. The urn *embraces* both but *is* only one; and this is equally true of the urn's observer. The question is, how far are the truths reconcilable in determining the *essential* nature of each? The opposed possibilities are the ideal stasis represented by the work of art and the organic process represented by the characters with which it is ornamented. Through the first three stanzas the essential differences in modes of being are increasingly emphasized: the urn shows but does not participate in intensity of mortal experience; the observer envies but does not participate in the ideality of experience objectified in the work of art that is the urn. The trees, piper, and lovers exemplify nature, art, and human affection—all capable of giving intense pleasure in human life, but all subject ultimately to the giving of intense disappointment, everywhere but in the unfeeling and unchanging existence that is theirs on the urn. Having reached this apparent impasse, the poet then, in his fourth stanza, reaches past the unequivocally mortal experience with which he has so far been concerned, to the one human possibility that goes beyond organic process, beyond the ephemerality of momentary passion, and beyond the static perfection of art, to a quality of experience capable of providing not only intensity but the promise of a human alliance with permanence—he reaches out to consider religion.[23] It is the logical culmination of the path he has been following, but it yields no more satisfactory answer to his problem. If the identity of the god, to whom the priest has dedicated his life and the townsfolk have piously dedicated their morning, must forever remain a mystery to later generations of men, then that god has forever ceased to have efficacy in the world. Either his original followers were deluded or we are being deprived of him, but if we have to ask the questions that the stanza asks, we must tacitly acknowledge that there is at some point a defect in religion's promise to elevate the willing seeker above the flux of temporality. There being no farther point to seek, the poet is obliged

[23] Not many commentators have chosen to linger on this stanza. Among the few who have, Cleanth Brooks [*The Well Wrought Urn: Studies in the Structure of Poetry*, New York (Harvest Books), 1947, pp. 161-62] seems to me more to have befogged than cleared the air by suggesting that here Keats takes up residence in the fantasy world he has created. Certainly the concluding stanza gives no indication of the poet's being lost in his own subjectivity, and Mr. Brooks makes no real attempt to show how such a possibility would contribute to the organic unity which he is willing to claim for the poem.

David Perkins [*The Quest for Permanence*, p. 239], by emphasizing merely the verbal ambiguities of the stanza (e.g. the greenness of the altar suggests life, while the description of the heifer's flanks as silken renders life in terms of art) and trying, rather haplessly, to sandwich in Brooks's irrelevancy, loses the opportunity to make the point his book is concerned with generally, this being the place in the poem where Keats makes the longest reach for permanence, and, failing, arrives at the summation of his experience which is rendered in the last stanza.

then to contract his range, return to the original object of contemplation, the urn as a total entity, and make the necessary inferences.

These are made in the concluding stanza. The urn is indeed "Fair," but the men and women, flowers and trees with which it is overwrought are, after all, marble, and the conditions of their existence cannot be equated with the conditions of ours. We are tantalized by the idea of eternity which they implant in our speculations, but finally we must acknowledge the coldness, for us, of their stone Arcadia. Whatever the work of art may suggest to the contrary, the fact is that old age *will* continue to waste the generations of men, that woe *will* continue to be the portion of mortal man, and that the urn has no truth to offer which can mitigate those hard facts. The work of art is a friend to man insofar as it stimulates speculation and contemplation of ideal experience as the sort of momentary escape from worldly problems which the creation of the poem illustrates, i.e. insofar as it exercises the imagination within proper bounds. But since, as the poem has progressively made more clear, there is no possibility of substituting the urn's ideal world for our real one, it is only the urn that can ground the principle of its existence in the formula, "Beauty is truth, truth beauty." Man needs to know, as the poet has just pointed out, that something more than that governs the condition of his existence on earth. The urn's statement, valid as it may be for the urn, cannot persuade the poet, who may be sorry that he cannot agree but who is nevertheless in possession of the knowledge that the exercise of the poem has forced him to define and elaborate. He therefore replies with the counterstatement, rooted in the knowledge of the speculative journey he has come, which places the urn's tempting half-truth in its only possible perspective.

As for the several kinds of punctuation for which there

is warrant in considering the two last lines, one factor remains constant in all: there is always a dash separating the beauty-truth assertion from the final statement.[24] In both published versions, over which Keats presumably had more control than he had over his friends' transcriptions, and in which he would presumably give more attention to the clarity of his meaning than he would in a working draft, there are even greater separations: in the *Annals of the Fine Arts* version, a period at the end of the beauty-truth statement; in the 1820 volume, the statement enclosed within quotation marks. Since these additional emphases serve the logic that the poem demands in its conclusion, one wonders by what demon of perversity so many good-hearted souls have been driven to a reading that has neither textual authority nor internal consistency.

The most frequent objection that I have heard is that "ye" is a plural, hence cannot be addressed to the singular urn. One answer that has been provided to this is that it is addressed to the marble *figures* on the urn,[25] a reasonable suggestion, though one burdened with the awkwardness (not absolutely debilitating) of coming as the climax to a unit of statement initially addressed to a singular "Thou" and including another reference to the "Thou" as "a friend." Another proposal, a bit more difficult, is that the "ye" of the concluding remark is addressed to mankind at large, all the readers of the poem, to whom the speaker turns from the urn in his final statement, and that what "ye know on earth" includes everything in the five last lines of the poem, beginning from, "When old

[24] A fact which is complicated by the presence in the transcripts of an additional dash after "Beauty is Truth." For perspective on this, and for a survey of all available textual evidence, see the following excellent note, which provided all the facts in this paragraph: Jack Stillinger, "Keats's Grecian Urn and the Evidence of Transcripts," *PMLA*, LXXIII (1958), 447-48.

[25] Robert Berkelman, "Keats and the Urn," *SAQ*, LVII (1958), 354-58.

age shall this generation waste."[26] I find the difficulties of adapting the undoubted singulars into this scheme even more awkward than in the previous case, though it is an attractive idea. But I think we can resolve the basic difficulty more easily. While "ye" certainly began its grammatical life as a plural, it had been used as a singular, with increasing frequency, since the thirteenth century,[27] and was so used in Keats's time—and, by Keats[28]—and, indeed, in this place in this poem. If one should pause a moment to consider that the urn is said to be speaking in its capacity as a "friend to man," and that the generic "man," or mankind, is singular (as distinguished from the individuating plural "men"), it immediately becomes clear that a purist reading of "ye" as plural is inappropriate to either possible referent, in any strict sense. Should one wonder why Keats suddenly broke from conventional distinctions, it ought to suffice to try out, on an ear attuned to Keatsian harmonies, the reading, "that is all / Thou know'st on earth, and all thou need'st to know."

The poem, then, accepts the urn for the immediate meditative and imaginative pleasure that it can give, but it firmly defines the limits of artistic truth. In this it is wholly consistent with all the great poetry of Keats's last creative period.

[26] Earl R. Wasserman, *The Finer Tone*, pp. 58-62.

[27] See the general discussion in the *NED*, and the examples given there under B2.

[28] Martin Halpern ["Keats's Grecian Urn and the Singular 'Ye,'" *College English*, xxiv (1963), 284-88] thoroughly canvasses Keats's poetry, to demonstrate that the singular "ye" is by no means unique in the Grecian Urn ode, and that Keats elsewhere, as here, used both "thee" and "ye" in reference or address to singulars. Mr. Halpern anticipates me in suggesting euphony as one reason for the "ye" construction in the Grecian Urn ode.

Index

Names of persons, and titles of Keats's poems. Names of persons include references to their works. Principal discussions of poems are given in italics.

PERSONS

Abbey, Richard, 13, 188
Abrams, M.H., 10, 58, 197n
Alfred (King), 78-82
Allott, Miriam, 246n, 281n
Aristophanes, 62n
Arnold, Matthew, 3, 14n

Bailey, Benjamin, 72, 114n, 137n, 187, 192
Bate, W.J., vii, 13n, 24n, 35n, 97-98n, 308n
Beach, J.W., 82-83n, 238n, 269-270n
Berkelman, Robert, 318n
Blackstone, Bernard, 77n
Bouquet, A.C., 9
Brawne, Frances (Fanny) 67-68, 246, 247n, 248, 305, 311
Bridges, Robert, 110
Brooks, Cleanth, 316n
Brown, Charles, 16-17n, 60n, 214, 268, 311
Brown, Leonard, 114n
Browning, Elizabeth Barrett, 25n
Burton, Robert, 248
Bush, Douglas, 17n, 19-20, 90n
Byron, George Gordon, Lord, 16

Clare, John, 15-16
Clarke, Charles Cowden, 59n, 63n, 108n
Coleridge, S.T., 135
Colvin, Sidney, 23n, 35n, 51n, 82n, 85n, 110, 153n, 198, 246n, 269n, 294n

Connolly, Thomas E., 308n
Courthope, W.J., 17-18

Dante, 247n
de Selincourt, Ernest, 23-24n, 110, 153n, 167, 168, 196, 205n, 227-228, 247n, 269n, 295
Dilke, Charles, 4-5
Donne, John, 87
Drayton, Michael, 93-94n
Dryden, John, 35n

Eliot, T.S., 14n
Evans, B. Ifor, 24n

Fairchild, Hoxie Neale, 9, 10, 209n, 291n
Fausset, H. I'A., 24n
Finney, C.L., 13, 23n, 35n, 37n, 51n, 82n, 85n, 93n, 97n, 115n, 117-124, 131, 137n, 153n, 246n, 247n, 256, 269n, 270, 276n, 278n
Ford, George H., 3n
Ford, Newell F., 121n, 143n, 150-151n, 153-154n
Foss, Martin, 76
Frogley, Mary, 43n
Frye, Northrop, 238n

Garrod, H.W., 24n, 37n, 59n, 60n, 62n, 101, 205n, 215n, 308n
Giovannini, G., 34n, 45n, 79n
Gittings, Robert, 55n, 247-249,

INDEX

Virgil, 33, 34, 255n

Ward, Aileen, vii, 13n, 24n,
  98n, 108n
Warren, Herbert, 17
Wasserman, E.R., 13n, 247n,
  254-255n, 256, 272-273n,
  291n, 318-319

Wells, C.J., 248
Wilson, June, 15n
Woodhouse, Richard, 37n, 43n,
  181n, 247-248, 249
Wordsworth, William, 39, 39n,
  137n, 188, 190n, 223, 248,
  260n
Wright, Herbert G., 13n

POEMS

"After dark vapours," 76
Apollo to the Graces, 49, 85n

"Bards of Passion," *258-259*,
  282, 309-312, 314

Calidore, 24, 59, 91, *94-95*, 100
"Cat! who hast pass'd," 177

Endymion, vi, 5, 6, 10, 15, 18,
  20n, 22, 23, 24, 24n, 25, 26,
  27, 29, 30, 46, 49, 50, 50n,
  51n, 55, 60-61, 62n, 69, 70-
  71, 72, 75, 76-77, 83n, *88-*
  176, 177, 186-187, 188, 223,
  225-229, 236, 238n, 239, 249-
  256, 261, 281, 285n, 289, 290

EPISTLES

To Charles Cowden Clarke,
  49, 56, 68, 69n, 80n, 82,
  97
To George Felton Mathew,
  40-42, 47, 51-52n, 61, 64-
  65, 80n
To J.H. Reynolds, Esq., *194-*
  211, 212, 218, 219, 235,
  242, 255, 259, 268, 281,
  296, 309
To My Brother George, 41-42,
  42n, 46, 47, 51n, 53n, 56,
  65, 68, 96, 102, 293
Eve of St. Agnes, 238, 242-243,
  247-249, 282
Eve of St. Mark, 238, 248, *302-*
  303

Fairy's Song "(Shed no tear")",
  310n
Fall of Hyperion, 5, 96, 238n,
  244, 278-279, *287-296*, 296-
  297n, 299
Fancy, 50, *309-314*

"Fill for me a brimming bowl,"
  67-68, 303, 309, 310n
"For there's Bishop's teign,"
  177
"Four seasons fill the measure
  of the year," 73-74, 76, 193

"Give me women, wine and
  snuff," 179, 310n
"God of the Meridian," *178-182*,
  185-186, 189, 214, 219-220,
  221, 255, 292
"Great spirits now on earth are
  sojourning," 245

"Happy is England," 56
"Hence Burgundy, Claret, and
  Port," 49, 71-72, *178-182*,
  214, 262
"How many bards," *37-39*, 37n,
  53-54, 57, 63-64
Hyperion, 10, 15, 16, 20n, 22,
  24n, 30, 46, 54-55, 104, 104n,
  225-243, 248, 265, 279-280,

[323]

ODES